S0-BAM-849

PEASANT CAPITALIST INDUSTRY

Piecework and Enterprise in Southern Mexican Brickyards

Scott Cook

WITHDRAWN

UNIVERSITY
PRESS OF
AMERICA

LANHAM • NEW YORK • LONDON

HD
9605
.M63
0233
1984

Copyright © 1984 by

University Press of America,™ Inc.

4720 Boston Way
Lanham, MD 20706

3 Henrietta Street
London WC2E 8LU England

All rights reserved
Printed in the United States of America

ISBN (Perfect): 0-8191-4322-7
ISBN   (Cloth): 0-8191-4321-9

All University Press of America books are produced on acid-free
paper which exceeds the minimum standards set by the National
Historical Publications and Records Commission.

JAN 1 5 1987

For Hilda

and

For the Ladrilleros

ACKNOWLEDGEMENTS

This monograph is primarily based on data collected during the final year of the field work phase of a research project in Oaxaca, Mexico initiated in June 1977 and completed in September 1981 (see Appendix 1). Between 1977 and 1978 funding was provided by the Social Science Research Council and by the University of Connecticut Research Foundation. Between September 1978 and September 1981 funding was provided under a grant (No. BNS 78-13948) from the National Science Foundation. Supplementary funding for data processing, analysis, and write-up between 1981 and 1984 was provided by the National Science Foundation (grant No. BNS 81-20103) and by the University of Connecticut Research Foundation.

The project was originally sponsored in Mexico by the **Dirección General de Artes Populares,** Alberto Beltrán, director; and subsequently by the **Dirección General de Culturas Populares,** Rodolfo Stavenhagen, director. Alejandro Guzmán was the liason person between these agencies and the project. Sponsorship in Oaxaca was provided by the **Dirección General de Desarrollo Económico** within the state government, Ing. Fernando Avila, director. Manuel Esparza of INAH, Pedro Arrieta of INI, Tito Cortés of FONART, Cecil Welte, and Arturo Solís provided assistance and friendship in Oaxaca.

As principal investigator during this period I spent approximately two and one-half years in Mexico. When the work-time of other members of the project is considered, several additional years of collective research were conducted. I wish to acknowledge the contributions of Hilda Cook, Leigh Binford, Pierre Bernier, Amelia Pacheco, and Ana Emma Jaillet to the brick industry study during 1980. Leigh Binford also made an indispensable contribution to the computer processing and statistical analysis of brick industry data between 1981 and 1984. I also want to express my appreciation to Binford, Bill Roseberry, Jim Wessman, and to an anonymous reviewer for the University Press of America for their critical readings of earlier versions of this manuscript and for the many helpful suggestions they made toward its revision.

Without the consent, cooperation, and hospitality of the elected officials and people of Santa Lucía del Camino and of Santa Cruz Amilpas--and especially of the brickyard men and their families--this study would not have been possible.

TABLE OF CONTENTS

vii

APPENDIXES

LIST OF FIGURES

LIST OF TABLES

LIST OF PHOTOGRAPHS

1. Scenes of a "gouged and cluttered landscape"

CHAPTER 1

INTRODUCTION: GLOBAL INDUSTRIALIZATION
AND MEXICAN SMALL INDUSTRY

The tendency to define industry as large-scale, capital-intensive factory production wrongly deprives much of past and present humanity of any direct involvement in industrial activity. Industry, in broader terms, refers to the systematic fabrication of commodities (on a scale embracing several production units) to satisfy a definite social demand, and its origin and significance in the human economy long pre-date factory production. Max Weber was correct to emphasize that industry "first begins to be interesting ... when production is carried beyond household needs" (1961:97). This industrial threshold was crossed by human societies in the Stone Age (see Cook 1976:399).

The so-called "Industrial Revolution"--the technoeconomic transformation beginning in 18th century England which represented the "first historical instance of the breakthrough from an agrarian, handicraft economy to one dominated by ... machine manufacture" (Landes 1969:1)--could not have occurred without a series of previous industrial happenings starting several millennia ago during the Neolithic period in non-european areas like Mesopotamia, India, Africa and China. In global diachronic terms, large-scale capital-intensive factory industry was an outgrowth of small-scale, capital- (and labor-) intensive forms which were antecedent to it.[1]

Gordon Childe (1951:74-81) was among the first modern writers to emphasize the importance of industrial commodity production in the Neolithic. He observed that "The outstanding common features (of many Neolithic societies) are woodworking, pottery manufacture, and a textile industry" (1951:75). Among political economists Ernest Mandel has also emphasized the importance of the emergence of industrial commodity production as a specialization in Neolithic village communities (1970:54-59). Recent archaeological findings in Third World regions like the Oaxaca valley, Mexico point to the presence of significant labor-intensive industrialization and commodity exchange at the intercommunity and interregional levels quite early in the sequence of sedentary village farming life (Blanton and Kowalewski 1981; Blanton et.al. 1981; Kowalewski and Finsten 1983).

1

Small-scale, non-factory forms of industry are thriving today throughout the Third World. Even in lesser developed countries where capital-intensive industrialization is often well-entrenched in some branches of production, labor-intensive forms are not disappearing as many expected on the basis of their understanding of the general effects of the "Industrial Revolution" upon craft production in Europe (e.g., Bottomley 1965). This situation in the Third World must be examined in the light of recent scholarship which has begun to uncover and document the extent to which labor-intensive forms of industry persisted long after the factory form had achieved dominance in the advanced capitalist economies of Europe, the United States, and Japan, and in some cases were either created by or integrated with it (see Tilly and Tilly 1971; Kriedte et.al. 1981). In short, the phenomenon of "industrialization within industrialization" (Cook 1984c)--that is, the process of the appearance, persistence, or expansion of labor-intensive forms of industrial commodity production within economies with a capital-intensive, factory-based sector--is very much present in the Third World today (see Goody, ed. 1982).[2]

Nevertheless, the significance of small-scale industry in lesser developed countries is often downplayed or overlooked. Anthropologists and other practitioners of "peasant studies", as well as specialists in rural economic development, have tended to "agrarianize" their approach to the Third World countryside. Rural peoples in lesser developed countries have been studied and written about as if they were exclusively agriculturists. There have been many studies of the "agrarian question" but only a handful dealing with the question of rural industry (Cook 1984c).

This neglect of rural industrial commodity production, given its well-documented importance in the development of capitalism in Western Europe between 1750 and 1850 and in Russia after the 1860s agrarian reform (Lenin 1964), is paradoxical. England is the benchmark case. One need only recall Maurice Dobb's (1963:ch.1; 1976) thesis of the "petty commodity" bridge between feudalism and industrial capitalism and the debate it engendered (e.g., Sweezy et.al. 1967; 1976) to confirm this. E.J. Hobsbawm (1969:29), in discussing the so-called "textile phase" in the industrial revolution in Great Britain starting around 1750, reminds us that at that time:

> ... a good deal--perhaps most--of the
> industries and manufactures of Britain
> were rural, the typical worker being
> some kind of village artisan or small-
> holder in his cottage, increasingly
> specializing in the manufacture of some
> product ... and thus by degrees turning
> from small peasant or craftsman into
> wage laborer.

In **Capital**, Marx recognized that the English
countryside was an arena of industrial as well as
agricultural development. Thus, with reference to the
rural direct producer in the transition from feudalism
to capitalism in England, he (1967:794) noted that:

> ... the new wants he acquires ... and
> the increasing assurance with which he
> disposes of ... his labor-power will
> spur him on to a greater exertion ...
> the employment of his labor-power is by
> no means confined to agriculture, but
> includes rural home industry.

Finally, Marx added with reference to rural industry
that "The possibility is here presented for definite
economic development taking place ..." (ibid.).

It should not be inferred from this discussion
that labor-intensive industries in underdeveloped
regions of today's lesser-developed national economies
like Mexico embody the same evolutionary potential for
capitalist development as did those in the European
past. Such a notion is an illusion created at the in-
tersection between our knowledge of capitalism's as-
cendance and the complexities and uncertainties of its
current combined and uneven trajectory as a global
phenomenon. For example, the processes of capital
accumulation and social differentiation in the contemporary Oaxaca valley appear to parallel the early
phase of regional capitalist development in many of
the advanced capitalist countries. Despite these similarities the national, international and world-
historical ramifications of such regional processes in
contemporary Third World countries cannot parallel
those of the European past (cf. Mintz 1964).

This is so because, in the world-historical
sense, the future of simple commodity production is
already buried in the history of capitalism. Simple

3

commodity production and small-scale capitalism in Third World regions like the Oaxaca valley are inevitably subordinated in an international capitalist system dominated by advanced forms of capital (which long ago sprouted from simple forms they eventually superseded). Thus, the conditions and consequences of the coexistence of simpler, less-advanced commodity forms with complex, advanced forms--and not the possible world historical implications of their appearance and persistence--are at issue.

Despite this world-historical evolutionary pattern, there are mutually reinforcing and compatible elements in simple commodity and capitalist forms of production which coexist in today's lesser developed economies. These elements are overlooked by those scholars who mistakenly portray peasant-artisan economies and their constituent household units as intrinsically non-accumulative of capital; and by those who, even more mistakenly, view them indiscriminately as non-entrepreneurial, irrational, and as presenting obstacles to capitalist development. The fact that peasant-artisan households aim for subsistence does not mean that they cannot also aim for capital accumulation; nor is their subsistence aim incompatible with reinvestment in commodity-producing operations.

Many Third World countries today, as in their precolonial past, provide ongoing testimony to the proposition that capitalist development need not be built on the graveyard of simple commodity production (Ghosh 1984:41; Krader 1975:327-339); and that, on the contrary, under the appropriate conditions simple commodity production deserves recognition as either a "pioneer of capitalism" in the Third World, a role which has been exclusively assigned to imperialism (Warren 1980), or a seedbed of capitalist development.[3] A brief look at the Mexican case provides an indication of what some of these conditions are.

Small Industry and Economic Crisis in Modern Mexico

The post petroleum-boom crisis in the Mexican economy which began at the end of the López Portillo regime (1976-82), with its much publicized deleterious internal and external ramifications, reflects Mexico's emergence in recent decades as an indispensable junior partner in the international capitalist system. Mexico has attracted massive foreign investment from the

4

United States, Japan, and various European countries to fund its industrial development program--especially in the petroleum sector, where it has become a leading exporter, but also in other extractive, manufacturing, and service sectors. It is the magnitude of the international financial stakes which has assured extensive media coverage in the metropolis of Mexico's continuing economic crisis.[4]

The importance of the Mexican economy to the United States can be highlighted succinctly. It has surpassed Saudi Arabia as the major foreign oil supplier to the United States (with 21% of the current import market), and is the United States' third largest export market, after Canada and Japan. Moreover, Mexico is the largest single supplier of cheap migrant labor to the United States--the flow of which is stimulated by high inflation and by the 1982 peso devaluation which caused wages in Mexico to drop to an average value fifteen times less than the average value of wages in the United States. Finally, half of the Mexican private and public sector's staggering multi-billion dollar debt is owed to U.S. commercial banks whose viability is dependent upon a solvent Mexican economy which can repay its loans.[5]

This is not the place to examine in detail the macro-statistical record of Mexico's economic performance since 1970. Suffice it to say that the strategic indicators are mixed. Its 1979 per capita income ranked only 45th in a list of 124 nations compiled by the World Bank, giving Mexico a position in the upper echelon of the so-called "middle income" nations. Yet its average annual growth rate in industry between 1970-79 was higher than that of Japan (6.4 to 5.6), which had the highest rate for the advanced industrial capitalist economies. Moreover, Mexico's average annual growth rate for manufacturing over that same period was slightly above Japan's (6.4 to 6.2) (World Bank 1981:137).

It is this type of macro-statistical performance in the world economic development arena which has earned Mexico a promotion from the pariah ranks of the "industrializing" or "non-industrial" economies into the ranks of the "semi-industrialized" (i.e., 58.9% of value added in commodity production in manufacturing, and has almost qualified it for membership in the prestigious club of the fully "industrialized" economies (more than 60% of value added in commodity production in manufacturing) (Hughes 1980:25-27).

Despite these strides in modern, capital-intensive industrialization, the Mexican economy is by no means free of the underdevelopment malady. Indeed, analysts of the dependency school argue that it is underdeveloped precisely because its industrialization is heavily tied to United States´ capital (e.g., Barkin 1975; Baird and McCaughan 1979). Regardless of one´s posture on the dependency thesis, the empirical record creates a consensus among all observers that the Mexican economy suffers from extraordinary extremes of wealth and poverty, and the scale of the latter places it solidly in the ranks of the "Lesser Developed Countries" (LDCs) (González Casanova 1980).

Whereas it shares a structure of inequality with the advanced capitalist countries--and, especially, with the United States--two structural features of the Mexican system differentiate it from them. First, as the 1982 bank nationalization reminds us, its central government has a more pervasive role in the economy than is characteristic of, for example, the United States, Canada, or West Germany; and its "Presidentialist" system is considerably more centralized and authoritarian. This means, among other things, that enterprise in Mexico is less "free" and "private", and its "democracy" is more of a sham than it is in any of the major capitalist countries. The Mexican system has been aptly described by an astute critic as one of "despotic bourgeois power" (Bartra 1978).

Second and most significant for purposes of this monograph, Mexican capitalism embraces a large sector of small-scale, labor-intensive, non-capitalist commodity producing units. This sector is organized and operates at the household and community levels in several provincial regions like Oaxaca (though present in the metropolitan regions as well, e.g., Lomnitz 1975; Eckstein 1977; Alonso 1983). It involves a sizeable urban and rural population of direct producers whose material reproduction depends to a significant degree upon production for own-use, or upon either a partial non-valuation or undervaluation of their labor-power (i.e., their labor-power is either unremunerated or is under-remunerated with respect to its cost of reproduction in terms of basic life necessities).

6

It is wrong to dismiss the economic subjects in this sector as passive, or as creatures of the Mexican State (Semo 1984:39). It is true that the government has sponsored handicraft production to stem the tide of rural migration, to promote tourism, and for ideological motives (Novelo 1976:30 et passim). However, the economic subjects in the craft and other small industry sector are active, and the sector has an autonomous dynamic with deep roots in the Mexican past (Semo ibid.).

On the basis of this characterization of its production organization, it is important to resist the temptation to divide the Mexican economy into a modern, urban, capital-intensive sector, on the one hand, and a traditional, peasant, labor-intensive sector, on the other. There is only one Mexican national economy which is unified, if for no other reason, through the functioning of the Party-State apparatus (Ramírez Brun 1980; Alonso,ed., 1982). Some of its provincial branches, like that of Oaxaca, do embody elements which are not capitalist but, even if these are quantitatively predominant at the regional level, they are contained within and are affected by forces originating at the national or international levels. Finally, as I will demonstrate in the analysis of the Oaxaca valley brick industry, capitalism is not necessarily a phenomenon external to or superimposed upon a provincial, regional economy. It also has an affinity with simple commodity production which has precapitalist roots there.

Small Industry, Peasant Economy, and Capitalist Development in the Oaxaca Valley

If Mexico is a land of breathtaking contrasts and startling contradictions, then the state of Oaxaca is its microcosm (see Figure 1). This is so regardless of one's perspective: geographical, ecological, social, cultural, or economic. Its 95,364 square kilometers encompass rugged mountain chains, expansive valleys, and broad coastal plains. The triumvirate of climatic zones--cold, temperate and hot lands with their diversity of plant and animal life--are found in juxtaposition in all directions from the center of this impressive mass of southern Mexican landscape. A majority of its three million inhabitants, dispersed among 571 municipalities in seven distinct regions, are still tillers of the soil who are involved in "minifundios" growing subsistence crops with family

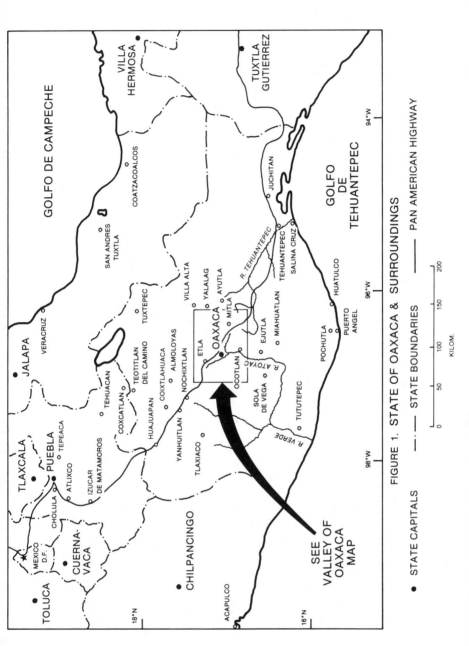

FIGURE 1. STATE OF OAXACA & SURROUNDINGS

● STATE CAPITALS   —·— STATE BOUNDARIES   —— PAN AMERICAN HIGHWAY

labor and/or in **"latifundios"** growing cash crops with hired labor. But there is a rapidly growing population of town and city dwellers whose occupational and class affiliations cover the gamut of those characterizing modern Mexican capitalism.

Oaxaca de Juárez, the state's capital and largest city centrally located in the Oaxaca valley, has grown fourfold since 1950 to a population of nearly 200,000. Its incoming migrants have emigrated from all corners of the state. Although internal rural-to-urban migration is caused by a variety of push-pull factors, widespread rural poverty surely heads the list (Hendricks and Murphy 1981:59-60). Oaxaca City itself, however, is among the poorest cities of its size in Mexico; 65% of its households have been estimated to have a "less than adequate income" (Murphy and Selby 1981:251). It is not surprising, then, that the state loses many of its residents annually through out-migration. One recent study estimates that 1-1/2 million Oaxacans between the ages of 15 and 65 have emigrated from the state in search of employment since 1960, with 47% of that total leaving between 1975 and 1980 (cited in Cook 1982a:395). Most of these emigrants go to the major industrial centers of central and northern Mexico, especially to Mexico City and Monterrey. This emigration translates into a chronic and, apparently, increasing rate of decline in the size of the state's economically active population.[6]

Paradoxically, as labor-power has emigrated from the state, big capital has moved in. The Isthmus region, for example, in the past few years has become a major site for the most sophisticated and capital-intensive form of industrialization in Mexico--petroleum refining. Yet, a painful fact of life for Mexican developmentalists who equate economic development with factory-based, capital-intensive industrialization is that Oaxaca's industry remains household-based and labor-intensive. Moreover, its capital-intensive industry (e.g., petroleum refining in the Isthmus or the paper industry in Tuxtepec) is located in enclaves from which profits are siphoned out of the state (see Wolf and Hansen 1972:12-13). It is not surprising that one consequence of the developmentalists' obsession with capital-intensive industrialization is the neglect of labor-intensive industry by most branches of government (except the tax collectors) from the census bureau to the economic planners, and by the financial sector (Cook 1982a:358-69).

9

Oaxaca's socioeconomic diversity and the signs of modernization in its commercial and industrial sectors nothwithstanding, the state still calls to mind the metaphor of a "living museum" of the traditional, provincial way of life. The southward journey by land across the U.S.-Mexican border evokes a sense of discontinuity rather than of continuity, of abrupt rather than subtle differences; it represents an existential leap across an economic, political and cultural barrier. Similarly, the 350 mile journey from Mexico City southward to Oaxaca evokes the impression of traveling "folkward" on Redfield's (1941) hypothetical continuum. While it is not a journey back in time, it is one from a hyperdeveloped metropolis to a lesser-developed provincial hinterland.

One perception which seems to reinforce this impression, in addition to the "peasantness" of Oaxaca's countryside, is the apparent "indianness" of many of its peasants. Indeed, the name of the state itself derives from a **Mexica** word; yet today's speakers of the **Mexica** language, Nahuatl, are but a tiny fraction of the large segment of the rural population of Oaxaca which speaks indigenous languages. According to the 1970 census, roughly 40% of Oaxaca's population over five years of age spoke one of the state's fifteen indigenous languages; and 30% of these indigenous language speakers were monolingual (Nolasco 1972). As it turns out, only a small percentage of the population involved in the brick industry of Santa Lucía del Camino, which is the focus of this monograph, are indigenous language speakers--and none of the latter are native-born Santa Lucians. This community long ago lost its original ethnic identity.[7]

The Oaxaca Valley (see Figure 2) has 256 populated places with a total of some half million inhabitants and covers 3,375 square kilometers. Since prehispanic times it has had an intercommunity division of labor and specialization with widespread industrial commodity production (Blanton et.al. 1981; Blanton and Kowalewski 1981; Kowalewski and Finsten 1983). Indeed, some commodities were produced in the prehispanic or colonial periods in the same communities where they are produced today (e.g., woven products in Santo Tomas Jalieza, pottery in Atzompa and in Coyotepec, wooden spoons and other wooden utensils in Santa Cecilia Jalieza--Taylor 1972). In other communities, however, industrial specialization is either of post-

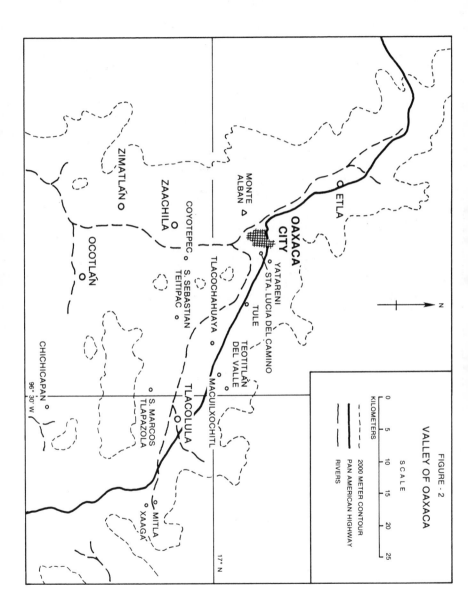

FIGURE - 2
VALLEY OF OAXACA

SCALE

KILOMETERS
0   5   10   15   20   25

- - - - - 2000 METER CONTOUR
━━━━━ PAN AMERICAN HIGHWAY
───── RIVERS

ZIMATLÁN

ZAACHILA

COYOTEPEC

OCOTLÁN

MONTE ALBAN

OAXACA CITY

ETLA

YATARENI
STA. LUCIA DEL CAMINO

TLACOCHAHUAYA

S. SEBASTIAN TEITIPAC

TULE

TEOTITLÁN DEL VALLE

CHICHICAPAN

96° 30' W

S. MARCOS TLAPAZOLA

TLACOLULA

MACUILXOCHITL

MITLA

XAAGA

17° N

11

colonial origin (e.g., brick making in Santa Lucía del Camino and in San Agustín Yatareni, metate production in Magdalena Ocotlán, embroidery in many villages in the district of Ocotlán, treadle loom weaving in Xaagá), or has assumed new forms in the postcolonial period (e.g., treadle loom weaving largely displacing backstrap loom weaving in Mitla and completely replacing it in Teotitlán del Valle). With few exceptions, valley settlements, including those with craft industries, are also substantially involved in agriculture on lands communally or privately possessed.

Among the most prominent rural industries in the valley and its dependent mountain hinterland--each involving many households in several communities--are treadle and backstrap loom weaving, pottery, embroidery, palm weaving, basketry, rope making, brick making, and mezcal distilling. Several industries restricted to fewer communities include wood carving, broom making, limestone extraction and processing, stone quarrying and metate making, and thread spinning. Most of these industries engage people of both sexes, and of a wide range of ages at some stage in the production or circulation of their respective commodities. They display varying mixes of family labor and hired labor together with different forms and scales of production organization. The production forms include independent household units with one or more family workers, independent household workshops with family workers and hired workers, and putting-out units consisting of a workshop with outworker households. They also differ with regard to variables like the level of investment in tools and equipment, length of production cycle, volume and value of sales, and level of earnings (Cook 1978, 1982b).

Many of these industries are integrated through a seven-day periodic marketplace system (Malinowski and De La Fuente 1982; Beals 1975; Cook and Diskin, eds. 1976). However, this system is bypassed in varying degrees particularly in the marketing of luxury crafts produced for tourists, but also in the marketing of utilitarian commodities produced for regional consumption. This implies that an important difference between craft industries lies in the nature of the market for the commodities they produce.

One group of industries (e.g., weaving and embroidery) produces "neo-traditional" luxury items (i.e., new products made according to `traditional' methods) to meet a tourist demand for handicrafts. This demand is a latent by-product of capitalist industrialization in the metropolis which capital-intensive industry cannot satisfy. It is here that multiworker manufactories and putting-out units tend to predominate.

Among the contradictory forces at work in the tourist-craft industries is one on the demand side and another on the supply side. The "creative destruction" (Schumpeter 1950) of capitalist accumulation in the metropolis essentially destroyed handicraft production there through its competitiveness and its economies of scale, both of which favored capital-intensive units and ruined labor-intensive units in many branches of industry (see Goody 1982). As nostalgia for the "good old days" spread among subsequent generations of the metropolitan middle classes, a demand was generated for handicrafts which are produced mostly in the Third World countryside where the "old ways" live on and where labor is still cheap and abundant. One predictable outcome of this has been the opening up of new markets for handicrafts and the increasing commoditization of noncapitalist products (cf. Littlefield 1979; Graburn 1976, 1982; Cook 1981; García Canclini 1982).

Another group of industries (e.g., palm plaiting rope making, metate making) produces traditional utilitarian commodities to meet a demand emanating mostly from other rural households in the regional economy. It is here that the independent household unit without hired laborers predominates; and it is also here where reciprocal labor assumes greater importance.[8]

Brick making is among those industries which do not fit into either one of the two groups just identified. It produces a utilitarian commodity to meet a demand from the construction sector (primarily urban and centered on Oaxaca City). Moreover, its production forms range from single household units with no hired workers and with relatively modest investments in tools and facilities, to enterprises that own and operate several brickyards, kilns, and flatbed trucks and employ many workers. By contrast, the woodcarving industry of Santa Cecilia Jalieza mentioned above produces utensils for sale to other rural households as well as "souvenir" items (e.g., combs, letter openers) for tourists. Here the independent household unit without hired workers predominates. Finally, in the multi-village basket industry there is a large production of reed basketry products for local, regional, national, and international markets. In this industry the household production unit prevails but it often becomes dependent upon credit (and sometimes upon raw materials) supplied by buying-up merchants who specialize in the export trade.

Village on the Urban Fringe:
Santa Lucia del Camino

What is the nature of the community matrix in which one of these industries, namely brickmaking, is located? The casual visitor to Santa Lucía del Camino who walks through the unpaved streets of its residential zone, or along the dirt paths and roads of its agricultural fields and brickyards, may easily develop an oversimplified and distorted set of impressions about its economic and social life. On the one hand, the living conditions of most of its residents are concealed behind high walls, hedgerows or fences while, on the other, its agriculture and industry appear, for the most part, to be archaic or technologically unsophisticated. Moreover, local industry and agriculture are portrayed to outsiders by their practitioners as entailing family-based, subsistence-oriented and relatively unproductive, unrewarding activities. In short, the casual visitor is likely to leave Santa Lucía with the impression that it is comprised mostly of peasant and working class families who differ from their counterparts in more isolated rural communities only by being more exposed to the enticements of city life.

In this section, the evolution of Santa Lucía from an agricultural dependency to a periurban agricultural and industrial community will be outlined, and its contemporary population will be analyzed to determine to what extent the casual visitor's impressions of homogeneity and simplicity give way to a reality characterized by heterogeneity and complexity.

From Dependent Peasant Village
to Periurban Industrial Center

The historical record suggests that Santa Lucía del Camino was originally a Mixtec-speaking community (Paddock 1966:373 quoting Villaseñor) but I have been unable to determine exactly when it was settled. We know that in 1660 the people of Santa María Ixcotel

14

(now a Municipal agency of Santa Lucía) became sharecroppers (**terrasqueros**) for Santa Lucía (Taylor
1972:78). In 1710 the inhabitants of Santa Lucía threw
rocks at Spanish officials who were attempting to make
boundary measurements (op.cit. p. 85). That they were
justified in their actions, but that these were fu-
tile, is clear from a statement excerpted from a
document in the Agrarian Reform archives which reads
as follows:

> The village possessed communal lands
> that, by order of Juan Privativo de
> Tierras, were transferred to the owner-
> ship of the Dominican Fathers of
> Oaxaca, with the village itself retain-
> ing possession only of the **fundo legal.**

In other words, as happened in so many other villages
in the Oaxaca valley, the bulk of Santa Lucía's communal land (most of which was arable) was confiscated
and incorporated into the domain of the good prelates
of the Dominican establishment in Oaxaca City. This
despoliation no doubt triggered the land dispute that
broke out in 1720 between Santa Lucía and its neighboring communities of Santa Cruz Amilpas and San
Sebastian Tutla (Taylor 1972:209). It is not clear how
long Santa Lucía's land remained in the hands of the
Dominicans but, in any case, it did not come into the
possession of the Santa Lucians again until the federal government, under Calles, recognized their peti-
tion for an **ejido** grant in 1925.[9]

Santa Lucía entered the 20th century surrounded
on the north, south and west by three privately owned
haciendas, **El Rosario** (a sugar estate with a large
sugar mill (**trapiche**) owned by the Mimiaga y Camacho
and Santibañez families who were the largest landlords
in the Oaxaca valley at the time), **Dolores**, and **Cinco
Señores.** A 1923 socioeconomic study by the Agrarian
Commission, preliminary to the expropriation, reported
a total population in Santa Lucía of 667 with 284
heads of household. However, the average household
size of 2.4 which these figures yield suggests that
they were incorrect. It was determined that 246 of
these households had no land at all and that 30 of
them had relatively little.

More specifically, the village encompassed 150
hectares (i.e., essentially the colonial **"fundo
legal"**) of which 30 comprised the habitation zone. Of

15

the remaining 120 hectares, 82 belonged to 18 individuals who were not natives of the village (including the **hacendados** themselves and some prominent Oaxaca city residents), three were absorbed by a railroad right of way, leaving 35 hectares which were distributed among only 38 of the 284 heads of household. By contrast, the three adjacent **haciendas** possessed 1424 hectares of which a significant proportion was prime irrigated land.

What these figures demonstrate unequivocably is that most Santa Lucía households in 1923 were landless. This, in turn, raises the question of precisely how they were making a living. Unfortunately, the Agrarian Commission's report does not provide us with a detailed answer to this question but it does provide a succinct one, as follows: "The inhabitants of the village of Santa Lucía del Camino **in their majority** (emphasis added) are dedicated to the fabrication of ordinary bricks and to commerce." The report suggests the possibility that some of these landless individuals may also have worked seasonally as agricultural wage laborers, with average wages of 50-60 centavos for a ten-hour day. It also indicates that none of them worked as sharecroppers for the landed villagers; but it does not tell us if any of them did so for the **hacendados** or for other outsiders who owned the 82 hectares mentioned above.

Official census data from around 1900 indicate that the brick industry was already well-established in Santa Lucía. It had ten kilns producing an estimated 360,000 bricks annually. No employment data is presented for the Santa Lucía industry but the neighboring Santa Cruz Amilpas industry (which had only four kilns) had 98 employees whose aggregate salary was estimated as 15,000 pesos, or almost one-half of the estimated 36,000 pesos value of annual brick sales. It is logical to assume, therefore, that the Santa Lucia industry had a substantially larger number of workers at that time.[10]

The following peculiarly worded statement in the Agrarian Commission's favorable recommendation in 1923 for an **ejido** grant seems to carry the implication that the brickmakers were also involved in agriculture:

> The residents of Santa Lucía have a right to and a need for land allotments, and the fact that some of them--

16

without hindrance to their agricultural
work--engage in the fabrication of
bricks, does not present an obstacle to
this. Apart from it not being shown
that on this account the village's need
for land disappears, sufficient data do
not exist to exclude these individuals
from the group which has rights to
benefit from the law.

Accordingly, the Agrarian Commission decreed (15 July
1925) that the 249 Santa Lucians with rights to an
ejido be granted 170 hectares from the lands of two of
the adjacent haciendas--thus culminating a process
that had been initiated in 1916.

It is clear that the 170 hectare grant was far
below the minimum needed to provide for the subsistence of the 246 landless households. By the Agrarian
Commission's own calculations a family of three required 22 kilos of shelled corn weekly or 1100 kilos
per year, as well as 104 kilos of beans annually
(with a combined market value of 108 pesos per year),
to survive. But the Commission also estimated that
each household required an additional income of 100
pesos to meet other needs.

Even if the ejido grant had included sufficient
land to enable each eligible household to be assigned
a one hectare allotment of 1st class (i.e., irrigated)
land, this would not have met the subsistence needs of
the typical household. As it turned out, the 170
hectare grant (comprising three types of land) would
have yielded an average allotment of only .7 hectares
per eligible household if it had been equitably distributed. Unfortunately, a report filed by the ejidal
zone chief (Jefe de Zona) to his superiors in Mexico
City, approximately one and one-half years after the
expropriation decree, documented the inequities of the
land distribution, and resulted in his intervention to
parcel out remaining land.[11]

Consequently, 100 hectares were distributed among
the 178 eligible usufructuaries "in a manner which assured that each one received a fraction near the
village and another more distant from it" (this means
that each eligible head of household received just
over 1/2 hectare of arable). The zone chief remained
frustrated by evidence of factionalism within the
community which, from his perspective, "made it impos-

sible to efficiently organize one of the best **ejidos** in the state of Oaxaca, on the edge of the city and with excellent conditions and lands." Unfortunately, factionalism has continued to plague life in Santa Lucia and, in recent years, has crystallized along party lines with the "**Priistas**" (i.e., followers of PRI, the ruling Institutionalized Revolutionary Party) in one faction and the "**Panistas**" (i.e., followers of PAN, the National Action Party) in another. Santa Lucia has a reputation throughout the valley, apparently deserved, as a base of support for PAN.[12]

It should be mentioned here that the brickyards were, from the beginning, located exclusively within the 120 hectares which were owned both by native Santa Luciáns and outsiders. It is likely that the pattern of "buying clay" ("**comprar tierra**") through which individual brickmakers paid a landowner for the clay extracted from a given parcel according to the number of bricks produced, had its origins in this skewed land distribution. Although the historical record is barren here, it is likely that some of the landowners were also brickmakers or, at least, hired brickmakers to work for them. Only recently has a small brickyard area opened up in a sector of Santa Luciá's **ejido**. Until this occurred the development of the brick industry involved only privately owned land (**pequeñas propiedades**), some of which was purchased in the 1920s and 30s from the owners of the Dolores hacienda.

It is probable that one consequence of the **ejido** grant was to reduce the participation of previously landless households in sharecropping or agricultural wage labor during the rainy season (April - October). However, given the increased need for cash associated with agriculture, it is also likely that dry season participation in the brick industry intensified among the new land-allotment households.

Two major events highlight the subsequent history of the **ejido** in Santa Lucía. First was the development of a limestone processing operation in a hilly, agriculturally marginal section of the **ejido**. Second was the expropriation by the government in 1970 of approximately 50 hectares, most of which was land that had once belonged to the **Cinco Señores** hacienda, for the purpose of constructing an urban housing development. Over the years the limestone business evolved from a relatively small extractive operation (usually through annual contracts with private operators for a set fee

18

plus a surcharge on each ton of limestone extracted) to the establishment in 1975 of a multi-million peso mechanized hydrated lime plant through a partnership between the ejido, the federal government, and a private corporation. Several Santa Luciáns are employed in this plant which yields a substantial annual revenue to the **ejido**. However, there appears to be no direct relationship between the brick industry and the limestone operation, although some households are involved in both.

In summary, it can be said that the development of the limestone business simply served to integrate Santa Lucía's economy even more completely with the urban construction industry. The expropriation represented the inexorable expansion of the city and was probably the first in what will be a periodic series of predatory land expropriations to satisfy the needs of the growing city. It is ironic that as Santa Lucía has industrialized to meet the needs of the urban construction market, it has collaborated in digging its own grave as a discrete corporate community.

A Heterogeneous, Urbanizing, Peasant-Industrial
Community[13]

With regard to the regional division of labor, Santa Lucians' are substantially involved in the urban economy. More than half of the households surveyed had at least one member in a non-agricultural occupation, whereas less than half were involved in agriculture. Approximately one-half of the households had one or more members in the brick industry; one-third were involved in commercial activity, most of these with small retail food vending or grocery businesses; one-quarter were engaged in the artisan trades (e.g., carpentry, tailoring, sewing, meat cutting, blacksmithing, plumbing); and just under one-quarter had members in transportation as bus, taxi, or truck drivers. One in every ten households surveyed had at least one representative employed in the hydrated lime factory, in government service, or as professionals. Finally, and surprisingly, less than 5% of the households had members employed in domestic service.

Although the community's reputation as a center of the brick industry is supported by the occupational data, so is the heterogeneity of its population. Furthermore, its heterogeneity is underlined by the fact that a majority of the household heads in the census

19

were not born there, as well as by the fact that 22%
of the households had bilingual speakers (either
Spanish-Nahua, Spanish-Zapotec, or Spanish-Mixtec).
Finally, a majority of the household heads completed
four years or less of schooling, but nearly 10% received a secondary or post-secondary education.

With regard to living conditions, Santa Lucía is
closer to urban rather than to rural standards in
Oaxaca. For example, 70% of the dwelling units in the
central residential zones (see Figure 3) were either
constructed of cement or brick, and only 30% were constructed of thatch or adobe. Although the majority of
households owned their house lots and the house itself
--which is also typical of rural communities--there
was a higher percentage of rental or loan housing
(22%) than one expects to find in rural communities in
Oaxaca. Finally, more than half of the households owned a television set, whereas even in the most affluent
rural communities of the Oaxaca valley this percentage
is much lower. To summarize, then, the degree of heterogeneity displayed in most of the variables reviewed
above is more diagnostic of "typical" urban, rather
than of "typical" rural, populations and living conditions in Oaxaca (see Nolasco 1981; Iñigo Aguilar
Medina 1980; Murphy and Selby 1981).

Mean household size in Santa Lucía (Table 1) is
quite large, and there is a low proportion of extended
households relative to the proportion found in rural
industrial communities (see Table 13). The labor-intensive nature of the local economy, combined with incomes which are low relative to expenditures, provide
incentives for large households. As will be documented
in Chapter 4 large numbers of male offspring are especially important in determining the productivity (and
income) of household units in the brickyards.

Income differentials in the community (Table 1)
are consistent with the pattern of inequality which is
characteristic of the wider social-economy. What is
striking about them, however, is the large spread
between the lowest and the highest reported incomes.
This is consistent with the occupational heterogeneity
already referred to, as well as with different class
positions among these households. In fact the median
reported weekly income was only 35 dollars, and only
9% of the households surveyed had weekly incomes
greater that 135 dollars. But, again, what stands out
here is the size of the income spread and the

20

Table 1. Means and Range for Selected Social and Economic variables for 56 Households in Santa Lucía del Camino in 1980*

VARIABLE LABEL	N	MEAN**	MINIMUM VALUE	MAXIMUM VALUE
Size of household	56	6.7	2.0	15.0
Age of hshld head	56	41.9	20.0	79.0
Weekly income of head (principal job only)	46	54	9	222
No. of paid working household members	54	1.9	1.0	5.0
No. of jobs in hshld	55	3.7	1.0	10.0
No. of jobs of head	55	1.6	0	3.0
Hshld income for week preceding census	53	55	0	390
Hshld expenditures for week preceding census	53	83	10	444
No. of months corn bought in 1979	27	8.8	1	12
Total area of land cultivated(has.)	31	1.1	.1	5.5
Total value of Agric. means of production	4	2,173	1,071	3,555
Cost of Rental of agric. means	21	59	2.25	373
Total value of farm animals owned	26	319	13	1,045
No. of person days of agric. hired help	7	13.3	2.0	44.0
No. of days worked as hired hand in agric.	2	6.5	5.0	8.0
Kilos of corn last harvest	19	696	80	250

All monetary values in U.S. dollars @ $1 = 22.50 pesos

*For the variables in row 3 and in rows 10-16 the mean has been computed only for those households reporting values greater than

21

inequality of income distribution.[14]

That many Santa Lucians are not involved in agriculture, or are only marginally involved, is borne out by the survey data (Table 1). Although it is true that more than half of the households possess arable which they cultivate themselves or with hired hands, three-quarters of these have only one hectare or less. Moreover, few households own agricultural means of production (e.g., oxen, plows, carts) and less than half rent them, which suggests that only a limited number of the landed households actually work in agriculture themselves. Most of these latter households do plant corn, but the average 1979 harvest of shelled corn was modest. It is no coincidence that the number of households which raise farm animals is almost identical with the number of households which cultivate their own land since fodder production, especially of alfalfa, is at least as important as food production in Santa Lucía's agriculture.

Given the high degree of landlessness, coupled with the relatively low corn yields among the agricultural households, it is surprising that only half of the households reported that they bought corn in 1979. This relatively low rate of corn purchase is primarily attributable to the fact that many households either buy tortillas or corn dough for making them, and no longer make them from scratch as is done in most rural households of the Oaxaca valley. In short, the data presented above generally support the portrayal of Santa Lucía as a heterogeneous industrial and commercial community in which the brickyards are a major foci of industrial activity. It is a community experiencing creeping urbanization where agriculture is only a supplementary occupation in most households that practice it. This overview of the household survey data sets the stage for an in-depth analysis of the brick industry.[15]

Background of the Brickyards Study:
A Personal Note

On countless occasions over the years dating back to 1965, I drove by the brickyards on the eastern outskirts of Oaxaca City heading for the Zapotec-speaking communities of peasant-artisans in the district of Tlacolula. My view of the gouged and cluttered landscape created by the brick industry was often obscured by dense clouds of black smoke spewing from the kilns.

It was usually necessary to exercise special caution at the driver's wheel in the traffic of flat-bed, brick-hauling trucks that frequently exit and enter the highway. At this point my thoughts would turn to the relative peace, quiet, and rusticity of the Zapotec countryside a few miles down the highway--with its unique array of villages that have fascinated generations of anthropologists and tourists. Given my exotic-sounding destinations--Mitla, Xaagá, Teitipac, Papalutla, Guelavía, Tlacochahuaya, Tlacolula, Macuiloxóchitl, Teotitlán, Matatlán, Tlapazola, Albarradas--I felt justified in passing by the brickyards even though my curiosity about them was aroused.

When I was in the city I was increasingly impressed by the ubiquitous evidence of construction activity, and especially by the large quantities of bricks and stones being handled. Through my work with the **metateros** (metate or quern makers) of the Teitipac villages (Cook 1982a), I became familiar with the quarries of Ixcotel (located immediately to the west of Santa Lucía proper between it and the city) where the **metateros** sometimes hired themselves out as piece rate quarryworkers as an alternative to work in their villages. I also learned that many men from the metate vilages worked seasonally in urban construction. While I never conducted systematic fieldwork in the Ixcotel quarries, I learned from my casual visits that they were the source of much of the stone used in the Oaxaca city construction industry. It was obvious that the brickyards, located a short distance east of the quarries, supplied many of the bricks to that same industry.

So, my involvement in economic anthropological studies in the Zapotec countryside brought me, in a roundabout way, into contact with the periurban industrial zone of quarries and brickyards in Santa Lucía del Camino. Given this background, it was inevitable that, as I became more and more interested in the dynamics of capitalist development in the Oaxaca valley, I would undertake the study which provided the basis for this monograph when the opportunity to do so arose.

With roots in the countryside, yet mass-producing a basic commodity for the city construction market, the brickyards provide an ideal arena for describing and analyzing the relationships between agriculture and industry, and between the rural and the urban

23

sectors of the regional political economy. Moreover, the brickyards offer a good example of peasant capitalist industry in provincial Mexican rural communities. In the following chapters it will be shown how indigenous industrialization differentiates peasant-artisan households, through the effects of capital accumulation and piece wage labor, as they are integrated into an industry such as brick making.

NOTES

[1] Max Weber's conceptualization of industry has influenced my thinking. One problem resulting from his emphasis on the "transformation of raw materials" is that extractive operations like mining and quarrying are arbitrarily excluded from the realm of industrial activity, as Weber himself notes (1961:97). Marx's notion of the "labor process" (1967,I:177-185) which includes the extraction or appropriation of natural resources, as well as their transformation by human labor power (and its instruments) into raw materials prior to their further transformation into finished commodities, overcomes this definitional deficiency.

I agree with Weber that "industry embraces all those economic activities which are not to be viewed as agricultural, trading, or transportation operations" (ibid.), with the proviso that agricultural commodities are industrialized when they serve as raw materials in the fabrication of derivative commodities (e.g., as when sugar cane is processed into sugar or distilled into rum, or when portions of the maguey plant are processed to form fiber products or to yield mezcal). The practice of agriculture, because of its unique relationship to the ecosystem, is excluded from `industry´ as I define it.

For a view of industry by an anthropologist which is diametrically opposed to mine see Slotkin 1960. He contrasts industry (in his terms "industrialism") to handicrafts and manufacture and argues that it is a Western invention. Its hallmark is the "use of complex technological equipment which can neither be owned nor operated by a single worker" (1960:13). In other words, according to Slotkin, the only way that industry enters the Third World is by diffusion.

[2]. Tilly and Tilly (1971:186) define "protoindustrialization" as "industrialization before the factory system" (cf. F.F.Mendels 1972). Given the exclusively European focus of their work their concept should be relabelled "protoeuroindustrialization." A comparable minimal definition of "intraindustrialization" is "industrialization within the factory system." The following more detailed definition is preferable: "Intraindustrialization refers to the dynamic appearance, persistence, or expansion of labor-intensive forms of industrial commodity production within inter-

stices or larger sections of a capitalist economy where, in aggregate, the capital-intensive factory form is dominant."

In a recent article Richard Tilly presents a much-improved definition of "protoindustrialization" as the "increase in manufacturing activity by means of the multiplication of very small producing units and small to medium accumulations of capital" or, alternatively, as an "increase in manufacturing without large producing units and great accumulations of capital"(1983:3). This definition clearly gives the concept a world historical applicability, although Tilly remains fixated on Europe. To his credit, Tilly is critical of the view which sets "peasant economy" against "industry" (and countryside vs. city). He now recognizes this view as being empirically and theoretically incompatible with our growing understanding of the process of European "protoindustrialization."

W.E. Moore´s **Industrialization and Labor** (1951) set an early post World War II precedent for a narrow, capital-centric conception of industry wedded to a unilineal, gradualist vision of economic evolution. This work also gives surprisingly little attention to non-factory forms of production (pages 55-58 and 223-226 essentially exhaust its coverage of the topic). For Moore, world history is divided into a pre-industrial and an industrial period, with the "industrial mode of production" (sic!) emerging with the Industrial Revolution (1951:3), and the Modern World has two major divisions: "industrial cultures" and "nonindustrial cultures." Consequently, for Moore, the basic dilemma of the contemporary world is unproblematic: "...either primitive and peasant societies will become industrialised, or they will be very substantially affected by industrialization elsewhere" (1951:6).

---

[3] Eric Wolf´s writings (1955:454; 1966:15; 1969:xiv) have emphasized the simple reproductive tendencies of peasant household economy, and have conceived of it in general as being diametrically opposed to market and commodity economy rather than as a form of it. His writings have underplayed the dual nature of the peasant household as both a domestic unit (i.e., producing with family labor products for own-use) and enterprise (i.e., producing commodities mostly with family labor but also with occasional hired labor)--see

Galeski 1972:ch.1. This tendency has reinforced the view, which in some situations is misleading, that commoditization (see Hart 1982) and capital accumulation originate only within external capitalism rather than also from within the simple commodity regime.

Likewise, Scott´s elaboration of his "safety first" principle (i.e., a "relative preference for subsistence security over high average income" 1976:29) makes it impossible for him to address the dynamics of capital accumulation, social differentiation, and class formation among peasantries. It provides a circular explanation of why poor and middle peasant households stay that way (i.e., because of their "safety first" propensities) but cannot explain how or why they might become capital accumulators (cf. Popkin 1979, 1980).

Robert Heilbroner, exemplifying the developmentalist posture of many liberal economists toward the Third World, portrays peasants as petty agriculturists and industrialists who are essentially "shackled to backwardness" by unproductive and irrational ways which prevent capital-creation (1963:ch.3 et.passim).

[4] It is troublesome that many educated, well-placed U.S. citizens either do not consider the capitalist identity of the Mexican political-economy to be significant (e.g., the most comprehensive study by a U.S. economist of the Mexican economy--Reynolds 1970 --makes no specific or direct reference to capitalism in its entire 468 pages), or sincerely believe that it is not capitalist at all (e.g., members of the U.S. Congress who have placed ads in **The New York Times** on May 5 and August 10, 1976 and most recently on October 9, 1981 which either explicitly claim or imply that Mexico is, in fact, a socialist or communist nation!).

[5] These facts and figures were culled from articles in **The Wall Street Journal** of 8/20/82 and in **The Latin American Regional Report** of 10/29/82.

[6] The Oaxaca valley, as the heartland of the "Central Valleys" region, lies approximately 350 miles south of Mexico City in the southern highlands of Mexico (Welte 1976). The Y-shaped valley has Oaxaca de Juárez

27

(hereafter referred to as Oaxaca City) at its center, with the towns (and their surrounding districts) of Tlacolula and Mitla in its eastern arm; of Zaachila, Zimatlán, Ocotlán, and Ayoquesco in its southern arm; and of Etla in its northern arm (see Figures 1 and 2).

Twenty-one percent of its total area is valley bottom or alluvium. A transverse profile of the valley "reveals four major ecological zones: the contemporary floodplain of the river (a narrow, relatively minor zone); a higher floodplain that lies above it and is the major area of the alluvium and key agricultural resource of the valley; the gently sloping piedmont; and the steep slopes of the surrounding mountains" (Sanders 1972:143).

The "central valleys" region encompasses the Oaxaca valley plus a large portion of the political-administrative districts of Ejutla, Miahuatlán, and Sola de Vega. It has a total of 142 municipalities (municipios) or 26% of the state total of 541. According to the 1970 census, the region had 549,560 inhabitants (27.3% of the state total) and an economically active population (EAP) of 102,812 (19.7% of the state's EAP), of whom about 71% were agriculturists. The region had a population density of 56.08 persons per square km. and a total surface area of 16,234 square kms. (17.2% of the state's total area). (See Moguel 1979 for a survey of various attempts over the years to "regionalize" Oaxaca.)

[7] The fifteen discrete languages spoken among the indigenous population of Oaxaca today are as follows (Nolasco 1972:17): Chontal, Mazateco, Chocho-Popoloca, Ixcateco, Mixteco, Cuicateco, Trique, Amuzgo, Chatino, Zapoteco, Chinanteco, Huave, Nahuatl, Mixe, and Zoque.

For my views on the ethnic factor in Oaxaca see Cook 1982a:379-82.

[8] Reciprocal labor is widespread in the Zapotec villages of the valley where it is known as "guelaguetza". I have described how its functions among the metate makers (Cook 1982a:213-16). The practice is also prevalent in the palm plaiting industry in the Albarradas villages where it is known as "golaneche". (See Martínez Rios (1964) for an analysis of reciprocal labor in valley agriculture.)

[9] Prior to the initiation of the agrarian reform during the second decade of this century as an outgrowth of the Revolution beginning in 1910, the term "ejido" referred to ancient communal lands subject to collective usufruct. After the codification of agrarian reform policy in article 27 of the 1917 federal constitution, the term **ejido** referred to a system of land tenure defined in clause X of article 27 (Title One, Chapter One) that says: "The population nuclei that lack **ejidos** or that can achieve their restitution through lack of titles, through the impossibility of identifying them, or because legally they have been alienated, will be granted lands and water sufficient to constitute them, in conformity with the needs of the population..." (1967:26 **Constitución Política de los Estados Unidos Mexicanos.** Mexico, D.F.: Porrua). It was through the procedure of **"dotación"** (grant) and not through **"restitución"** (restitution) that Santa Lucía del Camino was granted **ejido** lands (cf. Reyes et.al. 1974:434-466).

[10] The censuses consulted are included in the **Memoria Administrativa del Estado de Oaxaca,** (presented September 17, 1898 by General Martín González, governor) and published in 1899 in Oaxaca by the Imprenta del Estado; and in the **Memoria Administrativa del Estado de Oaxaca** presented September 17, 1900 also by General Martín González. The 1895 census (1898, **Ministerio De Fomento, Dirección General de Estadística. Censo General del Estado de Oaxaca** (1895), Mexico: Oficina Tip. de la Sec. de Fomento) lists a total of 229 brickmakers for the Centro district. It can be assumed that this figure pertains to the Santa Lucía del Camino and Santa Cruz Amilpas industries.

[11] Some additional insights into the nature and conduct of the agrarian reform process are embodied in this report. First, without explanation, the number of heads of household determined eligible to receive an **ejido** allotment had decreased to 178 by the date the report was filed. Next, we learn that the village official in charge of alloting the 170 hectares was himself not a tiller of the soil but a dairy farmer who rented out his own land to residents of Oaxaca city. The report describes this official´s management of the land distribution as follows:

Only 70 hectares near the habitation area were parceled out which left 27 eligible **ejidatarios** and residents of the village without a parcel and in the repartition 37 individuals were favored, among them the Executive (his father) who was granted two parcels and seven fractions; also various persons who had not resided in the community for several years were given parcels of land so that the official could rent it until they returned. The remaining 100 hectares were not distributed even though they are magnificent for agriculture and have always produced alfalfa, corn, wheat, beans, chickpeas, squash, and other crops , and others that are good pasture land."

[12] PAN has been succinctly characterized as a party of "privileged class composition" which serves as the "loyal opposition" to PRI (Levy and Székely 1983:73). See Cook 1984b for an exploration of some implications of recent electoral successes by PAN in several Oaxaca valley communities.

[13] See Appendix 2 for a discussion of some of the difficulties encountered in defining the community and surveying its population.

[14] At the time this study was conducted the peso-to-dollar exchange rate was 22.50. This is the rate employed in all peso-to-dollar conversions in this chapter and throughout the monograph unless otherwise indicated. For the reader's convenience I have converted pesos to dollars whenever appropriate throughout the monograph.

[15] Urbanization has intensified since the completion in 1982 of the widening and paving of the old "national road"("**camino nacional**") which transects the brickyard area and is a major traffic thoroughfare linking the **municipio** of Santa Lucía to downtown Oaxaca City (see Figure 3). See Appendix 3 for a statistical comparison of brick industry households with households in other craft industries.

2. "Brickyards in the Fields"

CHAPTER 2

BRICKYARDS IN THE FIELDS: THE SOCIAL
MATRIX OF PRODUCTION

Driving by day east from Oaxaca City on the Pan American highway one can often observe clouds of thick black smoke billowing skyward on both sides of the highway just beyond the city limits where the country-side begins. Sometimes the sources of this smoke are hidden from view but often they are clearly identi-fiable as kilns located in the midst of what looks like an ecological disaster zone. This gouged and cluttered landscape, upon closer examination, proves to be a labyrinth of clay pits interconnected by a network of paths and dirt roads which are plied by a constant traffic of flatbed trucks. Drivers on the highway, most without realizing it, are passing through the heartland of the Oaxaca Valley brick in-dustry. This is a zone encompassing several square ki-lometers both north and south of the highway within the territorial jurisdictions of Santa Lucía del Camino, San Agustín Yatareni, Santa Cruz Amilpas, San Sebastian Tutla and San Francisco Tutla.

The kiln-fired bricks produced in this industry have replaced sun-baked adobe bricks in urban con-struction thoughout the region; even though cement blocks and poured concrete are used in the regional construction industry this does not seem to have dam-pened the demand for hand-made, kiln-fired bricks. In recent years at least one major highly capitalized joint government and private venture into mechanized brick production collapsed. So, it appears that labor-intensive brick production is not in any immediate jeopardy from capital-intensive production. Its demise will ultimately have more to do with the supply of cheap labor than it does with the supply or the in-vestment of capital.[1]

From Peasant-Artisan to Peasant-Capitalist
Industry

There was agreement among my oldest informants that brickmaking has been practiced in Santa Lucía for generations but none had any precise idea of how far back its origins went. They all agreed, however, that in their lifetimes the industry had grown considerably and that the reason for this was the expansion of construction activity in Oaxaca City. Several of them

33

specifically noted that brick production expanded following severe earthquakes which destroyed buildings in the city. The oldest informant was 74 years old (and, incidentally, was still putting in a full day's work in the brickyards as a pieceworker at the time he was interviewed). When he entered the industry in 1925 at the age of 19, he recalled that there were eight brickyard operators and six kilns in Santa Lucia (which in the light of the census data for earlier in the century is probably a conservative estimate). He recollected that his starting wage was 50 **centavos** daily. Although he was unable to specify when the changeover to a piece rate occurred in the brickyards, he insisted that he had been paid at a piece rate per 1000 bricks produced for a very long time.[2]

A 63 year old informant said that he and other brickyard workers were paid a day wage of 75 centavos until 1955 when the piecework system was instituted at the insistence of the workers themselves. This story was not corroborated by any other informant, but is indirectly supported by a study done in the 1940s of the brick industry in Tlacolula de Matamoros (a district headquarters town located several miles east of Santa Lucia on the Pan American highway). This study indicates that brickyard workers were paid 75 **centavos** "for a workday which begins at 6:00 a.m. and lasts until 3:00 p.m." (Mendieta y Nuñez et.al. 1949:503). Another informant, who became a brickyard employer in 1945, insisted that he paid his workers on a piece rate basis from that date. Given the consensus that important changes began to occur in the industry after 1940 in terms of demand and transportation, it is reasonable to assume that brickyard employers would shift to the piece rate payment mode as a means for increasing productivity and profits.

The 74 year old informant remembered that in the early years of his brickyard career the demand for bricks was low and sporadic, and that **mileros** often went unpaid until bricks were sold. Another informant, referring to the 1940s when as a teenager he worked in his father's brickyard, had a similar recollection: "There weren't many sales, demand was low. We made bricks and piled them up. And then we couldn't work. One had to wait to see any money." Indeed, it was precisely this situation which led this informant to withdraw from brickmaking and seek other employment.

There was a consensus among informants that brickmaking has been practiced in conjunction with agriculture as far back as they can remember. Again to quote the 74 year old informant describing the situation in the industry when he entered it as a young man: "They did both things. In one place they opened a brickyard and in another they planted corn. Both bricks and corn were produced." In commenting on the low demand for bricks which obtained in the industry several decades ago, another informant observed that his father's household managed because there was sufficient land to cultivate. This complementarity between brickmaking and agriculture is still found today but is less prevalent than it once was. Market fluctuations, on the other hand, still plague the industry.

Prior to 1940 bricks were hauled from the village to the city in oxcarts. A cartful consisted of about 330 bricks. The increase in demand which began with a surge in construction activity in the city after 1940 coincided with the mechanization of brick hauling. There is disagreement among my informants as to the identity of the first truck owner in Santa Lucía, but most agree that trucks had replaced carts throughout the industry by 1945. The surge in brick sales and the subsequent growth of the industry is attributed to the construction of large buildings in downtown Oaxaca.

An informant who experienced this period of transition in the 1930s and 1940s recalled that when bricks from his father's yard were hauled to the city by oxcart that, "bricks were used only for decoration and that sales were low." "After 1935," he continued, "business picked up because people in the city began to construct brick houses, whereas before houses were made of adobe." His father was among the first Santa Lucians to buy a truck (cost 8,000 pesos) with cash raised through the sale of an ox team and two cows (2500 pesos as down payment with monthly payments of 500 pesos). By 1940 the price of bricks had risen to 50 pesos per thousand, **mileros** were paid 10 pesos per thousand, and the number of brickyards with kilns had grown to around twenty.[3]

One Santa Lucia informant recalled that his father and other brickyard operators initially began to pay workers a piece rate just to mold bricks, and that the clay preparation as well as the scraping and stacking was done by the operator. These original

35

piece rate brick molders were referred to as "destajeros". It was not until later--perhaps after the introduction of motor transportation and the increased demand for bricks from the city construction industry--that these employees began to perform all of the tasks in brick production and were paid per thousand bricks molded, scraped, and stacked. The term "milero" apparently gained currency under these circumstances.

The Industry Today

There is a marked contrast between a labor-intensive extractive and transformative industry like brick-making, which supplies a basic utilitarian product for the construction industry in Oaxaca City and elsewhere, and a labor-intensive transformative industry like weaving which supplies a basic luxury product for the tourist-oriented handicrafts market. This contrast is conveyed concretely by juxtaposing some of the things the two industries call to mind: picks, shovels, crowbars, pits, mud, kilns, smoke, fire, heat, bricks, storage sheds, and flatbed trucks , on the one hand, vs. skeins of thread, spinning wheels, spindles, looms, shuttles, and cloth, on the other. In essence, brickmaking evokes images of "heavy industry" (drudge work which transforms nature) whereas weaving evokes images of "light industry" (assembly work which alters raw materials but not nature itself).

This contrast may be carried further as a way of characterizing the uniqueness of the brick industry. If we follow the circulation of bricks from clay pit to kiln to consumer we are drawn into the guts of the Oaxaca valley's political economy, a location we bypass by following the circulatory routes of, for example, textile products. First, we must deal with a more crystallized and polarized class structure in the brick industry. Unlike weaving pieceworkers, the mileros comprise a true proletariat. They are landless and, since most of them are migrants, they are cut off from the social support infrastructure rooted in extended kinship networks. Also, the employer/employee relationship is more formalized in "class" terms in the brickyards than it is in the weaving workshops. This is so possibly because of the greater amount of start-up capital required in the brick industry which discourages the formation of new enterprises, as well as its greater dependency on outside labor. Second, in the brick industry we are confronted head-on with

36

powerful urban interests and a political-economic subterfuge involving millions of pesos in construction contracts which are up for grabs by politicians, bureaucrats, police, truck drivers, architects, construction bosses, and last but not least, the brick merchants themselves.

What this means is that the most successful entrepreneurs in the brick industry are those whose political contacts and generosity in the manipulation of kickback funds assure them of substantial shares in the brick traffic for urban construction projects. In other words, this is one of those cases where the appearance of small-scale industry yields to the reality of big-time money and interests.[4]

The Oaxaca Valley brick industry, comprised as it is of several community-based branches, is firmly rooted in local economies with their own specific conditions (e.g., land tenure and use patterns, cultural patterns, demography) which affect the industry's structure, functioning, and evolution. However, locally and regionally, it is also affected by forces external to it in the wider political-economic system. Not the least of these is the institutional strength of the private property and private enterprise regime in the national political economy, even if in a context of increasing statization with the significant presence of anti-privatistic, populist, and collectivist forces. Everything from employer-employee relations and credit to technical assistance and work organization, not to mention tax policies, in local small industries can be affected by decisions made in Mexico City.

For example, a decision made by the government to provide credit or technical assistance to brick producers through the **ejido** system could result in the demise of the Santa Lucía industry, which is primarily established on private lands, and the expansion of the Yatareni industry, which is established on **ejido** lands. Alternatively, the current labor and social security laws in Mexico could be locally enforced so that employers of pieceworkers would have to meet obligations such as providing safety equipment and various fringe benefits. The local enforcement of these laws would probably result in the radical transformation of the social organization of the industry, if not its demise (which might be possible given its complicated and fragile economics and if necessary accomodations between the government and the brickyard operators were not made).

Brickyard Social Categories and Statuses

Every person in Santa Lucia who is actively involved in the brick industry belongs to at least one of the following social categories: (1) family laborer (or in-kind laborer); (2) casual wage laborer not directly involved in brickmaking but in loading, hauling, or firing of bricks already made; (3) piece rate brickmakers (**mileros**) who are employed by brickyard (**ladrillera**) operators who may be owners (**dueños**) or renters (**arrendatarios**); (4) self-employed brickmakers (**ladrilleros por su cuenta**) who employ labor from their households as "owners" or "renters" of brickyards; (5) worker-employers (**ladrilleros patrones**) who rent or own the brickyard and who employ some combination of household and hired labor to make bricks; (6) employers (**patrones**) who own (or rent) one or more brickyards, regularly employ wage-laborers, and themselves perform mainly supervisory tasks; and (7) commercial intermediaries who buy bricks for resale and transport them on flatbed trucks to construction sites, and who are referred to interchangeably as businessmen (**comerciantes**), transporters (**transportistas**), or resellers (**revendedores**).

These categories cross-cut age, sex, and class position and encompass every dimension of the brick industry from clay extraction to the marketing of the final product. Men and women, young and old, rich and poor, regardless of the specific jobs they perform in the brick industry, fit into one or more of these non-mutually exclusive categories. The specification of an individual´s social category helps to understand the conditions and consequences of his participation in the industry. For example, **mileros** are more likely to regularly supplement their incomes by loading and unloading kilns and trucks for a wage, or by working as stokers, than are self-employed brickmakers or employers.

Since the household is the elementary social unit in Santa Lucia and functions also as the minimal economic unit for both labor and capital, it is appropriate to undertake an analysis of brick industry households according to the membership of their male heads in one of four mutually exclusive statuses. These are: (a) piece rate brickmaker who often depends

38

upon in-kind labor from other members of his household; (b) self-employed brickyard owner or renter using own or family labor only; (c) worker/employer using own, family, and/or hired labor; and (d) employer-operator who supervises workers.

Social and Economic Conditions of Brickyard Households

With the exception of one individual still going strong at the age of seventy-four, the pieceworkers and self-employed workers interviewed were generally younger than the employers. This age difference partly explains the larger mean family size among the employers, as well as their longer average period of involvement in the industry. Given the larger size of employer households (in comparison with non-employer households) it is not surprising that a larger proportion of them are extended. Extra-household ties, especially between patrilineally related males, often operate through inheritance to confer brickyard ownership as well as with regard to the use or ownership of kilns and trucks. In short, cooperation between members of the same household and between patrilineal kinsmen in different households is a basis for capital accumulation and enlargement of the scale of a brickmaking enterprise.

Data on birthplace confirm the validity of the label " avecindados" (new residents) which is regularly used by native Santa Lucians as a term of reference for brickyard proletarians. More than half of the latter were born and raised in outlying districts of the Central Valleys region or in more distant regions of the state. (During my first days in the brickyards I was surprised to meet two brothers from the Pacific coastal district of Pochutla, one of whom had been a fisherman, working as brickmakers.) However, on the basis of what was subsequently learned from several of the oldest informants, the brickyards have been a source of employment for migrants from the outlying regions since at least 1940.

It is also worth noting that brick making has spread to many villages throughout the Oaxaca valley and its mountain hinterland as a result of the efforts of returning migrants who applied the knowledge (and in some cases invested earnings) acquired by working in the Santa Lucía brickyards to start up new brickyards in their native communities. One such case was discovered in an isolated village some forty miles

39

from Santa Lucía in the mountains beyond the eastern end of the valley, and several others were found in the valley itself.

What has been the principal reason for the arrival in Santa Lucía of migrant laborers from other areas of Oaxaca? The majority of them, for one reason or other, enter the wage labor market as day laborers in agriculture or construction in Oaxaca City or its immediate rural environs, and by word of mouth learn of job opportunities in the brick industry. One **milero** from Zaachila who had worked for many years as a rural day laborer (**jornalero**) was told by his uncle living in Oaxaca City (who worked in the Santa Lucia brickyards) to start working with him there because the pay was better even though one had to pay for one's own food. Another **milero** from Sola de Vega who lived with relatives in a squatter's settlement near Oaxaca City and worked as a mason's helper (**peón de albañil**) in the urban construction industry explained that he came to work in the brick industry because he saw that it was work where one earned a decent wage.

In other words, the migration of labor into the brick industry is stimulated by the prospect of higher wages. An added incentive is the practice by employers of providing **mileros** and their families with rent-free (though rudimentary) living quarters in the brickyard. This practice has two distinct advantages for the employer. First, it provides him with a watchman and, second, it generally enhances the **milero's** productivity through the assistance of his wife, children or other dependents who, given the location of their living quarters in the brickyard, become a sort of captive labor force and perform various tasks in the process of producing unfired bricks. The specific economic significance of this family labor contribution will be examined in subsequent sections.

None of the brick industry men completed a high school education; and their average level of schooling is low. However, a higher percentage (45%) of the self-employed brickmakers and of the employers were able to finish elementary school than of the **mileros** (27%). On the other hand, one individual in each group had no formal schooling. The fact that the men who had more than six years schooling were born and raised in Santa Lucía is the only indicator of any educational advantage to residents derived from the community's proximity to Oaxaca City.

40

Employers are much more active in village civil and religious affairs than are the **mileros** and the self-employed brickmakers. Two factors, already mentioned, explain the inactivity in these areas of the latter two groups: (1) their relatively young age and (2) their immigrant status. Both of these factors operate to inhibit sufficient capital accumulation and the mobilization of support from kinship or reciprocity networks which are requisites for participation in these affairs. The **mileros´** participation in civic life is also inhibited by the fact that many of them reside in the brickyards which are located between the residential centers of Santa Lucia and of the neighboring village of Santa Cruz Amilpas (see Figure 3).

Given their residential isolation, the **mileros** and their families see themselves and are seen by other residents as occupying a status of second class citizens. This status, as pointed out earlier, is implicit in the reference to them by natives as "new residents." Finally, the fact that several employers have served in elected, executive civil posts and as sponsors of saint´s festivals (**mayordomías**) or in important church posts (i.e., the so-called "civil-religious hierarchy" or "cargo system") supports the thesis that these households represent the upper stratum in the local social economy (cf. Cook 1982a:82-4).

The larger average size of the employer households (see Table 2) does not translate into a significant difference between them and the **milero** households regarding the number of brickworkers per household. Likewise, the higher mean number of dependents per household for the employers in comparison with the **mileros** does not result in a lower consumer/worker ratio for the **milero** households--essentially because there are considerably more of them with only one paid worker in comparison with the employer households. This again reflects the fact that the employer households are older and, consequently, further along in the household developmental cycle (i.e., more adult or near-adult members--see Murphy and Selby 1981:255).[5]

The widespread landlessness of **milero** households places severe limits on their ability to engage in agriculture. By contrast, the employer households do, for the most part, have small amounts of arable which enable them to cultivate corn and other crops (e.g., alfalfa). However, only two of these households have capital invested in agricultural means of production

41

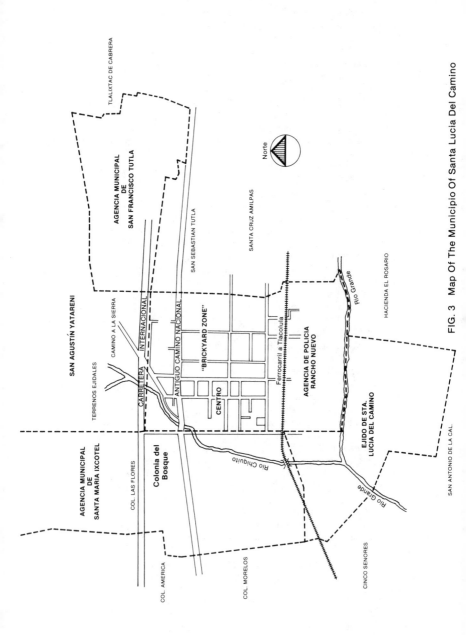

FIG. 3   Map Of The Municipio Of Santa Lucia Del Camino

42

TABLE 2. KEY ECONOMIC VARIABLES FOR 24 HEADS OF BRICK INDUSTRY HOUSEHOLDS IN SANTA LUCIA DEL CAMINO CLASSIFIED ACCORDING TO INDUSTRIAL ROLE CATEGORY.

Industrial Role Category	Case No.	1 Family Size	2 Family Type*	3 No. of Paid Working Family Members	4 No. of Family Brickworkers Besides Head	5 No. of Dependent Family Members	6 Consumer/Worker Ratio	7 Land Cultivated Seas.	8 Land Cultivated Watered	9 Tot.	10 Yrly. Rent Cost of Agric. Means of Prod.(pesos)	11 Yrly. Cost of Hired Agric. Labor (pesos)	12 Amt. of 1979 Harvest (Kgs.) Corn	13 Beans	14 No. of Mos. Corn Bought in 1979	15 Value of 1979 Cash Crop (pesos)	16 Total Value of Owned Animals (pesos)	17 Living Conditions Index
Employees (mileros)	1	8	N	1	4	7	8.0	0	0	0	0	0	0	300	12	0	11,300 (goats)	0
	2	7	E	3	1	4	2.3	0	0	0	0	0	0	0	12	0	0	4.0
	3	6	N	2	0	4	3.0	0	0.5	0.5	0	0	400	0	8	0	0	1.8
	4	5	N	1	0	4	5.0	1	0	1.0	0	0	0	0	12	0	2,500	2.0
	5	3	N	1	2	2	3.0	0	0	0	0	0	0	0	12	0	0	1.5
	6	6	N	1	4	5	6.0	0	0	0	0	0	0	0	12	0	0	
	7	5	N	1	3	4	5.0	0	0	0	0	0	0	0	12	0	0	
	8	3	N	1	3	2	3.0	2	0	0	0	0	0	0	0	0	1,500 (pigs)	3.0
	9	6	N	1	4	2	6.0	0	0	2.0	0	0	0	0	12	0	0	0
	10	7	N	1	3	6	7.0	0	0	0	0	0	0	0	0	500	0	0
	11	5	N	2	2	3	2.5	0	0	0	0	0	0	0	0	0	0	1.0
Self-Employed	12	12	E	5	3	7	2.4	1.0	0	1.0	2000	0	1000	0	2	250	900	5.0
	13	7	N	1	3	6	7.0	0	0	0	0	0	0	0	0	0	0	1.5
Worker-Owner Employers	14	13	E	3	7	10	1.5	0	0	0	0	0	0	0	12	0	0	3.0
	15	5	N	3	0	2	1.6	1.0	0	1.0	0	0	300	0	0	0	0	5.0
	16	6	N	2	2	5	6.0	0.5	0	0.5	1300	200	0	0	12	0	0	3.5
	17	5	E	4	1	1	1.3	0	2.0	2.0	4600	800	400	0	0	0	20,000	7.5
	18	13	E	1	1	12	4.3	0.5	0	0.5	2000	1000	300	10	4	0	5,800	10.0
Employer-Managers	19	6	N	1	3	5	1.0	1.0	0	1.0	800	N.D.	2000	300	12	N.D.	9,000	6.0
	20	12	E	3	2	9	4.0	1.0	1.0	2.0	2000	0	2500	0	N.D.	0	N.D.	N.D.
	21	4	N	3	2	1	1.3	0.8	0.3	1.1	3000	0	600	0	2	400	12,500	3.0
	22	6	N	2	2	4	1.2	4.0	1.5	5.5	6000	0	2500	0	3	0	2,300	6.5
	23	4	N	1	1	3	4.0	1.00	1.0	1.0	0	0	500	0	0	0	4,300	3.0
	24	11	N		0	10	11.0	0.8	0	0.8	2250	0	1500	0	7	0	4,800	6.5
Mean Employees (Nos. 1-11)		5.6		1.4	2.0	4.2	4.6	0.2	0.1	0.3	0	0	35.4	0	9.5	45.5	2,618	1.2
Mean Employers (Nos. 14-24)		7.7		2.1	1.8	5.6	3.4	1.0	0.4	1.4	1996	182	963.6	28.2	4.7	36.4	4,945	4.9

*N = Nuclear
 E = Extended

43

(e.g., oxen, plows, and carts). This suggests that most households are obliged to rent agricultural means of production. A handful of landed employer households employ some wage labor in their agricultural operations but most perform lighter agricultural tasks (e.g., weeding, cutting alfalfa, harvesting corn, planting) themselves.

The impact of agricultural involvement is shown by the fact that the employer households entered the market as corn buyers for substantially shorter periods in 1979 than did the **milero** households. Regarding animal raising, ownership of animals is more common among the employer households (80% of reporting households) than it is among the **milero** households (27%), a pattern which reflects the greater capacity of the former, because of their agricultural involvement, to provide fodder for animals. The agricultural involvement of these households is focussed more on the growing of alfalfa on irrigated land, for use primarily as fodder for animals (especially pigs and cows), than it is on planting corn, beans, and squash by the extensive, dry farming methods so prevalent in other areas of the Oaxaca Valley. What is striking, in retrospect, is not the small amount of land under cultivation by these households but, given Santa Lucía's location on the periphery of Oaxaca City, that they are involved in agriculture at all.

Last but not least, a Living Conditions Index (Table 2, col.17) was designed to give some approximation of the level of material well-being achieved by brick industry households. It was formulated by assigning different numerical values to contrasting house types (e.g., thatch, adobe, or masonry construction), types of house flooring (i.e., dirt, tile, or concrete), number of rooms, tenure status of the residence lot and of the residence itself (e.g., owned, rented, or borrowed), and possession or non-possession of a television set (which is a more accurate status indicator than the radio) for each household. The assigned values were then summed to arrive at an overall index value.

The fact that the mean of this variable is four and one half times as high for the employers as it is for the **mileros** is significant, and does accurately reflect the substantially greater affluence and higher standard of living enjoyed by the employer households. Reported income data confirm this difference between

44

the two groups. The mean weekly income(household head only) computed from informant estimates for the employers was approximately 90 dollars compared with 48 dollars for the **mileros**. These figures are in line with the mean total household income reported for the week immediately preceding our census which was 46 dollars for the **milero** households and 84 dollars for the employer households.

The Development of Family Brickyard Enterprises: Case Studies

Considering that most of the brickyard employers interviewed were born and raised in Santa Lucía, it is surprising that only Antonio and Ricardo came into the occupation--and the land on which their brickyards are currently operating--by inheritance. Most of the others grew up in landed peasant households with full-time agriculturist fathers. (The same is also true of one-third of the workers.) The employers had spent an average of 12 consecutive adult years in the brick industry (vs. 9.7 for the employed workers), and their mean age was a relatively high 48 years. In essence, the picture that emerges is one of diverse occupational histories with shifting fortunes but showing a trend toward increasing affluence and material success after brickmaking becomes their principal source of livelihood.

In some cases an early experience in the brickyards was interrupted by a series of other occupational experiences both within and beyond the bounds of the village division of labor. In others current involvement in the brick industry reflects either a progressive, though prolonged, passage through a series of stages in the development of the domestic enterprise or an abrupt, opportunistic entry into the industry at a fairly high level of commitment of time and capital.

These different trajectories can be documented through some case studies. The careers of Gilberto and Antonio exemplify the "interrupted" pattern of involvement in the industry. Coincidentally, as will be described, both of these individuals have experienced fluctuating fortunes involving, among other things, problems with the law.

45

The Atypical, Interrupted Career Trajectory:
Two Cases

Gilberto. Gilberto was born and raised in Rancho Nuevo where agriculture and animal husbandry were the predominant modes of livelihood. He described this earlier period of his life as follows: "... we had everything. We harvested beans, corn, chickpeas-- everything came into the house...to maintain us...We sold corn to buy clothing or whatever we needed. We had no other work." After his father died, Gilberto continued for a time working in agriculture and also began to learn brickmaking in Santa Lucia though he never became a bonafide brickmaker. Then he decided to leave the village and was able to get a position with the state police (**Policía Judicial del Estado**), an experience which turned out badly for him. He was involved in a case of "abuse of police authority", was tried, convicted and spent more than two years in the state penitentiary. He came out of the penitentiary with a new occupation learned behind its walls, basketmaking, which he pursued in combination with agriculture upon his return to the village.

Six years prior to the interview with Gilberto in 1980, he quit making baskets and took up brickmaking through the influence of a younger brother who was a **milero** in one of the major Santa Lucia brickyards. During the next five years, prior to his acquisition in 1979 of the brickyard where he currently works, Gilberto worked as a part-time **milero**, loader (and unloader) of kilns and trucks, and stoker with five different employers; also, he continued to cultivate his own agricultural parcels. One year prior to my interview with him, Gilberto made a decision to sell his remaining agricultural means of production (e.g., his ox team) and bought a brickyard. For several reasons, including his reputed propensity to overin- dulge in alcoholic beverages and a flood in the zone where his arable was located, he sold off his land holdings. He now refers to this sale regretfully as "that foolishness of selling my land cheap" primarily because, as a consequence of the sale, he lost the ability to directly produce part of his household´s food supply. As he expressed it:

> Working the land one doesn´t suffer for
> anything because everything comes to
> the house: beans, corn, chickpeas. So
> one doesn´t have to buy these. When

46

> some extra cash is needed you sell one,
> two or three bags of corn.

Even though his statements seem to belie this,
Gilberto insisted that he was not repentant for the
depeasantization in which he was a willing partici-
pant. But this seems to reflect his fatalistic acceptance of the irreversible nature of his move into the
brick industry, rather than his confidence or optimism
about the future. A major reason for his regret about
past decisions and for his pessimism about the future,
aside from the large family he has to support (though
the fact that he has six sons between the ages of
three and twenty-one assures him a labor supply over
the next decade and beyond), was his inability at the
time of his liquidation of his agricultural assets to
rent a kiln for firing the bricks he produced. It is
clear that he made the move because he felt that he
could earn more money in the brickyards than he could
in agriculture. Gilberto has subsequently not been
able to further capitalize his brickmaking enterprise.
Not being able to raise enough operating capital to
enable him to fire the bricks he produces, he operates
by selling unfired bricks to larger producers who have
kilns.

Antonio. The case of Antonio is more complex than
Gilberto's. His career began with a background in
agriculture and brick making, moved through a series
of intervening occupational experiences, and then
involved a return to brick making in combination with
agriculture.

Antonio's career in the brickyards began at the
age of five when his father gave him various light
tasks like scraping and stacking bricks. He began
within a few years to make fifty bricks a day and
progressed by stages to reach a daily output of three
hundred. By that time he was in his early teens and
had reversed roles with his father who was, by then,
helping Antonio rather than vice-versa. He described
the division of tasks between his father, himself and
his three brothers as follows:

> Some of my brothers went with my father
> to the fields while others of us
> remained in the brickyard. When there
> was a lot of work in the fields, like
> stripping leaves from the corn stalks,
> all of us would go to help. The rest of

the time, some of us would go with my
father to the fields and others would
work in the brickyard.

As the second oldest brother of the family, Antonio was expected to work to help finance the education of two younger brothers. He became fed up with
the brickyard routine by the time he was eighteen and
took an opportunity to learn to drive and to get a job
as a trucker in the nearby city. This job lasted for
ten years. In 1958, married and with one son, he left
Oaxaca for Mexico City to find a better paying job.
His first job in Mexico City was as a newspaper vendor. After 1-1/2 years he got a job in a pencil factory where he worked for eight years, first as a me-
chanic's assistant and then as a boilerman. He also
established and ran a snack business at the factory
for his co-workers. The factory was sold and his
seniority was lost under the new management so in 1968
he decided to return to Santa Lucía.

Antonio's first job after returning was as a
truck driver and route salesman for a bottled water
company in Oaxaca City. He quit this job after two
years when he decided to lease-out a parcel of arable
he had inherited from his father. With the proceeds
from the sale of the lease, he made a down payment on
a used flat-bed truck. Thus he embarked on a career as
a brick hauler and reseller which was to last for four
years.

Much to his regret, in 1970 Antonio was elected
to the office of municipal president. He explains how
his involvement in local politics helped his fledgling
brick hauling business as follows:

> When I was president some good oppor-
> tunities came my way. I not only hauled
> bricks but I also resold them. Since I
> was born and raised here many people
> had confidence in me. I didn't have any
> capital but I would stop at the kilns
> in my truck and tell the producers
> that I had arranged a contract in the
> city of 25,000 bricks. Then I would
> make them a pitch: "I'll take your
> bricks and when the contractors pay me
> I'll pay you." As I said, I didn't have
> any capital but I did have the possi-
> bility of supplying orders. So with the

bricks I hauled I earned my hauling fee
plus an additional profit. In that way
I began climbing rapidly. I was lucky.

Antonio emphasized that his business success
derived from his use of the prestige of the municipal
presidency and of his knowledge of the brick industry.
He bought and sold only prime quality bricks and built
a steady clientele among building contractors in the
city. He explains how his success led to his acquisition of a second flat-bed truck:

> Some gypsies offered me a Chevrolet for
> 6000 pesos. I took money that I had
> earned from the bricks which the pro-
> ducers had consigned to me. Then I
> would tell them: "Look, the contractors
> still haven't paid me the full amount
> they owe for the bricks so all that I
> can give you now is a partial payment."
> But, in reality, I had all of the con-
> tractors' money in my hands so I was
> able to pay cash to the second truck
> which I knew would help me make more
> money to pay off the producers. So I
> started to work both trucks; we'd load
> up one and then the other. We hauled
> lots of bricks.

Within a year of the purchase of his second truck
he purchased a third truck in the same way:

> By taking money from others because I
> didn't have any of my own. One guy
> would consign to me his entire firing
> of bricks; I would take his and those
> of many others. I would owe 1500 pesos
> to one, 1000 to another, 2000 to a
> third, and so on. I would explain to
> them: "Within two weeks I'll get your
> money to you." I had already calculated
> that I'd pay one back first, then an-
> other, and then the third and so on.

But the burdens of local political office began
to take their toll. Antonio had to hire drivers and
helpers as his business grew. But the burdens of
office gave him less and less time to devote to the
business and he lost direct contact with his clients.
His clientele began to dry up. Near the end of his

term he sold one of his trucks, called in a lease on his land, and (for the first time since he was 18) began making bricks himself. Then he became embroiled in a controversy regarding his handling of a local school construction project. He was accused of illegally expropriating land from a private owner for constructing the school, was sued, and ended up in prison for a two-day stint. He had to sell another of his trucks to meet his bail and legal expenses.

Antonio came out of this situation essentially broke and humiliated; he was faced with the necessity of starting from scratch in the brickyard to earn his livelihood. As he put it:

> To raise myself up again in the brick business, since I was broke, I started making bricks myself. My wife and children came to haul the clay and to scrape and stack the bricks, although sometimes I worked alone. We completed the first kiln-load, loaded the kiln; then I asked the guy who sells sawdust to advance me a load so that I could fire up the kiln. I told him that I'd repay him as soon as the bricks were sold. He agreed. Afterwards I paid him in bricks since I didn't have any money. It took us three years working that way to raise ourselves up again.

He did recover sufficiently to put his eldest son through law school and to support his second son in medical school, though both of his sons worked in the brickyards whenever their schedules permitted. The last time this family was visited they were together in the brickyard; Antonio, his wife, his medical student son, and his two teenage daughters were working diligently as a coordinated team to load the kiln.

The Typical, Uninterrupted Career Trajectory: Four Cases

While the cases of Gilberto and Antonio provide dramatic illustrations of the fluctuating tides of fortune in the careers of some brickmakers, the more typical pattern of development may be represented in the cases of Porfirio, Hermilo, three brothers (Raymundo, Juan, Rodolfo), and Máximo. Their occupational backgrounds are somewhat more prosaic and traditional, if still involving diverse experiences, and their careers in the brick industry evidence slow, systematic, and steady progress in expanding the scale and productivity of their enterprises. In other words, a scrutiny of their career trajectories should disclose a developmental cycle for the family brickyard—one which is unilineal and progressive regarding scale and capitalization (even though all units do not pass through each of the stages).

Porfirio. The case of Porfirio spans a 17-year period and passes through all of the principal stages in the developmental cycle. Aside from its exemplary status, it is also illustrative of a pattern of residential and socioeconomic mobility which, I believe, is no longer realizable to the degree that it was in the past. Porfirio was born and raised in a traditional Zapotec peasant village located a few miles to the southeast of Santa Lucía in the district of Tlacolula. His father, a landless agricultural proletarian, died when Porfirio was nine and his destitute mother placed him in the care of a better-off peasant family. He earned his keep by tending animals and later, in his teens, by working as a field hand.

At the age of 19 Porfirio left the employ of his village **patrón** and got work on a highway construction crew where he earned five times the daily wage that he had been paid in the village. He worked on highway construction for about a year and then returned to his mother's house in the village where he took up basketmaking. This occupation was thriving there under the influence of an American expatriate who had established an export business specializing in reed baskets produced by hundreds of peasant households throughout the Oaxaca valley. Porfirio married a local woman and worked on a piece rate basis for this American merchant for the next fifteen years. In his words: "I made all kinds of baskets. I made baskets for the United States. I even made baskets for dogs to sleep in."

During those years Porfirio also acquired a second occupation as a butcher. Then in 1960, as a result of political factionalism and violence in his village (which is endemic in that section of the valley), he accepted an invitation from his **comadre** (ritual coparent) to move to Santa Lucía. He describes that troubled period as follows:

> I never liked trouble and I left my
> village because it was divided into two
> camps. They wanted me to join sides. I
> didn't have any reason to arm myself
> because I didn't have enemies. But I
> decided to get away from people who
> were troublemakers. I came to visit my
> **comadre** and she encouraged me to stay
> here and let the troublemakers stew in
> their own juice.

He worked at his two trades, basketry and butchering,
in his adopted village but his sons soon started to
work in the brickyards and they convinced him to try
it out.

Porfirio worked with his sons as a **milero** in a
Santa Lucia brickyard for five years but then decided
to pay the owner of a clay pit (**barranca**) for the clay
extracted per 1000 bricks--an arrangement known as
"**comprar tierra**." He rented a kiln, fired the bricks
and sold them directly to the clients who arrived.
Porfirio worked on this basis for three years. Next he
leased an abandoned clay pit from the widow of a
deceased brickmaker, put it back into operation, built
his own kiln on the leased property, and became a de
facto brickyard operator. At the end of his three-year
lease term he was presented with an opportunity to buy
a parcel of land suitable for establishing a brickyard; he bought it outright for 25,000 pesos which he
obtained by making a secured loan at a Oaxaca City
bank through the good offices of his ex-employer, the
American basket merchant. With hired hands and his
remaining sons (his oldest sons had migrated to Mexico
City), Porfirio dug a clay pit, constructed a kiln and
began operating his own brickyard. He repaid his bank
loan in two years and immediately applied for another,
this time for 50,000 pesos to enable him to buy a used
flatbed truck for hauling bricks.

Porfirio still makes an effort to grow subsistence crops on a small parcel (.5 ha.) of arable and
admits to liking agricultural work, especially because
it helps to cut down food and fodder expenses. Nevertheless, he considers brickmaking to be a less risky
and more profitable occupation. He emphasized that
bricks which are not sold one day can be sold the next
and noted that, "working as a peasant...a bad season
comes along with no harvest and one loses the money
invested."

Hermilo. Hermilo, as a native born Santa Lucian, has been involved in the brick industry since his late teens when he started working as a **milero**. He combined this with agricultural work over a period of twenty years until he began to "buy clay" from landowners and to fire his bricks in a rented kiln. About fifteen years ago he bought a brickyard (without a kiln) with money accumulated from the sale of several farm animals (including two ox teams), a decision triggered by the fact that he had four sons to work in the brickyard alongside him. Five years later he built his own kiln. Then a few years ago his eldest son bought a used flatbed truck and began to haul bricks in a joint venture with Hermilo. (A 1978 highway accident deprived Hermilo of his son and the truck but his brickyard has remained productive.)

Three brothers: Raymundo, Juan, Rodolfo. The next case involves three brothers—Raymundo, Juan, and Rodolfo—who, like Gilberto, were born and raised in **Rancho Nuevo** and who started working in the brickyards as **mileros** in their early teens (their father had died when they were young). They worked for several different employers. In 1977 a brickyard owner offered them the opportunity of working with him on a share (**a medias**) basis. As one of them expressed it: "The boss supplied everything. We supplied the labor and we got half of the output." By 1979, with saved earnings from this share operation and with additional cash raised from the sale of some farm animals, they made a down payment on a brickyard (with kiln). Within a year they were able to pay off the balance owed on the brickyard and with saved earnings, together with cash raised through the sale of a plot of arable inherited from their father, they made a forty thousand peso down payment on a used flatbed truck which Rodolfo operates full-time to haul his brothers´ bricks and to haul for hire.

Máximo. Máximo, the last of the cases to be considered, was born and raised in Santa Lucía in a peasant family. He had only sporadic experience in the brickyards until around 1970 (three years after marrying) when he decided to enter the industry through the "clay buying" arrangement. Like Porfirio he fired his bricks in a rented kiln. Máximo explained his decision to become a brickmaker as follows: "We couln´t get by on agricultural work. I began to make bricks to help meet household expenses." The "clay buying" arrangement worked as follows:

53

> They sold clay to me by the thousand.
> From my earnings I had to pay for the
> clay, for hauling the bricks to the
> kiln, for the firewood, and for the
> kiln. I had to save up and I had to do
> the work myself in order to make ends
> meet. I began to work little by little.
> It took me two or three months to make
> enough bricks for a firing. I saved
> money by doing everything myself. I
> took out a little to live on but saved
> the rest. The corn that I always had in
> the house helped too.

As this statement indicates Máximo took up brickmaking
as a supplement to agriculture; the viability of his
brickmaking operation, at first, depended upon the
success of his agricultural activities. Within three
years after entering the brick industry, he had accumulated sufficient savings from brick earnings and
animal sales to enable him to buy a piece of land
suitable for establishing a brickyard. He subsequently
built his own kiln . Máximo's children were too young
to be of much help in the brickyard or in agriculture,
so he often employed hired help.

Summary of the four typical cases. This completes
a brief review of four cases of gradual, progressive,
phased development of brickmaking enterprises by individuals from peasant backgrounds whose involvement in
the industry began either in wage labor, share
production, or some form of rent arrangement, and
gradually evolved into full-fledged proprietorship and
employer status. In three of the four cases, capital
accumulation was accomplished through the sale of farm
animals; and in all four cases work in the brickyard
was combined with agricultural work.

Newcomers to the Employer Ranks

The cases of Marcelino, Guadalupe, and Artemio
illustrate the pattern of abrupt, opportunistic entry,
at the level of proprietor-employer, into the brick
industry by individuals with no prior history in it.
These cases are different from the others because of
their relative brief period of involvement in the
industry (two-four years), as well as in the fact that
their entry was at the level of owner-employer. This
means that, from the beginning, the success or failure
of their brickyards rested heavily on hired labor.

54

Marcelino, alone among the three, works full-time and employs only part-time help in his brickyard. Guadalupe supervises the work of his two sons and of two **mileros**; and Artemio, who like Guadalupe is not himself a brickmaker, supervises the work of his **mileros** (he has no children). Guadalupe, who first entered the industry at the age of fifty-eight after spending most of his working life in the mining industry, is the only one of these three who has invested in a flatbed truck (which is driven by one of his sons).

Summary of Employer Career Trajectories

Given this review of several cases of the development of owner-employer units, how can the process and its significance for the organization of production in the brick industry be summarized? One point which bears emphasizing is that the statuses of self-employed and of owner-employer have been achieved, in a majority of cases, through hard work and experience in the industry from the ground up. For the most part, today's owners and employers were yesterday's pieceworkers and, in several cases, as natives of the municipality they have been around the brickyards since childhood. It must be kept in mind, however, that most of these men have had a variety of work experiences outside of the brick industry, and that several of them either came to it relatively late or returned to it after substantial experiences in other lines of work.

Another point is that, although no single, sequential line of development has been followed by all of these units, most of them have evolved through a stepwise process. First, there was the acquisition of private ownership or use rights over the land (or a brickyard). Next came the construction of a kiln. Last but not least, was the acquisition of a flat-bed truck. The combination of brickyard, kiln, and flat-bed truck is the most productive and profitable type of enterprise in the industry. Of course, not all units achieve this level of integration. Its achievement requires the presence of several conditions (assuming motivation, health, and luck to be equal) including inputs from agriculture to household subsistence or capital accumulation, labor inputs from nuclear or extended family, and the willingness and ability to obtain outside financing (e.g., loans from credit institutions).

NOTES

[1] In their survey of brick manufacturing in the Third World Keddie and Cleghorn conclude that, "Over a wide range of developing country circumstances, the least-cost brickmaking techniques are found to be generally labour-intensive, and to have low investment costs" (1980:4). They further note that, "Some exceptions to this tendency are found under a high wage regime for labour, notably at larger scales of output; but only in the earlier stages of the process do the more highly mechanised techniques appear to be competitive, even in those conditions, with manual labor" (ibid.).

[2] For expository convenience and precision I will use the Spanish term **milero** to refer to an employed brickmaker who is paid a weekly wage calculated on the basis of a rate set per thousand bricks molded, sun-dried, and stacked. The literal meaning of this term is roughly "maker of a thousand" and it is the term most commonly used in the brickyards to refer to employed brickmakers. Other terms used more or less synonymously are **destajero** or **destajista** which mean "pieceworker", and **ladrillero** which is a cover term for brick producer and does not distinguish between employer and employee in the brickyards.

[3] There is a general consensus among historians and architects in Oaxaca with whom I have talked that fired bricks were used in building construction in Oaxaca by the Spanish in the sixteenth century. Castañeda Guzman, a leading Oaxaca historian, told me that he had found references to the existence of brick production during the colonial period in the **barrio** of Xochimilco, which is usually associated in the literature with spinning and weaving. Neither he nor other historians have found references to brick production in Santa Lucía del Camino during the colonial period. Nor are there references to brick production in the papers of the Mimiaga y Camacho family (who owned the Rosario hacienda for several decades until the Agrarian Reform) which would confirm the opinion expressed by some informants that brick production originated in Santa Lucía to meet the needs of the hacienda.

Aside from the increasing size and height of buildings, another reason for the trend toward the substitution of kiln-fired for adobe blocks in city construction was a growing concern to make buildings as durable and earthquake resistant as possible. Architects in Oaxaca agree that, whereas some bricks were used in colonial construction projects in Oaxaca City, bricks were much more widely used after 1900. All agree that after the 1931 earthquake bricks became even more popular as a construction material.

[4] I should point out that, for obvious reasons, I have no hard data to support this generalization regarding kickbacks. This is an educated guess based on insinuations by informants and inferences from what was implied, but not directly stated, by some informants. Also, such practices are "rumored" to exist--especially with regard to lucrative government contracts (e.g., public housing, school construction).

[5] For all of the 998 households surveyed by the project there is a regular tendency for increases in agricultural means of production to be accompanied by increased family size (Cook 1984c). This type of relationship raises the problem of ascertaining whether family size is a relatively independent variable, in which case Chayanov's (1966) approach becomes applicable, or whether it is a function of other factors. If the latter is the case, more family members per household will be a function of pre-existing economic means for their support. This line of argument essentially contends that some households are larger because they are more affluent in contrast to the Chayanovian thesis that their greater affluence is a function of their larger size.

A principal finding for all groupings of households in the Oaxaca valley is that larger families bring more material advantages than disadvantages in the labor-intensive regional economy, although the consumer/worker ratio at early stages of the household developmental cycle (see Medick 1976) seems to reduce the favorable balance. Unpaid family labor makes a very significant contribution to income among the households in our survey, especially in households with five or more members where it accounts for roughly one-third of all labor performed. It is plausible to infer from this that factors which increase the level of material well-being of households also contribute to their capacity for capital accumulation.

3. Brickyard Activities
   above: kneading clay
   rt. upper: unloading sawdust
             at kiln side
   rt. lower: molding bricks

CHAPTER 3

THE LABOR PROCESS OF BRICK PRODUCTION:
ITS FORMS, DYNAMICS, AND RESULTS

In its initial stage the labor process of brickmaking belongs to the extractive industries along with quarrying and mining. Like these activities, and unlike agriculture, it consumes the land by transforming it into raw materials. Whereas agriculture tends to participate in or manipulate the ecosystem--and uses land as a means to enter and alter it--industries essentially disrupt the ecosystem and have no inherent interest in manipulating it. Agriculture may cause ecological transformation, and may even damage the land when badly practiced, but its effects are rarely as drastic as those wrought by the extractive industries which literally destroy nonrenewable land resources. Nevertheless, in Santa Lucía agriculture and brickmaking are practiced in juxtaposition and, ultimately, are complementary both ecologically and economically rather than mutually opposed as they appear to be.[1]

Having noted this complementarity, the larger truth is that the labor process of brickmaking creates real contradictions which are directly visible to all observers. On the one hand, the land is irreversibly altered by the process. This is reflected in the gouged landscape created by clay extraction. Yet, there is also a transformation and reordering of the land which results from this destructive intervention of human labor. The geometric symmetry of the brick stacks, of the kilns, of the bricks laid out to dry on the patio, and the almost manicured smoothness and cleanliness of the latter, attest to the creative, constructive, and organized force of human labor-power. The brick industry, in essence, provides an excellent example of the contradictoriness of the labor process in the Oaxaca valley economy.

Although Santa Lucía is located near Oaxaca City and is partially urbanized, the self-employed and employer households remain involved in agricultural production. This is not surprising when one considers that the primary natural resource in the brick industry is land--or, more specifically, a particular type of clay soil which is the basic raw material for brick fabrication. The typical brickyard lies on flat arable land so that its downward and lateral expansion occurs

59

at the expense of the arable topsoil which, in effect, is consumed through the process of developing and working a clay pit (**barranca**).

The land is permanently pitted by the extraction of clay, but it is not permanently removed from the agricultural ecosystem. As it turns out the lower limit of excavation is set by the water table. At a point a few feet above the latter (which varies from 15 to 30 feet below the topsoil depending upon the exact location of the excavation) clay extraction ceases and the remaining soil (which is often irrigable) is recycled back into agricultural production (usually planted in alfalfa). Ironically, the now humid parcel is often more productive agriculturally than it was under seasonal, rainfall cultivation before it was excavated.[2]

A combination of ecological and economic factors determine land use patterns in Santa Lucía. The brickyard zone is confined to an area of seasonal or rainfall arable (**temporal**) with poor topsoil for agriculture but having soil with a high clay content. Economically, it seems that this land is more productive as a source of raw material for brickmaking than it is when planted with seasonal crops such as corn or castor beans. It is also possible for a given parcel of land to support a dual pattern of land use, with one portion converted into a brick yard and the remainder cultivated on a seasonal or year-round basis usually through well irrigation. Under these circumstances there is the possibility for complementarity rather than conflict in the two land use patterns on any given parcel, at least for several years.

Indeed, the juxtaposition of extensive seasonal or irrigation agriculture with year round clay extraction on the same parcel is quite common. However, there are significant areas of unutilized land (**baldio**) within the brickyard zone. This is mostly comprised of land which has been earmarked for future development of brickyards; it also includes land which has already been used for brick production but has not been recycled back into the agricultural ecosystem.[3]

Figure 4 shows the layout of a typical brickyard (**ladrillera**) located on a parcel of agricultural land. First it should be noted that the parcel covers fifteen thousand square meters with approximately five thousand square meters (one-third of the total surface

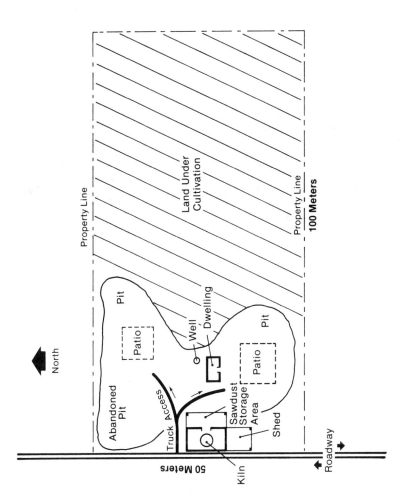

FIG. 4   Layout Of A Typical Agricultural Parcel With A Brickyard (Ladrillera) — Sta. Lucia Del Camino.

61

area) occupied by the brickyard and the rest by arable under extensive seasonal cultivation. This brickyard, together with its kiln (**horno**) and fired-brick storage shed (**galera**), is strategically positioned on one end of the land parcel along a road running north-south which sets the parcel's western boundary. The location of the kiln and brick storage shed along the road is standard throughout the industry since it facilitates the unloading of sawdust which is the principal fuel, as well as the loading of fired bricks. Many brick-yards also have clay pits and work patios (i.e., flat, smooth area where bricks are molded and laid out to dry in the sun) which may be located some distance away from main roads but are always accessible by truck paths so that unfired bricks can be hauled to the kiln.[4]

One **milero** defined the clay pit succinctly as the place within a brickyard where one "digs up earth and makes clay", and the patio as the place where "one cuts and lays out bricks." So, the brickyard is mini-mally comprised of a clay pit and a patio but its most complete form also includes a kiln and a storage shed. It should be noted that the patio, in some brickyards, is located on ground level above and outside of the clay pit, so that the excavation of the latter may actually eat away the patio and make it necessary for the brickmaker to prepare a new one. As shown in the diagram, a typical brickyard has several clay pits and patios where separate production units work, as well as abandoned or exhausted clay pits. Likewise, it is common for a brickyard to have at least one shanty for a resident **milero** family and a well to supply water for the preparation of clay and for human consumption.

Another important element of the ecology and so-cial geography of the brickyards is illustrated in this diagram, namely, that the limits on lateral ex-pansion of clay extraction are socially determined by property lines, in addition to being ecologically determined, both laterally and downward, by the water table and by soil quality and texture. The brickyard diagrammed in Figure 4 has expanded laterally to its social limits on its northern, southern, and western sides and can expand eastward only at the expense of the arable. I might also point out with regard to property lines that one source of ill-will among brickyard owners is the question of right of ways. Some brickyard owners whose property does not have an outlet to a public thoroughfare are often requested to pay right of way fees to property owners whose land must be crossed by trucks which haul bricks from the kiln or bring loads of sawdust.

Although it was not possible to make a systematic study of the ecology of the brickyard as it relates to the economics of production, it is clear that the industry depends upon the extraction of an exhaustible or non-renewable resource, the supply of which within the community's territorial jurisdiction is fixed and non-expandable. It is also clear that many land parcels of the kind shown in Figure 4 have been exploited to their limits, and are either overgrown with weeds and grass or have been planted in alfalfa. Even though the industry has experienced intensive growth since 1930 with irreversible and shocking effects on the rural landscape, it has a sufficient unused supply of soil to sustain its output at current levels for several decades--perhaps beyond the time that the technology and economics of the construction industry will make it feasible or necessary.

From Raw Clay to Sun-dried Bricks

On any given day during the year (weather conditions permitting), bricks are made, though much of the activity is hidden from the casual ground-level observer who does not venture off the roads. This is true for two reasons: first, many of the brickyards are located away from the roads, are hidden behind thickets or stands of reeds (**carrizo**), and can be reached only by following truck or foot paths; and, second, much of the observable activity (especially that related to the extraction and preparation of the clay) occurs below ground level in open pits. In other words, the would-be observer must look downward as he walks along to see clay pit activity and must descend by path or ladder to get close to the workers.

What are the nature and order of operations in the labor process of unfired brick production, the stages in the transformation of clay to bricks, and the tools and equipment required (see Table 3)? The tool kit is typical for labor-intensive, earth moving and transforming industries: the shovel is the only tool which appears throughout the sequence, closely followed by the bucket; equally important at particular steps in the sequence are the crowbar or pinchbar (**barreta**), the pick (**talache** or **zapapico**), wooden brick molds (**marcas**) and the scraper (**raspador**). Ap-

63

TABLE 3. LABOR PROCESS OF BRICK PRODUCTION

	EXTRACTION OF RAW CLAY	PREPARATION OF THE CLAY		FABRICATION OF BRICKS		
	1. Pry, dig and scoop soil from the walls and floor of the excavation ("Tumbar y quebrar la tierra del banco o paderón y del piso o suela de la barranca"); sift gravel from clay (if soil rocky)	2. Make the clay paste ("Hacer el barro") A. Wet the loosely piled raw clay to form a thick muddy paste ("Mojar la tierra para hacer el barro") B. Mix the clay paste; stir or turn over the muddy paste repetitively to insure that it is uniformly wet; remove rocks and debris ("Voltear el barro")	3. Knead the clay paste ("Componer, amasar or manotear el barro") Work the clay mass into a smooth, uniform mixture; add some water and sawdust and remove remaining gravel and debris; must be done immediately prior to molding bricks.	4. Prepare the brickyard floor ("Hacer el patio") Wet lightly with water, then sprinkle sand and smooth it out (spread it) with raspador ("arena")	5. Mold bricks ("Hacer ladrillos")	6. Scrape and stack sun-dried bricks ("Raspar y encadenar")
NATURE AND ORDER OF OPERATIONS						
TOOLS AND EQUIPMENT REQUIRED	crowbar (barreta), pick, (zapapico), shovel (pala), sifter (criva)	well (pozo), bucket (cubeta) / shovel (pala)	shovel, bucket, crowbar	metal scraper (raspador) sand (arena)	molds (marcos) 2.0 liter tin cans (botes) shovel; shallow tub (tinaja)	metal scraper (raspador) plastic cover
STAGES IN MATERIAL TRANSFORMATION	Native clay soil in ground is extracted by excavation	From "barro crudo" to "barro amasado" or "compuesto" (loosened clay soil is watered, cleaned of gravel and debris, and piled into mound of 'clay mud')	From "barro crudo" to "barro amasado" or "compuesto" (loosened clay soil is watered, cleaned of gravel and debris, kneaded with sawdust)	From kneaded clay to molded, sun-dried, unfired bricks ("ladrillos crudos")		
WORK ORGANIZATION	individual or cooperative male (rarely female)	individual or cooperative male (occasionally female)	individual (usually male, sometimes female)	individual male (sometimes female)	individual male (rarely female)	usually cooperative, both sexes, all ages
DURATION OF OPERATION	Range between 1 3/4 – 6 1/3 hours depending upon work organization and upon prevailing pit and soil conditions (e.g., gravel content, wetness)--Mean = 4.7 hours for extraction and preparation of the clay			Mean ¾ hour	Mean 4 3/4 hours	Mean 72 min.
AMOUNT OF SOCIAL WORK IN HOURS OF 'COOPERATIVE' LABOR TIME	4.7 hours x 1.4 (mean of the means of combined individual and cooperative labor expended in extraction and preparation of clay for 291 events reported by informants) = 6.58 hours			.25 hour + 4.75 hour + 2.64 hour = 7.64 hours for fabrication (mean of the means of combined x 1.8 individual and cooperative labor = 13.75 individual and cooperative labor expended in brick fabrication for 319 events reported by informants)		

6.58 + 13.75 **hours of cooperative labor time** to produce average output of 497 unfired bricks

parently it was not until around 1950 that the tool kit assumed its present form. The major changes were the replacement of straight hoe (**coa**) by the crowbar and the pickaxe for extracting clay, and the replacement of clay pots (**cántaros** and **apasles**) by factory-made buckets and tubs.[5]

One of the oldest **milero** informants who experienced these changes describes the traditional tool kit as follows:

> We used to work with a hoe--a tool with a wooden handle with a wide metal blade on one end. We used it to dig soil and to prepare a batch of clay. To wet the clay we used a clay pot. We didn´t have buckets like we have now. We also used **apasles** (shallow clay containers) to wash the molds. (See Mendieta y Nuñez 1949:502-07 for photos and a description of the use of this technology in the Tlacolula branch of the industry.)

This same informant described the changes in this tool kit and their effect on production as follows:

> Around 1950 the tools began to change. We saw that it was quicker with the crowbar than with the hoe and all of the bosses began to buy crowbars. It was not the same as it was with the hoe and the clay pot. With the hoe one could only make 200 bricks daily because one could not dig the clay easily; the hoe didn´t dig well. We could make 400 bricks daily but during the two days that we prepared clay we earned nothing.

This **milero** worked four days a week and said that he produced only 800 bricks a week before the tool change and 1600 a week following the change. These changes in brick production technology, productivity, and increased earnings occurred concomitantly with the growth of the industry and the mechanization of truck transport. They should be understood as reflecting an intensification of the struggle between the brickyard employers and the brickyard proletariat over their relative shares of the income generated from brick sales.

65

Each brickyard owner must invest in a complete tool-kit if he expects to operate successfully. The crowbar and pick are employed to loosen soil from the sides and bottom of the clay pit and then to pulverize large clods which have been broken loose. Then, if the soil is high in gravel content a sifter (**criva**) is used to remove the gravel. Next the pulverized earth is shovelled into a mound against the wall of the pit. A hole or depression is scooped out in the center of the mound of loose clay and then water is added; the clay and the water are mixed until they take on a thick, mudlike consistency. There are two mixings or "turn overs" (**volteadas**) of the wet mass; during the second of these, sawdust and sometimes sand is added to provide the desired consistency.

The strategy of the worker during this process is to avoid, as much as possible, extracting soil with a high gravel content. When veins of gravel are encountered during the initial phase of clay extraction, the workers shift their efforts away from the gravel or work around it. There is no efficient way for them to extract clay and process it when the gravel content is high since the sifting process is very time consuming. Consequently, especially rocky sections of clay pits are abandoned. One **milero** informant described how gravel presents an obstacle to efficient clay extraction and how it may increase the employer's costs:

> Our problem is that at times we run into a lot of gravel. Wherever it is we have to move it or move to another area of the pit. That slows us down. If one complains to the boss, he says that he doesn't have time to clear away the gravel. He tells us to clear it out.

As the excavation deepens, another problem which confronts the workers is the possibility of a cave-in of a section of the pit wall. In order to avoid this, care is taken to shear off protruding areas. This often necessitates the use of ladders to climb up the wall or, more dangerously, entails efforts to loosen protruding sections of the wall from ground level above (and on the edge of) the pit. The danger here is obvious since a cave-in will usually take the worker with it to the bottom of the pit.

Once the mound of clay is uniformly wet then the task of the worker is to clean out remaining debris and to knead the clay into a smooth, uniform mass. Timing is crucial here. Typically, clay is won and processed in the afternoon, after a morning spent in molding bricks from a clay batch prepared the day before. The final kneading process must occur on the same day the bricks are to be molded and not more than two hours before the molding begins. Clay which has gone through a second mixing, as well as preliminary cleaning and kneading, is covered with a layer of sawdust (to avoid drying out in the sun) and is left to stand overnight. The following morning it is ready for the final kneading which involves the folding in of some additional sawdust and water. The addition of sawdust prior to molding produces an essentially self-firing brick (cf. Keddie and Cleghorn 1980:9). If this final kneading is not done properly many of the bricks produced from the batch will crack or split even before they are fired, so a great deal of effort is expended to do it right.

The main reason for the time limit on the kneading process prior to the initiation of molding has to do with the consistency or pliability of the clay. If the clay is too dry, is poorly mixed, or contains gravel or other debris, it will crumble; and if it is too wet it will not hold its shape as the mold is removed. The judgment as to when the clay batch is ready for molding is strictly up to its preparer. Finally, it should be noted that too much gravel or large pieces of gravel cause bricks to break before or during firing. As bricks dry, water evaporates and air spaces form around the gravel. These may result in immediate cracks. If not they expand when the bricks are fired and they break then.[6]

The fabrication stage is initiated with the preparation of the patio which is a flat, smooth surface adjacent to the clay pit where the clay is molded, the freshly molded bricks are laid out to dry (with the distance between them being only the width of the mold), after which the dried bricks are temporarily stacked. This preparation, which takes one person about fifteen minutes, involves the wetting down of the patio surface, followed by the spreading of a thin layer of sand to keep the freshly molded bricks from adhering to the patio surface during the drying process.

Brick fabrication is the most demanding phase of the production process; it requires physical dexterity, strength, and perseverance--and can be mastered only through a fairly extended period of apprenticeship. The operation encompasses five discrete activities: 1) molding or forming--beginning when the kneaded (or tempered and pugged) clay hits the mold and ending when the mold is removed from the freshly molded clay; 2) washing and placement of the mold on the patio floor ready to receive the next batch of clay (begins when the mold is pulled off the freshly molded clay and ends when the worker takes a step in the direction of the off-patio supply of kneaded clay); 3) travel to the off-patio clay supply to obtain a fresh bucket load (begins when the worker takes a step in the direction of the clay supply with his bucket and ends when he arrives at the clay supply); 4) fresh clay procurement (begins when the worker enters the clay mound and ends when he refills his bucket with kneaded clay; this may entail some last minute kneading or pugging); and 5) return trip to the molding area on the patio (begins when the worker takes a step toward the patio from the clay supply and ends when the newly procured clay is dumped into the mold).

It should be emphasized that the five steps in brick fabrication are performed in a continuous and rapid manner--the average time for each complete sequence being four minutes (mean time for seven cases observed for one hour each). Since kneaded clay may lose its required consistency through the effect of insolation, the workers are under constant pressure to mold the entire batch as quickly and efficiently as possible. The longer the fabrication process takes, the more extra kneading will be necessary to keep the clay supply at its required consistency.

The principal tool for molding is the wooden frame mold (made by carpenters in Santa Lucía) which comes in two, four, six, eight, and ten brick sizes. There are two basic frame widths which mold bricks of two different thicknesses: the **mediatabla** or "ceiling/flooring brick", and the **tabique** or regular wall brick which is the thicker of the two and is the most widely produced. The choice of mold size is largely one of the personal preference of the worker. Most apprentices (especially children) use the two-brick mold, although there are a few full-fledged brickmakers who prefer this size. Children at the age of six or seven start out working with the two-brick mold and by the time they have reached their teens, they generally have begun using the four-brick mold (though some do move directly to the six-brick mold which is the most popular size among the brickmakers. A few brickmakers prefer the eight-brick mold which, due to its large capacity, requires that its user carry a maximum load of fresh clay on each trip from patio to the clay batch. It is not surprising that the use of this mold is limited to workers in prime physical condition since it permits its user less flexibility in pacing his work.

The six-brick mold is preferred by a majority of brickmakers because it can be filled with less than a maximum load of clay, is somewhat easier to remove after the bricks are molded, and has a relatively high yield of bricks. This enables its users to alternate between carrying full loads back to the patio and spending more time molding, and carrying less than capacity loads and spending less time molding. Such a trade-off is impossible for the eight- or ten-brick mold user who, other things being equal, will finish molding the same number of bricks in less time or a larger number of bricks in the same time, if he can match the 6-brick mold user trip for trip to the clay batch and back carrying a full load. The observational data show, however, that there is no significant difference in hourly output between the eight- or ten-brick and the six-brick mold users. There is a one hundred brick per hour average for producers in the late teens/early twenties age group regardless of the mold size used.

The molding process itself involves three separate activities: 1) filling the mold by, first, dumping the clay directly into the mold from a bucket or can and, then, packing and tamping the clay into the mold by a series of downward thrusting actions with the extended fingers of both hands to assure that all air spaces to the bottom of the mold are filled; 2) levelling off the excess clay with a motion in which the extended hand sweeps across the top of the mold; and 3) smoothing out the clay in the mold (after the worker cleans his hands in water) to assure that the exposed side of the molded bricks will be smooth and flat to match their unexposed sides (i.e., which are on the bottom of the mold facing the patio floor).

The analytical results of a systematic and detailed observational study of twelve brick makers for a cumulative total of fourteen hours in May 1980 show than an average brick fabrication cycle requires four minutes and twenty-one seconds. This time is allocated as follows:

	no.of seconds	% of total time
molding	111.31	42.7
washing and placement	52.65	20.2
travel to clay supply	11.97	4.6
clay procurement	70.32	27.0
return travel to patio	14.09	5.4

These data show that the typical worker completes the molding sequence in just under two minutes, and that this consumes about 43% of the 4-1/3 minutes of labor-time expended in the average five-stage sequence of brick fabrication. Some 63% of his time is spent on the patio, either in molding bricks or in washing and placing the mold, and the remainder is spent at the clay supply site or in traveling between it and the patio.

It is worth noting here that the proportion of time spent in clay procurement varies considerably over the sample: ranging from a low of 10% to a high of 41%. This means that some brickmakers attempt to mold bricks by spending a mimimum amount of time in the preparatory kneading of clay so that kneading and molding activities overlap (see Table 3). The brick-makers who do this are operating under a less stringent set of quality control constraints since an inevitable result of skimping on the kneading operation is poorer quality bricks. It is also conceivable that the variations in clay procurement, like the variations in clay preparation time itself (range from 1-3/4 to 6-1/3 hours), are a response to variable soil quality in different clay pits.

Cooperative and Individual Labor-Time:
the Social Average

The observational study of twelve brick producing units provides the most reliable source of quantitative data dealing with work organization, labor-time allocation, and brick output. But it is encouraging that the results of the analysis of labor-time allocation and output data (recorded daily by selected informants on project forms) are in line with results obtained from the direct observational study. The data indicate that the daily output of the majority of brickmaking units is a result of joint rather than individual labor. The average cooperative labor coefficient for the twelve units is 2.7 which, when averaged together with the coefficient of 2.2 from additional units participating in the self-reporting program, yields a coefficient of 2.5. This means that the bricks produced by these production units were made by an average of 2.5 persons per unit per day.[7]

Underlying this statistic is the fact that the number of brickmakers in the study units ranges from one to six, and that they are both family workers and hired pieceworkers. This translates into considerable variation within and between units for variables such as productivity and work time per day. The values of these variables are, in turn, a function of the age and sex composition of the unit's work force. Thus, in one father and son unit, which produces an average of 78.5 bricks per hour, the father's hourly rate is only 60 bricks per hour compared to his son's rate of 97. In other words, the productivity of the unit rests disproportionately on the work of the son.

Another way of expressing this is that those units whose members put in the longest work days per capita are not necessarily the most productive ones. As a general rule, production units with the highest number of brickmakers in their teens or early twenties are the production leaders. On the average, the hourly rate of brick production is at least twenty-five bricks higher for this age group than it is for men in their thirties or forties. The empirical record of output variability within and between production units will be examined in the next section.

By focussing exclusively on the molding process which is dominated by young men in their teens and twenties, it is possible to underestimate the important contribution to daily production made by women and children. This contribution is most critical in the final finishing stage of trimming and stacking the dried bricks. Trimming is an activity which involves stooping, picking up the dried brick, trimming off rough edges with a metal scraper and then placing it on its side, ready to be picked up for stacking. Of the three separate periods of trimming observed, two involved the twenty-five year old wife of one of the brickmakers. On one occasion she trimmed 504 bricks at a rate of 453/hour and, on another occasion, 510 at a

rate of 518/hour; this compares favorably with the
trim rate of 487/hour achieved by two boys, aged ten
and fifteen, who worked interchangeably in trimming
568 bricks.

In another **milero** family unit which was studied
over a period of five weeks, the thirty-four year old
wife of the brickmaker-head participated in trimming
and stacking bricks on thirteen separate occasions
(for a total of 16.7 hours or 3% of the family total).
More significantly, the twelve year old, ten year old,
and seven year old sons of the head spent a combined
total of 258.5 hours (or 43% of the family total of
603.75 hours) over the thirty-six day observation
period in tasks ranging from clay extraction and
preparation to molding, trimming, and stacking bricks.

Table 4. Allocation of Labor-time in a Family Production Unit*

Household Member	Age	Labor-time (hours)	% of Total	Tasks**
T	46	123.65	20.4	EPT
I	34	16.7	2.8	T
son	15	194.75	32.2	EPMT
son	12	168.10	27.8	EPMT
son	10	97.60	16.0	MT
son	7	4.70	.8	T
	TOTAL	605.50	100.0	

* Six Workers and 123 Tasks Observed Over a 36-day
Period in June and July, 1980

**E = clay extraction; P = clay preparation; M =
molding bricks; T = trimming and/or stacking

Table 4 presents the results of a tabulation and
analysis of daily labor-time reports submitted over a
thirty-six day period in June and July, 1980 by this
same **milero** household which will be referred to as
the Tomás unit. Several of the results of this exercise merit discussion. First, the predominant contribution to brick production by young males, which was
already demonstrated in the analysis of the observational data, is confirmed here. Tomás'fifteen year old
son was responsible for 32% of the total family work
time over the report period and, together with his

twelve year old brother, accounted for 60% of the total family work time spanning every stage in the production process. By contrast, Tomás himself accounted for just over 20% of the total work time--and did not contribute at all to the critical molding process which was performed exclusively by his sons (except the youngest who was only occasionally involved in trimming and stacking along with his mother). It should be noted, however, that Tomás does work as a stoker sometimes as often as twice a month (18-20 hour stints) to bring in additional income.

Tomás' wife, Irma, was also observed on one occasion participating in clay preparation but this occurs infrequently. Women seldom participate in the preparation of clay where there is an adequate supply of male labor. On the other hand, in non-employer households without boys twelve years or older, the productive role of the housewife becomes much more important--especially in clay preparation. There are exceptional cases in which husband and wife participate jointly in all stages of the labor process, including molding. This case illustrates the typical division of labor by age and sex in family brick production units and exemplifies the truly social nature of the labor process in this industry--a characteristic which will be emphasized as we move on to examine the nature and sources of output variability (or productivity differentials) in the next section.

Variation in Productivity and Output:
Causes and Patterns

It has already been suggested that the size and composition of brick production units are crucial determinants of productivity. Two-thirds of the multiple-worker units had members at work in the brickyards for six or seven days a week (33% for six days vs. 29% for seven days), whereas only 50% of the solo units worked this often. A documented progressive increase in mean daily output from the solo to the four-worker units, can be attributed to the capacity of the larger units to mobilize more labor-time per week.

This proposition can be examined in more detail (see Table 5). All of the multiple-worker units involve family cooperation. More specifically, average hourly output per unit increases as the number of workers in the unit increases. This is accompanied by

4. Milero molds bricks while his young son observes and a peasant plows in the background

5. Milero supervises his sons in clay
extraction and preparation

6. Milero and son molding bricks

an increase in total output (except in the four-worker units because of their low average per capita work time), and a decrease in hourly productivity per worker. What is demonstrated here is the positive effect of family cooperation in the labor process upon unit productivity, and also that increases in the latter are, in most cases, achieved together with decreases in per capita work time (except in one of the three-worker cases where the work observed was leisurely and inefficient, perhaps because the workers were grandsons of the relatively prosperous owner, their widowed grandmother). The data, in any case, bear out the generalization that, for the great majority of the cases observed, as unit size decreases workers put in longer hours and produce more bricks per hour worked.

Table 5. Output and Work Time for Eleven Brick Production Units over 24 Observation Periods

No. of observations	No. of workers per unit	Hourly output per unit	Mean total unit output per day	Hourly mean output per worker	Mean work time per person	per unit
14	1	89.16	386	89.16	4.33	4.33
3	2	108.16	395	63.36	3.65	7.30
2	3	115.30	628	49.13	5.45	16.35
5	4	208.82	485	51.47	2.32	9.28

Having considered some factors associated with differential productivity, as measured by mean output in various production units, it is appropriate to seek more specific causes for output variability within and between production units. These units will be designated by the first name of their principal worker. The figures (see Table 6) are presented in rank order from the lowest to the highest average weekly output i.e., 2,300 for the Pedro-unit to 5,720 for the Gilberto-unit.

In all of these units the division of labor by age is the key to their productivity. All of them combine a middle-aged head with one or more male workers between the ages of ten and twenty-one. The Gilberto-unit had the highest average weekly output (see Table 6 and Figure 5). Observational records show that it was only between June 9 and June 22, the weeks of highest output, that both **mileros** were regularly employed by Gilberto--thus giving his unit three work-

ers in their late teens or early twenties in addition
to Gilberto himself and his fifteen year old son.
During the remaining three weeks the unit consisted
primarily of Gilberto, his son, and his son-in-law
with irregular work by only one milero.

All of the output curves, given the relative age
composition and size of these work units, suggest that
their capacity to achieve sustained periods of high
output resides in the productivity of their younger
workers. In the Pancho unit (Figure 6), for example,
Pancho's mean hourly output is seventy bricks compared
to his son's rate of 102; his son also prepares the
clay batch for both of them unassisted each day. The
multiple-worker units also have distinct advantages
over solo units regarding participation in the supplementary cash, short-term job market. This includes the
jobs of stoker (**atizador**) and loader (**cargador**) which
not only provide **milero**s with a change of pace but
also enable them to earn cash more quickly than they
can by making bricks (for which they are paid only on
Saturdays).

Table 6. Work Organization, Work Time, and Output for
Four Multiple-worker Brick Production Units

Unit	C o m p o s i t i o n	Avg.output per week	Avg. Agg. work time per week
G	G(age 50)+ son(age 15) + son-in-law(age 21) + 2 mileros (late teens)	5,720	184.7
T	T(age 46)+3 sons(15,12,10)	2,963	109.0
C	C(age 44)+3 sons(18,16,10)	2,445	88.5
P	P(age 49) + 1 son (18)	2,300	67.0

A case in point is provided by the Carlos unit
(Figure 7) where the head, together with at least one
of his older sons, works once or twice a week in
loading or unloading kilns or trucks. He is able to do
so without appreciably affecting the unit's weekly
output because one or both of his younger sons remain
at work in the brickyard. Also, his oldest sons have
the capacity to intensify their pace of work to compensate for lost brick production time. In a similar
fashion, Tomás (Figure 8) is able to work periodically

78

as a stoker without diminishing the output of his unit which, in any case, is heavily dependent on the labor of his sons.

The male age composition of a production unit affects output daily and does so throughout the year. However, an important factor which affects output only seasonally is rainfall. Its impact on brick output is well illustrated in the time series. The earliest significant rainfall during our period of study occurred on May 27; this is confirmed by the 0 values for output on that date for the Carlos (Figure 6) and the Tomás (Figure 7) units. The heaviest rains occurred on June 20-22 and 24-26. Consequently, the lowest points on the weekly average productivity curves (upper curve) occur for the week ending June 22 in two cases (Pancho unit and Tomás unit) and for the week ending June 29 in the other two. In all four cases the drop in output is drastic and reflects wet brickyard conditions which forced work suspensions.

Interestingly enough the data also show that the four brickyards were not affected similarly by the rainfall: two of them managed to produce above average outputs during the first rainy week (Carlos unit and Gilberto unit), whereas the output of the other two plunged to its lowest average for the period during that week; and during the second rainy week the performance of these units was reversed. This differential response to rainfall refects a combination of factors having to do with the physical layout of brickyards and with worker strategies for coping with rainfall. Rain usually falls during the afternoon and evening so those workers who finish their molding operations in the morning are usually able to trim and stack their bricks before the rain begins. The largest units have a decided edge here.

If, on the other hand, the rain is especially heavy and continues into the evening then the clay supply may be flooded and will be too wet for molding on the following day. In such cases, or on those days when it begins to rain in the morning and continues into the afternoon and evening, all production is suspended. Some workers will reduce their morning output during the rainy season in anticipation of afternoon rains; others will simply arrive in the brickyard very early in the morning to finish a normal day's output before the rain begins.

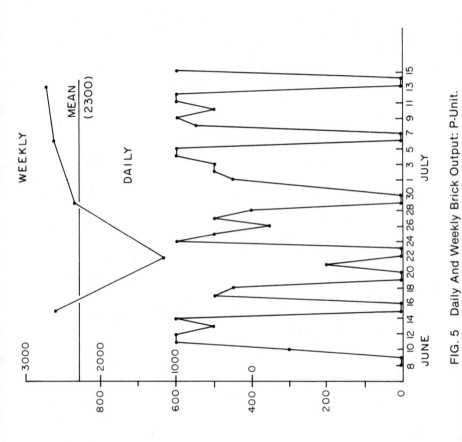

FIG. 5   Daily And Weekly Brick Output: P-Unit.

80

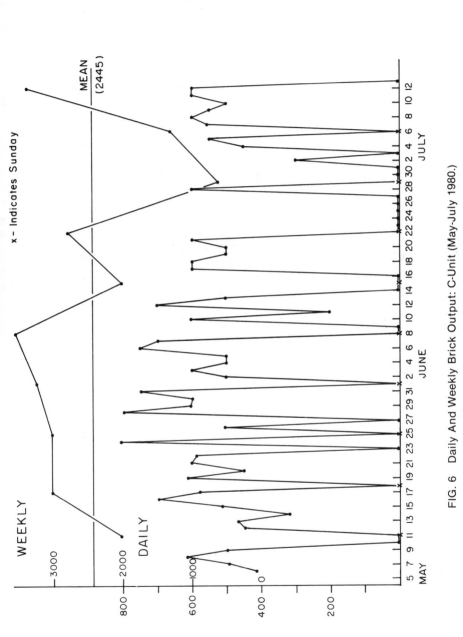

FIG. 6   Daily And Weekly Brick Output: C-Unit (May-July 1980.)

81

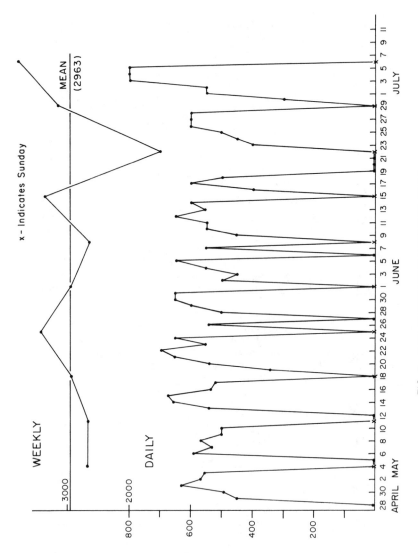

FIG. 7 Daily And Weekly Brick Output: T-Unit.

82

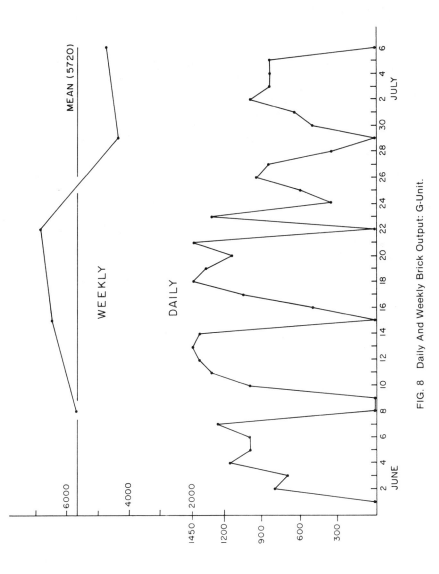

FIG. 8 Daily And Weekly Brick Output: G-Unit.

83

Rainfall may be the answer to every peasant's prayers but it is often the brickmaker's scourge. Consequently, there are several ways that the they try to limit its deleterious effects. Some workers dig channels or employ a form of terracing in the clay pit to facilitate a faster runoff or drainage of rainwater. Most workers will begin extracting clay in more elevated sections of the pit to avoid the effects of flooding. Plastic sheets are used to cover freshly made clay mounds so as to protect them from rain. Likewise, freshly molded bricks which are laid out on the patio to dry, or are stacked near the patio in the open air, will also be covered with plastic sheets when rain threatens. However, these efforts may be to no avail if the rain is heavy and is accompanied by high winds. There is always the possibility that an entire day's output can literally be washed away.

These problems serve as a testament to the wisdom of the seasonal staggering of industrial work in peasant communities throughout the Oaxaca valley where, in contrast to the situation in Santa Lucía, brickmaking--like adobe making and construction work in general--is customarily restricted to the dry season. In Santa Lucía the emergence of year-round production in what was (and still is in outlying rural communities) a minor, seasonal peasant industry (see Cook 1982a: Ch.2) went hand-in-hand with capitalist development. On the supply side, this involved depeasantization and proletarianization (which created the supply of **mileros**). On the demand side, it involved urbanization; construction activity associated with Oaxaca City's growth provided the stimulus for the expansion of brick production.

The daily output curves (Figures 5-8) show another pattern which is pervasive but which has two different manifestations, namely, the weekend hiatus indicated by the steep plunge from a Saturday high to a rockbottom Sunday. In the Pancho unit this hiatus involves both Sunday and Monday throughout the series, a pattern which is also found three times in the Carlos unit series (May 10-11, June 8-9, and June 15-16), twice in the Tomás unit series (May 4-5, 11-12), and once in the Gilberto unit series (June 8-9). Since Saturday is payday in the brickyards, weekly output is targeted accordingly with Saturday itself culminating the weekly production cycle. On the other hand, Sunday is traditionally a day on which heavy work is not scheduled. As the time series show there is no molding

84

7. Brickyards in the rainy season

of bricks on Sunday. Our field notes report only one instance of Sunday molding by one of the most destitute **mileros** who had just recovered from an illness and was debt-ridden.

Typically, a new unfired brick production cycle is initiated on the same day that a preceding one is completed. This means that a standard daily schedule of tasks in the brickyard is as follows(selected at random from the daily reports of the Pancho unit):

Time	Task	Personnel
6:30-7:30 a.m.	knead clay batch	Pancho
7:30-7:45 a.m.	clean patio	Alvaro
7:45-9:30 a.m.	mold bricks	Pancho/Alvaro
11:00-2:00 p.m.	prepare clay batch	Alvaro
2:00-3:00 p.m.	scrape bricks	Pancho/Alvaro
3:00-4:00 p.m.	stack bricks	Pancho/Alvaro

The first task each day is to knead the clay batch which was prepared in the afternoon of the previous day. It is a standard rule of brick production that a newly prepared clay batch must stand overnight prior to its final kneading. Or, put differently, bricks should not be molded from a clay batch prepared on the same day. This rule of thumb is rarely violated.

This cycle is broken each week on Saturday afternoon when a new clay batch is not prepared as it must be on every normal work day. Most units will produce their first clay batch of the week on Sunday afternoon to begin molding on Monday morning. So, for a majority of brickmakers "never on Sunday" applies only to molding bricks, not to extracting and preparing clay or to scraping and stacking bricks produced on Saturday. The Pancho unit is in a minority with its practice of avoiding clay preparation on Sunday (though they sometimes trim and stack Saturday's bricks on Sunday afternoon) and of initiating weekly production on Monday by preparing a batch of clay for molding on Tuesday. They are on a five-day rather than a six day schedule.

How does the performance of solo producers compare with that of the joint producers? The first thing that strikes one as being significant about their performance profiles (see Figure 9), in comparison with the multiple-worker unit profiles, is that the hiatuses tend to be longer (though the series are too

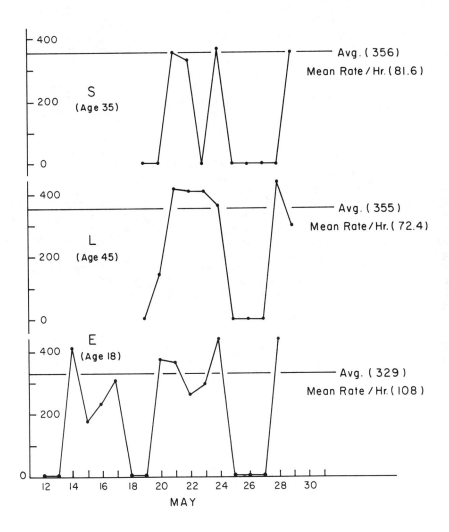

FIG. 9   Daily Brick Output Of 3 Solo Producers.

short to be conclusive). To the extent that this is true, it would support the argument that the physical demands of the labor process of brickmaking are such that it is not possible for solo workers to sustain high levels of output for as many consecutive days as can the multiple worker units. The impact of the age factor on output is also illustrated by these cases, since their average hourly rate of output declines progressively as their age increases. The decline in hourly productivity with age seems to be an iron law of brick production which is most apparent in solo units where it cannot be offset through the division of labor.

Production Strategies and Tactics: the Scheduling and Disposition of Labor-Time

Given the structure of production in the brick industry, with the **patrón/milero** relationship being predominant, most decisions about what to produce are made outside of the brickyard by the employer and are transmitted to the **mileros** either on Saturday (payday) or at the beginning of the week. The only exception to this is the case of the independent worker-operators who are themselves involved in daily production. Except for the occasional production of specialty bricks, this decision boils down to whether flooring bricks or regular wall bricks will be made. Not all brickyard operators need to make this decision simply because they or their workers lack the skill or patience to make the thinner, more delicate flooring bricks or lack the prime clay (minimum gravel and lime content) to produce them.

About one-quarter of the operators interviewed made only one of the two types of brick; and only two of them made flooring bricks exclusively because, as one of them put it, "...it's less work; they are thinner and one can mold them quicker." The other, who also owns a kiln, justified his preference for making this type of brick by pointing out that, "one is in a hurry and they can be made more quickly" and also noted:

> The flooring brick is more delicate. Many clay pits are no good for flooring bricks because the soil has a lot of gravel and limestone. But if the soil is good, it's better to make flooring bricks. More of them can be loaded into the kiln and one earns a little more.

88

The regular brick producers, nevertheless, avoid flooring brick production precisely for these same reasons: either they don't have access to prime clay or
they say that flooring bricks are too difficult to
make.

For the majority of informants who produce both
types of bricks, the following is a typical response
to a question as to how they decided which type (or
which proportion of each type) to produce week by
week:

> According to the market. If one sees
> that regular bricks are selling better,
> then one makes more regular bricks
> That's done on the basis of talking and
> keeping one's eyes open. It's all ac-
> cording to demand. Whatever is selling
> best that's what we make.

Another informant was more specific and expressive in
his answer:

> It's very simple. I go around and see
> what is happening. I talk with my
> friends: `How goes it? How are sales?´
> And I do the same with the resellers.
> `What are you hauling?´ `How goes it
> with you?´ And they reply: `Listen,
> there's going to be an order for floor-
> ing bricks.´ `When?´ I ask. `I'll have
> them ready on such and such a day.´ I
> return to the brickyard and I tell my
> **mileros** to start making flooring bricks
> because there's going to be a big or-
> der.

Another reason, apart from marketing considerations, for shifting production from regular bricks
to flooring bricks was illustrated concretely when one
of our observation units abruptly shifted from its u-
sual pattern of making flooring bricks and, instead,
made regular bricks. The explanation for this switch
was that two thousand regular bricks were needed by
the boss to place in the bottom layers of his kiln
which was being loaded for a firing. It turns out that
the firing of a kiln load of flooring bricks requires
several bottom layers of the thicker regular bricks
which can better withstand the more intense heat at
the lower levels of the kiln.

The operators whose brickyards can produce both types of bricks, keep abreast of current market conditions through an informal information network; this provides them with a guide for planning their production. There is always some risk in attempting to predict future demand so some operators attempt to minimize risk by regularly producing both types of bricks. As one operator who does this expressed it:

> If flooring brick sales stagnate we have to make only regular bricks. The day that flooring bricks begin to pile up then we start making regular bricks. But if we make only regular bricks that´s no good either. For that reason one tries to make a mixture of both.

The output of unfired bricks is geared to the operator´s kiln capacity--usually 10,000 to 12,000 bricks depending upon the mix between regular bricks (fewer required per firing because of greater thickness) and flooring bricks. The interval between firings in a one-kiln operation depends upon worker productivity. Considering differences in dexterity, work pace, and stamina among workers, the key to brickyard output, to reiterate, is the size and composition of the production unit. The highest weekly outputs and, therefore, the shortest kiln-firing intervals occur in those brickyards with the largest number of workers. When the operator finds the production of his own yard lagging or if there is a shortfall of bricks as a designated firing date approaches, he can purchase unfired bricks from other producers or complete his kiln-load from the yard of a relative.

How do the direct producers themselves view the problem of scheduling their labor time and pacing their work? Once the worker knows which type of brick to produce (keeping in mind that this is not always optional), it is up to him to determine how many to produce and how to produce them. For all practical purposes the pieceworker is his own boss when it comes to the labor process. He is provided with the necessary tools, possibly with his living quarters, with access to a brickyard, and with his pay by the employer. Yet, in the daily work situation, the **milero** himself determines the disposition of his own labor-power and that of his household dependents.

There are, in essence, only two types of work organization in the brickyards: one type in which an employer (who may or may not be a brickmaker) hires **mileros** to produce bricks for him or with him and supervises their work; and a second type in which the **milero** (or the worker-operator) works together with members of his household and directs their work. All cooperation in brick production occurs within one or the other of these contexts; there is little spontaneous or voluntary reciprocal labor in the brickyards. Cooperative work is either directed by an employer or is a routinized aspect of a household-based division of labor where the male head is the task master.[8]

The observational and interview data show that every production unit, regardless of its composition, initiates each week's production with a self-assigned target output for the week and adjusts daily work schedules accordingly. One worker-operator who works alone explained his mode of working as follows:

> Each week I have a work plan. I follow that plan in order to know how many bricks I'm going to make each week. I make the plan mentally, nothing more. I think about how many I can make on Monday, Tuesday, Wednesday and so on-- a total of how many I can make in a week.

When I asked this same informant to relate this general statement of strategy to the coming week he responded: "I intend to work every day, from Monday to Friday, more or less 300 bricks each day, that will come out to 1200 or 1500 for the week." He told me that he didn't plan to make more bricks because,"That is the time that I have scheduled to work. I work eight hours daily. If I work longer than that I get too tired. I don't make more bricks because I get too tired out."

What this comes down to is that each batch of clay is prepared with a specific yield of bricks in mind. Daily output counts show that there is only a small margin of error between the producer's estimate of yield when the clay is being prepared and the actual yield. One **milero** drew an analogy between the brickmaker and the baker to explain this:

It's in one's memory or in his faith in his work. It's an art. It's like the saying: what I say is what I do. If I say that a clay batch will make so many bricks, it's from sight alone--like the bakers that weigh the flour in order to estimate how much bread they will bake. Here in the brickyards we are better than the bakers (**"Somos mas chingones que los panaderos"**) because we say: from that clay batch such and such a quantity of bricks will be made. And it always comes out--from sight alone, an educated guess, real know-how!

It is through such statements that the craft dimension of brickmaking is expressed.

The Kiln Firing Process

Unlike the adobe block (which is still made throughout rural Oaxaca and remains the principal type of man-made construction material there --see Cook 1982a:55), the **ladrillo** is not a finished product when it is picked up from the patio and stacked. The strength, durability and appearance which set it apart from adobe as a basic construction material derive from its passage through a kiln firing process. Control over this process is an important axis of differentiation among producing units, and is the culminating step in the entire brick production process. It is, at one and the same time, the most demanding step in terms of technical know-how and the most physically dangerous to the workers. Moreover, on its outcome depends the market value of the labor power amassed in the unfired bricks (cf. Lackey 1982:113).

The proportion of unfired bricks that come out of the kiln in first class, second class, or discard condition depends upon how the kiln is loaded and how the firing process itself is conducted. Informant estimates run from an average of a fifty-fifty split between first and second class bricks per firing to an average of 87%-13%, with the mean for all informants being a 72%-28% yield (roughly one brick in four will be second class). About 5% of the unfired bricks loaded into a kiln will be broken during the firing process and can be sold only as waste for a minimum price. These figures indicate that even an optimum performance by the human labor component in the kiln loading and firing process cannot overcome the limitations of the unmechanized firing technology which is used throughout the industry.

In Santa Lucia there are about thirty-five operating kilns, distributed among some thirty owners, which range in firing capacity from 10,000 to 18,000 regular bricks (or from 12,000 to 20,000 flooring bricks). Most kilns are in the 10,000 - 12,000 range; of the ten kiln owners interviewed, eight had kilns in this category and only two had one with a larger firing capacity. The owners, in most cases, participated in the construction of their kilns but many of them relied upon the expertise of a mason to construct the interior arches which separate the combustion or firing chamber from the heat chamber or oven proper.

The arches are constructed lengthwise (from specially made wedge-shaped bricks) and are spaced at equal intervals of some twenty centimeters from the front to the rear of the kiln. One informant said that the spacing between the arches, as well as their height from the kiln floor, has been worked out by trial and error over the generations. The arches, in any case, are carefully constructed since they not only must withstand the intense heat of firing but also must repeatedly support the weight of full loads of 10,000 or more bricks. Each kiln has either five or six arches.[9]

It is precisely the periodic need to reconstruct these arches that represents the major maintenance cost of a kiln. Several informants estimated that the expected lifespan of a kiln varies between fifteen and twenty years but this may vary considerably with the pattern of use and upkeep. In the most active kilns, arches must be rebuilt annually and deteriorating wall sections are rebuilt when necessary so that from one year to another the typical kiln is partially reconstructed. The external walls of the kiln are constructed with a combination of adobes and regular bricks. A kiln is rectangular in shape, measures about ten feet on each side and is approximately twenty-five feet high. A parabolic arch-shaped opening for fuel is located in the bottom middle of one side of the kiln and measures about three feet wide along its base. Its internal construction is such that the combustion or firing chamber occupies the first six feet or so of the kiln's height, so that the lowest layer of bricks must be loaded about fifteen feet down from the top of the kiln on the flat topside of the arches.

Before the kiln is loaded the arches and firing chamber are cleared of ashes and debris remaining from the previous firing. The loading must be done with considerable care and is usually conducted under the supervision of the kiln owner (or the owner of the load of bricks to be fired). The basic strategy for loading is that the thicker and/or poorer quality bricks are loaded in the lowest two layers and the thinner and/or better quality bricks are loaded in the middle and upper layers. This is done because the lower layers are most likely to be over-fired and, consequently, to be either burnt or broken--and will be sold as second class or waste products. If the firing goes according to plan, the middle layers of bricks are the ones most likely to come out with the highest proportion in first class condition (the top layers will usually have a somewhat lower percentage of first class bricks).

The key to the proper loading of a kiln lies in the positioning and spacing of the bricks, and special care is taken to assure that each brick is properly positioned. Each layer of bricks is loaded in the opposite direction from the one which preceded it. The bottom layer is placed lengthwise, at even intervals of eight centimeters or so between each brick, so as to bridge the space between contiguous arches, and from one side of the kiln to the other. The second layer is then placed crosswise in a domino figure of five pattern. Since the kilns are of the updraft type, there must be a trade-off between assuring the upward circulation of superheated air and loading as many bricks as possible into the heating chamber.

This trade-off is achieved by loading the first six rows with spaces between them to permit air circulation. The remaining rows, however, are packed tightly; pottery sherds are used to wedge the rows of bricks as tightly as possible against the walls of the kiln. In a standard size kiln, each layer in the top half of the kiln contains about 390 regular bricks or 550 flooring bricks compared to the bottom six layers which because of spacing have about 350 regular bricks or 500 flooring bricks. On the average, the loading of a kiln takes eight workers about eight hours; but three workers were observed to load a kiln in twelve hours.[10]

8. Early stage in "setting" unfired bricks into a kiln: views from above

9. Setting unfired bricks into a kiln

The loading process itself is a marvel of coordination and timing, involving as it does the tossing of bricks in twos and fours from worker to worker--each strategically positioned in what amounts to a human conveyor belt. The kiln is loaded from the bottom up; there are rectangular openings on three sides which permit workers to convey bricks for the bottom layers from a position about halfway down from the top of the kiln. This shortens the distance which the bricks must travel through the air into the hands of the workers doing the layering. As the layering direction alternates, the position of the workers in the kiln shifts accordingly.

As layer after layer is laid in, the loaders literally build their way out of the kiln. The key worker in the loading process is the relay man who stands in one of the rectangular doorways, receives bricks (either carried or tossed) in serial fashion from one or more workers who are at the supply stack (usually a truck bed), and then tosses the bricks down to the workers doing the layering. The loading doors in the sides of the kiln are sealed with bricks and mud after the kiln is fully loaded and before the fire is lit.

A fire is lit through the stoking hole at the base of the kiln with old inner tubes being used as kindling. As the inner tubes ignite and begin to burn intensely they are spread around the floor of the firing chamber with a long stick. For the first three hours of ignition and heat-up of the fire box only inner tubes and old tires are burned. It is this ignition and initial firing that produces the billowing clouds of thick black smoke that are the most visible clue of the presence of the industry to travelers on the Pan American highway which serves as the northern boundary of the Santa Lucía brickyard zone. This dense black smoke from the burning tires diminishes as sawdust (which comes from a plywood factory and from lumber yards in Oaxaca City and is trucked into the kiln area) fed into the firing chamber by the stoker, replaces tires as the principal fuel.

Sawdust is fed into the firebox continuously for about nine hours before the kiln is judged to be sufficiently hot to place the first cover (**primera tapada**) on the top layer of bricks in the kiln. The process of placing the first covering layer of unfired bricks is initiated when it is judged by the kiln owner that the bricks positioned four or five layers from the top have become well heated (**"ha subido la lumbre"**). This determination is made by pouring water down into the kiln and listening for the telltale hisses as it hits the heated bricks. The cover is applied gradually with the hottest sections of the kiln being covered first. Typically, a period of 1 hour to 1-1/2 hours is required to complete the placement of the first cover.

The purpose of this operation is to achieve a uniform pattern of heat distribution throughout the kiln. It is said that by covering up the hottest sections first the heat will be pushed into the less heated areas. Stokers are instructed to keep fuel evenly distributed in the firebox to promote a more even distribution of heat in the kiln. The kiln is said to be heated-up when the first covering is completed. However, it is recognized that the hottest part of the kiln is the area surrounding the arches.

Once the first cover is in place, the stoking strategy is one of feeding the fire continuously until the temperature level throughout the kiln reaches the superheated level of the arches. Usually two stokers alternate by one- or two-hour shifts and a helper brings sawdust from the main supply area to the stoking area.

As indicated above, the major strategy during the post heat-up period is to feed the sawdust into the firebox with enough frequency and in sufficient volume to superheat all areas of the kiln. The boss, together with one of the stokers, constantly checks the top of the kiln to make sure that heat is distributed evenly. At night-time, by peering down through the layers of bricks in the kiln, they look for a tell-tale reddish glow that indicates to them the internal temperature and the upward progress of the fire. During the day-time the upward progress of the heat is measured by extending an outstretched hand over selected sections at the top of the kiln and also by carefully examining the widths of the gaps which open up between the brick layers and the walls of the kiln (i.e., the unfired bricks shrink as they are fired).

If the upward movement of the temperature is detected to be uneven by these means, then instructions are given to the stoker to feed more sawdust into that section of the firebox where the temperature is judged to be insufficient. The temperature may be raised by increasing the tempo of stoking and the pattern of sawdust dispersal (i.e., more sawdust is fed into a designated section of the firebox). The purpose of this activity is to **"darle punto al horno"** which essentially means to get the kiln temperature built up to a desired level and to maintain that level over a sufficient period of time to fire the bricks.

When a judgment is made that the upper layers of bricks are reaching the critical temperature, the order is given to begin sealing off the stoking hole (**"parar la puerta del horno para que no entre el aire"**) to avoid flaming at the top of the kiln. Then, section by section, an additional covering layer of bricks is placed across the top of the kiln (the **"segunda tapada"**) by one or two workers. This is the culminating activity of the firing process and marks the end of stoking activity. From this point on nature takes its course as the heat completes its rise to the top layers in the kiln and the bricks bake at a uniformly high temperature. The second cover is usually in place some twenty to twenty-two hours following the ignition of the fire.

The superheated kiln remains completely sealed for a period ranging from twelve to twenty hours after the placement of the second cover. The exact time lag depends upon the judgment of the kiln owner as to whether the top layers of bricks are properly or sufficiently fired. This is determined primarily by their color (i.e., burnt orange). The process of uncovering the top of the kiln is conducted under physically punishing circumstances by two workers who dance across the glowing, sparking, and smoking surface. The upper layers of bricks are red hot and can only be removed with specially made long-handled shovels. The heat is so intense that the workers grimace in constant pain and sometimes suffer burns while performing this task.

The side doors of the kiln are opened about six hours after the top is uncovered; the stoking hole will be partially opened within twenty-four hours and will be completely opened some thirty-six hours after the top is uncovered. If the stoking hole is opened too soon, the bricks in the layers nearest to the arches will split when the cool air hits them. A minimum of three days following the uncovering (**destapada**) is required before the bricks inside the kiln have cooled off enough to permit unloading.

The Stokers

One thing that should be clear from this description of the firing process is that the job of stoker is dangerous and physically demanding. Indeed, in my judgment no job in the entire village-based division of labor in Oaxaca is more physically punishing and hazardous than this one. The men who perform it work under prolonged exposure to intense heat, smoke, and dust--with only primitive, improvised forms of protective clothing (e.g., long-sleeved shirts, rags wrapped around hands and arms, bandanna covering the nose and mouth, a makeshift apron over their trousers). They are always in danger of being seriously burned or incinerated when sudden downdrafts or turbulence force flames out of the fire box into the stoking area where the highly flammable sawdust, or the stoker's clothing, may ignite.

Most stokers retire from the job by the time they reach their forties. The average age of the stokers interviewed was thirty-one. Out of sixteen brickmakers interviewed, seven had not worked as stokers--citing reasons ranging from fear of getting burned to a lack of success in learning how to do the job (**"No llegué agarrarle el pulso al horno"**). A kiln owner who has never attempted to stoke succinctly explained his reasons for avoiding it: "It's really a bother; it bothers one's vision and, then, with the live flames to climb up on top of the kiln to seal it, that really screws you up (**"Es una chinga"**)."

Of the nine informants who worked as stokers, two worked once or twice a week and the rest worked two or three times a month. Since a stoking session lasts about twenty-four hours and because of the effect of the intense heat on the body, stokers usually take one or two days off before resuming other duties in the brickyard. Most of these physical effects seem to be temporary with the exception of the problem of impaired vision which often is permanent and is the most common complaint mentioned by stokers and ex-stokers. It apparently is a consequence of the need for the stokers to visually inspect the fire periodically in order to ascertain its intensity and position in the firebox which provides them with information on which areas should be stoked.

100

How does a brickyard worker get his start as a stoker? The forty-nine year old head of the Pancho unit, who had retired from stoking only six months before he was interviewed, explained how he got his rather traumatic initiation to the occupation:

> My boss, who has a kiln, one day he didn't have a stoker and he said to me: `Listen Pancho, you're going to stoke, right?´ `Don't bother me´, I replied, `I can't do it.´` Well, here you're bothered´, he told me, `Either you stoke or you won't get paid next Saturday!´ Well, he threatened me, right? I replied: `What do you think? I don't want to stoke because I don't know how, not because I don't want to do it. It's that I don't understand how to do the job.´ `Here, you will learn how,´ he told me. `Get going.´ He gave me the shovel, and I began to shovel sawdust without knowing what I was doing.
>
> Well, I couldn't stand it there next to the flame, not even two minutes, because I felt that the flame was on me. I wasn't used to it. The boss laughed at me. And when it came time to seal off the top of the kiln at three a.m., my partner helped me to climb up on top. I was told to do it. I climbed up and said I can't do it. But they only laughed at me. And there I was standing in the live flames! It was like hell. The flames were shooting out the top of the kiln! I yelled at him to bring the ladder. He said no that what I was up there for was to seal off the kiln. Well, I couldn't stand the heat and I began to jump around. And my buddy laughed at me. That's how they punished me on the job.

This same informant emphasized that learning to stoke is one thing but learning the whole technique of firing is quite another:

> It took me five years to learn the basics. Once I learned the basics, once

10. A kiln in the early stage of firing

11. Stokers at work

12 . Upper left: sealing the stoking hole
Upper right: placing the "first cover" over kiln
Above: uncovering the kiln to promote cool-down

I learned about the flash point and
about how the flame moves up the kiln,
well, then I lasted about 9 years in
the job. It was only about a year after
I finally learned everything about it
that I quit.

And he mentioned some of the physical complaints common to stokers: " My eyes couldn't hold up any longer.
My liver became inflamed. I felt deep inside as if I
was being cooked." He also told how he narrowly escaped incineration on one occasion, the only close
call he had over a nine year career:

Blessed be the lord. I was a stoker for
nine years and I wasn't burned once.
And in that job there have been lots of
deaths. When the flames shoot out and
ignite the sawdust it burns you up;
there you stay, roasted once and for
all. It's just like a strip of beef
that shrivels up when its barbequed,
that's how a Christian shrivels up. I
used to stoke when I was drunk. I was
stupid and nothing happened to me.

Once I was inside the firebox with the
flames all around me! It happened this
way. The fire died out and the boss
told me to check it out. I climbed into
the firebox to rearrange the tires with
the intention of relighting the fire
afterwards. The fire had been burning
well but for some reason had died out.
So I got inside the firebox right where
the flame burns. When I picked up a
tire that was buried in the sawdust, I
heard a noise like an explosion--
BROOOM!--and suddenly the whole roof of
the firebox was burning, the arches,
the corners, everything. On the floor
where I was standing it didn't burn. I
lunged toward the stoking hole, shout-
ing to the boss: `Pull me out!´ And he
pulled me out, he dragged me out. I was
so scared that I had lost my strength.
After I was out and was sitting down
outside the kiln I asked the boss:
`Weren't you scared?´ And he snapped
back: `You bastard, you're damn right I

was scared! I thought the **Chingada** had taken you away!'[11]

Other stokers who were interviewed had less dramatic initiations to the job and none reported he had experienced a close call of the type narrated above--though all made reference to the fact that several stokers had been burned or incinerated in the past. A typical way of becoming a stoker was described by another informant as follows:

> I was working as a sawdust shoveler so I began to observe how the stoker worked. That's how I learned to stoke. Then the first time that the boss could not find a stoker I had an opportunity to see if I could take the heat. I was able to stand it so I began to stoke more often.

The main incentive to work as a stoker is economic since it is the highest paid job in the brickyards. A stoker is paid twenty-two dollars (500 pesos) for ten to twelve hours work over the twenty to twenty-four hour period he is at the kiln, and is also provided with food and drink. The disadvantage is that even a full-time stoker can work only a maximum of three firings a week, given the physical rigors of the job. Few individuals work at the job on a full-time basis for extended periods. As discussed earlier, the preferred pattern is to alternate stoking with brickmaking and loading.

Future Changes in Firing Technology?

Though economic rather than humanitarian motives are involved, several of the kiln owners interviewed expressed an interest in replacing the current fuel and firing system with an oil burning system. One of them, in fact, had invested in an oil burner which he tried to adapt unsuccessfully to his kiln. These kiln owners are aware that such burners are used in kilns in Oaxaca City pottery manufactories but their skepticism about the feasibility of their application to the larger brick kilns has been reinforced by unsuccessful experiences like the one referred to above. The difficulty with the changeover to oil burners is that it requires a period of experimentation, which is costly both in terms of the investment in money and time and also of the bricks which may be lost in the process.

106

The consensus among the brickyard operators seems to be that, given the present fragmented organization of the industry with each producer for himself, a basic change in firing technology is not feasible. It might become so, they agree, if a producers' cooperative or association were established which could then apply for technical and credit assistance from the government or some private source. On the other hand, the availability of sawdust and cheap stoker-labor are disincentives for technological innovation in the industry. Consequently, it is unlikely that any major change in technology will be made until a diminished supply or an inflated cost of labor necessitates it.

[1] The concept of "labor process" views the economic
field of human activity as a purposeful, socially
organized process of producing and supplying material
needs and wants with products, commodities, and services. Reduced to its basic elements this process may
be conceived as a series of relations between material
objects in nature (natural resources), others partially or completely transformed from natural resources
(i.e., raw materials and tools), and human labor
power. I have discussed this concept more fully elsewhere (Cook 1982a:29-30 et.passim) on the basis of my
reading of sources like Marx (1967,I:177-185),
Harnecker (1971:19-32), and Cohen (1978: esp. Chs. II
and IV).

   Keddie and Cleghorn describe the brickmaking process as follows: "All processes for making
fired clay bricks share the same broad outline. The
basic raw material is ... clay, which must be ´won´
from the earth. After more or less preparation of the
clay, it is formed into undried `green´ bricks, which
must be dried before they are finished by firing them,
using a very considerable energy input, in kilns.
Though this outline is the common denominator of
brickmaking, there are an almost infinite number of
variations pertaining to particular processes and
works; variations of product, of raw material, of
energy source, of technique" (1980:6). They also characterize the wastes created from this process: "With
the exception of the airborne products of combustion,
the wastes of brick fabrication are inert, if unsight-
ly. They consist of topsoil (which should eventually
be replaced, where brickmaking has temporarily displaced agriculture), overburden from the clay beds,
ashes, clinker, dust, rejected bricks and brick rub-
ble" (1980:9).

[2] Keddie and Cleghorn report that clay is extracted
from deposits close to the surface at all the brickworks they visited in the Third World. They point out
that the extraction process, technically referred to
as "winning", begins "with the removal of topsoil and
overburden" and continue: "Winning methods are influenced by numerous technical factors including the
hardness, water content and thickness of the clay
deposits. On flat sites, a high water table may restrict the depth of winning if drainage is not practi-

cable. The depth of winning may...be legally restricted, as in many parts of India, by the requirement that
the land must be readily redeemable for agricultural
use" (1980:14-15). There are no comparable legal re-
strictions governing the winning process in Oaxaca.

The basic distinction in Oaxaca valley arable is
between that which is watered (either irrigated from a
catch basin via channels or from a well, or high water
table land or land which tends to have a high moisture
content as, for example, after flooding) and seasonal
(**temporal**) land which is unwatered and is dependent on
rainfall to support plant growth. (For more detailed
discussions of land taxonomies in the Oaxaca valley
see Cook 1982a:35-40 and Kirkby 1973.)

[3] According to Kirkby's (1973:65-70) calculations
rainfall-dependent arable in the Tlacolula arm of the
Oaxaca valley (where Santa Lucía is located) has an
average annual corn yield of between 0.2 and 0.4
metric tons per hectare which at the going price for a
kilo of shelled corn in 1979 of 3.50 pesos would have
a cash yield of from 700 to 1400 pesos. Considering
that in 1979 one thousand unfired bricks, which one
man can produce in two or three days work, sold for
about 1000 pesos, it is clear that there is a substantial reward in cash earnings for converting dry arable
into a brickyard (even if we assume that either beans,
squash or cash crops like castor beans are cultivated
along with, or in substitution of, corn).

[4] I prefer to gloss the term **ladrillera** as "brickyard"
rather than "brickfield" which Keddie and Cleghorn
define as "the neighborhood of a clay deposit and the
brick factories built upon it" (1980:126). The common
term for a brick factory is "brickworks" (ibid.) but
this usage is inappropriate for a labor-intensive
industry of the type I am dealing with in Oaxaca. My
dictionary (**Random House Dictionary of the English
Language**, unabridged edition) defines "brickyard"
concisely as follows: "A place where bricks are made,
stored, or sold."

"**Ladrillo**" is a cover term for any type of fired
brick. Keddie and Cleghorn define a common brick as "a
brick produced for ordinary structural work, with no
special attention paid to its regularity or colour"
(1980:126)--a definition which they adapt from Rees

(1912) who noted that "The common brick is of use for ordinary structural work. Appearance is of minor importance. Bricks are made without much regard to color, smoothness of surface or sharpness of edges" (quoted in Keddie and Cleghorn 1980:4).

In Oaxaca , the **tabique** is the "common brick" although some attention is paid to its regularity and color--and these characteristics have some bearing on the saleability and selling price of **tabiques**. As Keddie and Cleghorn point out, "the prime need in developing countries is for ordinary or general-purpose bricks" and, given their focus on appropriate technology, it is more significant to "question the choice of the fired clay brick as an appropriate building material vis-a-vis alternative materials than to try to distinguish between different kinds of brick" (op.cit p. 1). These authors list the following possible alternative materials: hollow fired-clay building blocks, unfired sun-dried bricks (adobe), stabilized rammed-earth bricks and blocks, sand-cement blocks, pre-cast concrete, wattle-and-daub, stone, various kinds of frame-and-matting construction, and some novel low-cost composite materials (ibid.).

[5] Our scheme, arrived at independently and inductively, approximates that of Keddie and Cleghorn who isolate the following six successive "readily distinguishable events" in brickmaking (together with handling of the bricks between stages): winning the raw material (typically clay), carrying the clay to the brickworks, preparing the clay for brick forming, forming the bricks, drying the bricks, firing the bricks (1980:11).

For expository convenience, I will use the term "bucket" to refer not only to the artifact which most commonly is associated with the term (plastic and galvanized varieties) but also to the 20-liter rectangular cooking oil can which is widely employed as a clay or water container in the brickyards. A distinction between these two types of containers is made by the brick workers: the bucket is referred to as a **cubeta** and the can is called a **bote**.

[6] Keddie and Cleghorn note that the wet method of clay preparation and brick forming is the only one available for labor-intensive preparation. They make the

110

following observations regarding the latter: "Clay that still contains stones, pebbles, lumps, roots, etc. or varies significantly in its plasticity, on its arrival at the forming stage will certainly make inferior bricks...Human moulders are obviously more discriminating than forming machines in this respect, but their productivity still suffers to some extent if they have constantly to interrupt their molding rhythm to accomodate variations in clay plasticity. But there is a reported tendency of human clay preparers, if not adequately supervised, to ease their task by adding water to soften the clay to the point where it no longer holds its shape properly after molding" (1980:16). Given the piecework system operating in the Oaxaca valley brickyards, bricks which are improperly molded will not be accepted and paid for by employers. Consequently, pieceworkers have a material incentive to temper and pug their clay carefully.

[7] This cooperative labor coefficient was calculated by summing up for each week the total number of persons who put in a full day´s work in a given brickyard and dividing by the number of workdays in the brickyard per week. For example, in the case of the G-unit over a period of five seven-day work weeks (i.e., 35 days) a total of 132 person-days were worked. This yielded a cooperative labor coefficient of 3.8 (132/35) which means that during the 35-day period an average of 3.8 persons worked per day in Gilberto´s brickyard.

[8] This contrasts markedly with the stone quarrying phase of metate production where spontaneous cooperation between independent quarry workers is common (Cook 1982a:206-16). Informal reciprocity relations are also prevalent among the **metateros,** as well as among weavers, palm plaiters, and others.

[9] The kiln used in the Oaxaca valley brick industry is the "intermittent chamber" type. According to Keddie and Cleghorn, the use of this type of kiln is "favored in circumstances where continuous kiln operation is impracticable, either because demand is below the level at which a continuous kiln can be economically run, or because demand itself is only intermittent" (1980:18).

[10] This process is referred to as **"meter cuñas."** Each layer is referred to as a **"daga"** and the task of layering is known as **"endagar"** or **"pararse la daga"**; each row of bricks is called a **"tendida."**

These capacities indicate that a kiln should hold half again as many **mediatablas** as **tabiques**--some 15,000 for a 10,000 **tabique** kiln. **Tabiques,** however, are narrower than **mediatablas** so the latter have fewer layers when loaded in the kiln thus reducing the number that can be loaded (i.e., typically around 12,000 in a 10,000 tabique kiln).

In the technical jargon of the brick industry, the placement of green bricks into a kiln is known as "setting" and their removal after firing is known as "drawing" (see Keddie and Cleghorn 1980:126-127).

[11] One example of the difficulties in translating colloquial Mexican Spanish to English is provided by the imaginative use in the former of variations on the uniquely Mexican verb **"chingar"** -- a slang expression which roughly means "to screw." The derivative term **"la Chingada"** alludes derogatorily to the Indian noblewoman-translator-mistress of Cortés, the Spanish conquistador, who bore him an illegitimate **"mestizo"** son. Known by the nickname "La Malinche", she has been transformed in the collective unconscious of the Mexican people into a symbolic "Whore-Mother" of all **mestizos.** This topic has been dealt with provocatively by Octavio Paz (1961: esp. Ch.4) and by Carlos Fuentes (1969) among others.

CHAPTER 4

DISTRIBUTION RELATIONS: PIECE RATES, PROFITS, AND CLASS MANEUVERS

There is no more fundamental controversy in political economy than that dealing with the proper way to approach and explain how the total social product in capitalist economies is allocated among their populations. At the risk of oversimplification, two diametrically opposed postures in this controversy can be identified: one which treats income distribution as the "result of social institutions (e.g., property ownership) and social relations", and another which treats it as being determined by the "conditions of exchange" (Dobb 1973:34). The first posture found its earliest systematic expression in the classical school and, especially in Marx who argued that income distribution occurred outside the process of market pricing (or the relations of exchange) and was determined by prevailing social conditions and class forces (i.e., the relations of production). Marxism asserts that capital exploits labor by appropriating its surplus product.

The second posture is associated with the marginalist school. It views income distribution as derivative of the "general pricing process--as a constituent set of equations in the total equational system of market equilibrium" (Dobb 1973:35). In other words, marginalism considers income distribution to be a process which is "independent of property institutions and of social relations: as something supra-institutional and supra-historical so far ... as income-distribution between factors is concerned" (ibid.). Marginalism, contra marxism, asserts that capital and labor are partners in production and are justly rewarded by profits and wages (see Hunt and Sherman 1975:241-42).

This high-theoretical controversy is paralleled, if less sharply and somewhat obliquely, in economic anthropological discourse and practice. Most economic anthropologists either operate in the marginalist tradition or, by theoretical default, view the distribution of value abstractly as a process through which factors of production (and exchange) are rewarded according to economic functions performed. Distribution, by implication, involves culturally-mediated "transfer events" (LeClair 1968:205) and is conceptu-

113

alized as an exchange process; so long as a "factor" adds value or contributes, materially or immaterially, to the production/exchange of commodities, that factor earns an appropriate reward. Value is added by the contribution of any factor (from bearers of labor-power to bearers of symbolic tokens like money or bank drafts). To the extent that marginalists are concerned with the creation of economic value, they view it in the context of circulation or demand. Their inclination is to reduce value either to utility or to price. The marxist thesis that value is created in the labor process, and even the neo-ricardian thesis that labor is the "ultimate factor of production" whose role "within the production process remains worthy of emphasis" (Gudeman 1978:6-7), is either anathema or incomprehensible to marginalist thought.[1]

A central problem for the marginalists in economic anthropology is to find increasingly sophisticated ways of measuring the flows of factor incomes which are considered to be results of factor performance through firms. Firms, in turn, are defined as units (individual agents, and enterprises of all sizes) operating in a competitive environment in which risk and uncertainty are postulated to be principal constraining parameters in a perpetually equilibrative process. In other words, the marginalist economy is socially and politically disembodied; economic behavior, for marginalists, involves abstract agents like factors and firms, or quantitative variables (e.g., price, output, marginal productivity and utility, elasticity) which are indices of these agents' "behavior". The results of marginalist analysis, regardless of their human implications, are uncritically accepted as rational and functionally justifiable. The ahistorical and asocial abstractionism of the marginalist approach legitimizes its empirical results, and is self-perpetuating.

There may be legitimate disagreement as to whether capital, operating through small enterprises like those in the brickyards, is parasitic or if its profits are gratuitous or unmatched by the contribution of productive services. For marginalist analysis this is hardly a concern since it views factor returns as being determined in the market via supply and demand. What workers earn as wages for their labor power, what investors earn as interest for their money, and what capitalists earn as profits, are seen as results of various price-determining market processes. Moreover,

114

with reference to the process of material production, marginalism considers the various factors of production to be productive in proportion to their measurable inputs--without regard to the forms these assume. Since labor is freely contracted by the capitalist to work for a price determined in the market, the wage is considered to represent, more or less, just compensation. Perceived inequities between returns to labor and capital are viewed as temporary, and as being balanced out in the long-run through negotiations (e.g., Baumol and Blinder 1982:ch.32 & 33).

There is probably little disagreement among most economic anthropologists about the proposition that the degree to which returns to capital are unearned or excessive requires empirical determination at the level of the specific enterprise. This is especially true of the role of intermediaries about whom it has been argued that they render specific services for which they merit remuneration. Mintz stated this argument as follows: "The services are not imposed on customers; they are salable because buyers and sellers require them. Intermediaries transport, process, accumulate stock, break stock, grant credit to agricultural producers and to urban consumers, pay taxes, keep truckers employed, and contribute much else to the ready functioning of the economy" (1964:4).

One clear implication of such an argument seems to be that direct producers in a commodity economy are not entitled to the whole surplus product of their labor simply because the commoditization of those products requires intermediary services; and that the providers of such services (which may or may not add value to commodities already produced) are entitled to a share of the value created by direct producers. However, the same functionalist rationale can be applied to other forms of capital, so that an argument which is not intentionally or formally marginalist or apologetic for capital becomes so by implication.

Marxists find some sympathy, and substantial indifference or outright opposition, from other economic anthropologists for their belief that the relationship between capital and labor--whether in Oaxaca brickyards, West Virginia coal mines, or Japanese factories--is characterized by exploitation. This simply means that capitalists get more work out of their workers daily (or weekly in the case of the brickyards) than they pay them in wages. In formal marxist terms this is expressed by saying that the economic forces of capitalist society assure that there is "a difference between the exchange value of labor power and the exchange value of what is produced by its employment (that is, the exchange value of the product); and this difference is the source of the capitalist's profit" (Howard and King 1975:42). The Santa Lucía brickyards, in any case, provide an interesting setting in which to examine--if not resolve--some of the issues raised above.[2]

Costs and Income

The main purpose of this chapter is to describe and analyze how the brick industry's income is distributed among its workers, employers, and commercial operators, and to discuss the implications of this distribution for the socioeconomic life of these groups. With thirty-five active kilns, and assuming an average kiln capacity of 10,000 bricks with an average firing interval of one month, the Santa Lucía industry has a minimum average monthly production capacity of approximately 350,000 bricks worth about 25,000 dollars. This translates into a potential annual gross income of 300,000 dollars, a significant figure for a village-based, labor-intensive industry in the Oaxaca valley.[3]

Given the wide variety of conditions operating to differentiate the nature and scale of brick production units, it is not easy to arrive at a characterization of the economics of the typical unit. For example, the owners of some brickyards inherited them, whereas others had to purchase them; also, some units have a much larger family or in-kind labor supply than others which may have none. These conditions have different implications for cost accounting and the comparative analysis of economic performance (e.g., profit calculations). Moreover, most of the brickyard enterprises do not operate according to standard cost accounting procedures. For the most part fixed overhead costs (e.g., land, kiln)--unless representing a current cash drain--are not considered in brickyard accounting, nor are in-kind labor costs factored in according to their wage equivalents. These are only three examples of many possible contrasts between brick production units.

Observational and interview data on the costs (see Table 7) and results (see Table 8) of kiln fir-

116

ings suggest that the average firing of 10,000 bricks costs about 400 dollars (9,000 pesos), and yields 70% firsts and 30% seconds. This amounts to a market value of 709 dollars (15,960 pesos) and yields an average profit of 352 dollars (7,909 pesos) per firing (Table 8).

In order to put this exercise in proper perspective several factors require discussion. First is the predominant role of labor as a cost factor in the daily operation of these units. With the exception of the L-unit which relied entirely on family labor, labor cost comprises an average of 85% of the total

Table 7. Estimated Costs Per Firing for Eight Kilns (values in pesos)

Cost Category	A	P	G	H	R	M	J	L
Sand	0	150	0	0	0	67	175	0
Old tires	10	333	0	0	25	200	0	0
Sawdust	1,400	1,333	1,300	867	1,200	1,300	1,300	1,300
Mileros	6,025	6,500	5,000	6,000	5,000	6,000	6,000	0
Loading	360	600	450	600	750	600	600	0
Stoking	950	1,150	750	575	1,150	1,150	0	0
Unloading	240	600	450	450	300	600	600	0
TOTAL	8,985	10,666	7,950	8,492	8,425	9,917	8,675	1,300
Labor cost	7,575	8,850	6,650	7,625	7,200	8,350	7,200	0
% of Total	84	83	84	90	85	84	83	0

Table 8. Profit Estimates per Firing for Eight Brickyards (values in pesos)

Name of Unit	Market value	Operating costs	Profit
L	15,960	1,300	14,660
G	"	7,950	8,010
R	"	8,425	7,535
H	"	8,492	7,468
J	"	8,675	7,285
A	"	8,985	6,975
M	"	9,917	6,043
P	"	10,666	5,294

117

total operating costs (i.e., of circulating capital in marxist terms) for the seven cases (range of 83-90%). If the average profit per firing is recalculated excluding the L-unit, the estimate is significantly reduced to 309 dollars (6,944 pesos). This demonstrates unequivocally the crucial role of the wage bill in the economics of the industry.

A second factor which must be considered is that of overhead costs which are incurred to facilitate each firing. Means of production such as tools, equipment, and the land itself are essential to each production cycle but entail cash expenditures only periodically, perhaps at intervals of several months or years, or not at all. Such expenditures, if incurred, are difficult to assign per thousand bricks fired and, in fact, many brickyard operators do not accurately account for them in figuring their costs and profits.

This means that the economics of the brick industry cannot be fully understood by considering only its current, short-term costs and benefits. Factors such as the history of the acquisition of critical means of production (e.g., land, kilns, trucks), and the level of current financial commitment regarding their payoff or replacement, must also be considered--with the proviso that these may not affect operating decisions in particular brickyard enterprises.

The typical brickyard operator has between 75-100 dollars invested in tools (shovels, crowbars, picks, buckets, cans, molds, and plastic sheeting). Given the wear and tear on these it is reasonable to assume a fifty percent annual replacement rate. This means an expenditure of from 38 to 50 dollars annually for tool replacement, which would reduce profit accordingly. Of the brickyard owners interviewed, one-third inherited the land on which they operate their brickyards, and another third purchased it prior to the 1976 devaluation at an average price of 1,700 dollars each. The remaining third purchased their land in the late 1970s and paid anywhere from one to four dollars per square meter, with an average investment of about 2,400 dollars each. Two operators still owed a balance on this investment when interviewed, so that payments for land cut significantly into their profits on each firing. Nevertheless, in the last analysis, it is not the fixed cost of the land which is most crucial in understanding the economics of the industry (or, in most cases, in determining the decisions of the brickyard operator) but, rather, the cost of the labor-power required to extract the soil from the land, to transform the latter into clay and, finally, to mold bricks from it.[4]

In addition there is the matter of expenditures for fixed capital assets which are necessary to transform the land into a viable brickyard. Most brickyard owners construct sheds to store unfired bricks. Sheds with a storage capacity of 10,000 bricks cost between 90 and 130 dollars in material and labor. Then there is the cost of the kiln. Only two of the eleven informants had new kilns. These had been constructed about one year prior to the 1980 interviews and cost 870 dollars and 1,100 dollars respectively. If we assume a fifteen to twenty-five year life span for a kiln, then its rate of depreciation would vary from a minimum of thirty-five dollars annually (870 dollars cost and twenty-five year life) to a maximum of seventy-two dollars annually (1,100 dollars cost and fifteen year life). If these amounts were spread over twelve annual firings (the average for all units), from three to six dollars per firing should be deducted from profits as payback (or replacement cost) on the original investment.

Another cost not included in the average profit calculation is that of the transport of bricks between the patio and the kiln in the brickyard. The logistics of brickyard layouts are such that, in many cases, it is not feasible to carry bricks by hand from the patio to the kiln. As previously noted, this carriage used to be handled by ox cart but the latter began to be displaced in the brick industry in the early 1940s and is now handled only by flat-bed truck. Consequently, yard operators without their own trucks must rent them at a fee of four dollars per 1000 bricks (or forty dollars per firing of 10,000 bricks). This expenditure, when incurred, reduces the level of average profit by fifteen to twenty percent.

Even those brickyard operators who own trucks incur some cost when their kiln is not close to the patio since the truck itself is a capital good which depreciates. Four of the ten kiln owners interviewed also own flat-bed trucks. In all cases these were purchased used at prices ranging from 1,400 dollars to 7,000 dollars. Brickyard operators who own trucks are in a position to defray replacement costs even if they do not use their trucks to haul bricks outside of the

brickyard since they can engage in patio-to-kiln hauling for truckless brickyards. Bricks can be loaded,
unloaded and transported from patio to kiln at a rate
of one thousand per hour (for a fee of four dollars
per thousand, with labor costs being paid by the
brickyard operator), and truckers can earn extra money
daily in this manner.

Therefore, the average rate of profit estimated
earlier is subject to various deductions, either for
replacement of means of production already purchased
or to complete the payoff of those still unpaid. Informant explanations of how they calculated costs,
indicate that only a few keep written acounts. After
their large debts are repaid (e.g., those for the
purchase of land or a truck), other brickyard-related
overhead and replacement costs are dealt with on an ad
hoc basis. Such costs recede into the background in
comparison with current operating costs which are the
critical factor in the typical kiln owner's evaluation
of how he is doing financially from one firing to
another. The longer fired bricks go unsold or payment
for a load of bricks is deferred, the greater is the
strain on the brickyard operator's cash flow. His
mileros must be paid weekly and, in addition, often
request cash advances against future work.

This dilemma is illustrated in the case of one
informant who said that when cash is short from brick
sales he keeps the brickyard going with cash raised
from the sale of alfalfa. Another informant said that
when short of cash on two occasions in the past, he
was forced to sell unfired bricks to raise sufficient
money to pay his **mileros.** As still another informant
put it, probably to minimize the profit-yielding potential of his business, the aim of each production
cycle is to get "some earnings to keep the work
going." Whether or not their business is as consist-
ently profitable as they would like, it should not be
overlooked that most of the brickyard operators have
alternative sources of income to fall back on in hard
times.

Only one of eight operators interviewed had no
agricultural land and produced none of his own foodstuffs; six kept farm animals (average value per informant of 236 dollars). These figures contrast sharply with those for **milero** households. Only three of ten
mileros interviewed had farm animals (average value of
114 dollars). Moreover, the brickyard employer house-

holds rank much higher in terms of the living conditions index (see Table 2) than the **milero** households.
Another indication of the relative affluence of the
brickyard operators vis-a-vis the **mileros** is their
estimated weekly income for the week preceding the
interview: 132 dollars (3040 pesos) vs. 42 dollars
(970 pesos) for the **mileros.**

This latter figure should be kept in mind as
income data (for the same producer households covered
in the section on output variability) are examined.
The observational study recorded the income of eleven
milero households (from brick industry employment
only) for periods of from one to eight weeks each in
April and May, 1980 (see Table 9). The mean weekly
income of 48 dollars weekly is more reliable than (but
in line with) the estimate of 42 dollars derived from
the survey.

It is no coincidence that the households with the
highest number of male brickworkers have the highest
average weekly incomes (which is also a reflection of
their status as the most productive units). The simple
fact is that such households can mobilize more labor
power to produce bricks and to participate in other
income-yielding jobs in the brickyards than can those
with fewer male workers. It is significant to note in
comparing the income column (which follows a rank
order from highest to lowest) with the output column,
household by household, that there are several cases
in which the income order does not correspond with the
output order (e.g.,the Cirilo and Tomás units are 1-2
for income but 2-1 for output). This reflects the
tendency among some units to supplement brickmaking
with other jobs in the brickyards such as loading and
unloading kilns and trucks or stoking.

A further breakdown of the income data for a
selected group of household units (Table 10) shows
that the high average income ranking of the Tomás unit
is partially attributable to its participation in jobs
other than brickmaking. This factor is also significant, to a lesser degree, in those units which have
advantages in scheduling work because of the favorable
age composition of their male workers. In short, the
14% average percentage of total brickyard income derived from work other than brickmaking is indicative
of several conditions in the brickyards: 1) the significance of a non-brickmaking labor market; 2) the
tendency among **mileros** to seek work alternatives to

Table 9. Income and Demographic Data Derived from the Observation of Eleven **Milero** Households

House- hold ID	Age of head	Hshld size	No. male	of female	workers total	Weeks obsvd	Avg. income	Avg. output
C	42	6	4	0	4	3	1,809	2,682
T	46	8	3	1	4	4	1,695	2,935
P	49	5	2	0	2	2	1,257	2,460
Pf	nd*	7	1	0	1	1	1,154	1,673
G	30	6	1	1	2	5	1,100	1,925
E	18	3	1	0	1	2	1,054	1,423
L	45	nd*	1	0	1	1	1,046	1,763
J	21	3	1	0	1	2	864	1,048
A	20	3	1	2	3	4	815	1,358
S	35	4	1	0	1	1	787	1,062
M	30	5	1	1	2	4	613	1,283
MEAN	42	5	1.5	.5	2	2.6	1,108.6	1,782.9

* = no data

Table 10. Income from Brickmaking and Other Brickyard Activities for Six **Milero** Households (in pesos)

Household ID	No. weeks observed	Total Income	Brick income	Other income	% other
M	4	637	487	150	23.6
T	4	1696	1321	375	22.1
P	2	1257	1107	150	11.9
G	3	1338	1153	185	13.8
C	3	1809	1609	200	11.1
A	4	814	814	0	0.0
MEAN	3.3	1259	1082	177	14.

brickmaking because of (a) its drudgery and (b) the need for quick cash during the week; and 3) the industriousness and labor-time planning skills of these working class households.

Average income and expenditure data from the reports submitted by four **milero** and one worker-employer household (Gilberto's) in June and July, 1980 (Table 11) yields an estimate of mean weekly income which is almost identical to the estimate derived from the observational study. This is, of course, substantially less than the 215 dollars average reported by the Gilberto unit which had neither a kiln nor a truck and, at the time of the study, still owed a balance of 890 dollars on its brickyard. The discrepancies between reported income and expenditures apparently reflect incomplete record keeping regarding expenditures since, in most cases, these are substantially lower than the reported incomes. Other data indicate that none of these units is accumulating capital at a rate as high as the income-expenditure gap suggests.

Regarding the level of weekly expenditures for **milero** households, the reports for the Cirilo and Tomás units (Table 11) are the most complete and reliable. The combined weekly mean expenditure for these two households is 57 dollars (1,316 pesos). Tomás´ household is the only one with any significant capacity to raise cash outside of the brickyard. Over the years, Tomás has managed to accumulate a herd of goats which he keeps in a pen alongside his brickyard shanty. The occasional sale of a goat, and regular sales of goat cheese, provide a significant supplement to brickyard income.

Table 11. Reported Income and Expenditures for Five Brick Industry Households (in pesos)

Household ID		June 1-7	June 8-14	June 15-21	June 22-28	June 29 -July 5	July 6-12	MEANS
G	income	5,000	6,800	4,000	nd	4,000	nd	4,950
	expend	3,535	3,735	2,833	nd	2,790	nd	3,223
C	income	2,000	1,500	2,580	1,500	1,950	2,040	1,928
	expend	1,767	760	830	1,067	925	1,067	1,070
T	income	1,500	1,700	750	1,575	1,900	1,825	1,542
	expend	1,353	1,669	1,481	1,323	2,324	1,225	1,562
P	income	nd*	1,000	700	nd	1,000	1,000	925
	expend	nd	510	185	330	341	358	345
M	income	675	nd	nd	600	600	800	669
	expend	875	nd	nd	561	667	595	675

* nd = no data

The above discussion may be summarized by concluding that brickyard employers fare much better than **mileros** in the distribution of revenues accrued from brick sales. This is reflected in the higher standard of living of employer households. Such a conclusion must be weighed, however, against the substantial amount of capital each employer invests in fixed and operating costs to keep his brickyard in business. These costs do significantly reduce the level of gross profits. Given the widespread failure to apply precise cost accounting procedures--including not accounting for in-kind labor, differential rent, value of clay, depreciation of kilns and other means of production-- it is clear that the **modus operandi** of brickyard capital is cost-defective rather than cost-effective. Nevertheless, combined with this accounting naiveté of brickyard capital, a key to the viability of the industry is the cheap labor supplied by multiple-worker households in which everyone but the very young, the aged or the infirm performs a productive role in the labor process of brick production.[5]

Patrones and Mileros: the Piece Wage Nexus

Marx considered the piece wage to be merely a version of the time wage (1967:553). However, in the period before the rise of "machinofacture"--the stormy youth of Modern Industry" at the end of the 18th and the beginning of the 19th centuries--Marx emphasized that the piece wage operated as a "lever for the lengthening of the working day, and the lowering of wages" (1967:556). His discussion of the topic is supported by documentary material extracted mostly from factory inspection reports on industries such as spinning and weaving, tailoring, and pottery. According to Marx, the source of the leverage for lengthening the working day resided in the piece wage's enhancement of the individual worker's material incentive, making it in his "personal interest ... to lengthen the working-day, since with it his daily or weekly wages rise" (1967:554). Under a piece wage regime, the value of the piece is not measured by the working time incorporated in it; rather, the working time expended by the laborer is measured by the number of pieces he has produced (1967:552-553).[6]

In essence, under the piece wage regime, labor is structurally propelled toward self-exploitation which is ideologically represented as enhanced "liberty, independence, and self-control" (Marx 1967:555). The individual worker is encouraged to believe that he is master of his own economic destiny, and that he will earn in direct proportion to his product.

Marx also argued (1967:555) that the piece wage system promotes competitiveness among individual workers in a given branch of production; but it has the material effect of raising individual wages above the average as it tends to lower the average itself (i.e., cheapening the cost of labor-power to capitalists). How, specifically, is this outcome accomplished? Marx's answer anticipated the arrival of Taylorism or "scientific management" to capitalist industry. The practice of "scientific management" by employers does not prevent workers from temporarily increasing their pay through piecework incentives but it does assure that production times of the faster workers will be used by employers to cut rates, thus lowering the wage for all workers (Lamphere 1979:261; Braverman 1974:98-99).

For example, the determination of piece rates by Taylorian methods in the contemporary costume jewelry industry in Providence, Rhode Island has been described as follows: "Through analysis of the time and study data and other inputs...management determines that 200 rings...can be produced per hour. By lining up this hourly production rate with the hourly rate of pay, i.e., 200 rings for $2.70, management determines a piece rate: $1.35 per 100. Through this method management has effectively predetermined that the company will have to "pay out" little extra piecework money" (Shapiro-Perl 1979:289-290). However, when a few fast workers master a job and begin "making money", management has the job re-timed and the piece rate lowered -- a practice commonly known as "rate busting" (Shapiro-Perl 1979:292).

How does a marxist analysis of the piece wage system fare when set against the situation in the brickyards? The incentives built into the piecework system are viewed by brickyard employers as providing the best stimulus to **milero** productivity. Aside from employing additional **mileros**, or replacing inefficient **milero** units with more efficient ones, there is little that an employer can do to increase brick output. When asked why he didn't impose a weekly production quota on his **mileros**, one employer responded: "That would be to demand that they work harder, but they are free. We can't force them. We aren't in charge of them so that they have to do what we order. They make what they can." When asked how he compared the piece wage with the time wage this same informant responded:

> The piece wage is better because if the
> **mileros** want to speed up work they can
> do so. It´s also better because one
> doesn´t have to lose time supervising
> them. They come to the brickyard as
> pieceworkers and what they make is what
> they get paid for.

Another employer expressed the following view: "**Mileros** are pieceworkers. The day that they want to make 200, 300 or 500 bricks they make them; it´s up to them. They work according to a piece rate, not by the day or week." In short, unless confronted with a deadline, the brickyard employers essentially adopt a laissez-faire policy regarding **milero** productivity.

There is a similarity of views on the piece wage vs. time wage issue between employers and **mileros**. This is illustrated by the following statement by a **milero** who, before coming to work in the brickyards, had worked on a time wage basis in Oaxaca City:

> I like the piece wage better because
> one is not forced to work continually.
> Tomorrow, if you want to work you do
> so; if you don´t want to work you don´t
> have to. On the jobs I had in the city
> it wasn´t like that. You had to work
> daily by force or the boss would fire
> you. Here in the brickyards it´s diffe-
> rent. No one forces you to work. If you
> want to make 400 or 500 bricks daily,
> well, you can make them. But, if you
> don´t want to make any, you don´t have
> to.

In addition to this emphasis on the fact that piece work permits them to work at their own pace, and according to their own schedule without close super- vision, two other aspects of the piece wage system emerge from an analysis of interviews with the **mileros** --all of which turn out to be compatible with Marx´s analysis. These are that: (1) **mileros** prefer the piece wage to the time wage because it permits them to earn more for increasing their productivity; and (2) there is competitiveness among **mileros** working for the same employer in contiguous patios. (Employers foster this dissension by by playing on individual **milero´s** pride in craftsmanship and productivity.) **Mileros´** views are well represented in a statement by Pedro, author of

126

the colorful narrative on becoming a stoker which was quoted in the preceding chapter:

> One is paid by quantity, never by day. We get paid once a week but according to the quantity that we produce. I prefer to be paid by quantity. That way I have a bigger lump sum of take-home pay. I work almost on my own account. We work for a wage but it's almost like we worked on our own because we make what we can. Around here it doesn't matter to the boss if I make 100 or 200 bricks on a given day. What counts is how many I make in a week. The boss will ask me: "How many did you make?" I answer: "I made 1,000, or 2,000."

> The more you screw yourself, the more money you make. If you don't screw yourself, you make no money. (**"Entre mas se chinga, mas dinero hay. Si no se chinga, pues, no hay dinero."**) That's the reason the boss likes me and my son because we supply him with more bricks than the two **mileros** who work for him in the patio next to ours. Those bastards (**cabrones**) make bricks on some days but not on others. Sometimes they go on drinking binges for a week. So, the poor boss counts on us two, and we do our best for him. I tell my son: "Let's get to it" and we make 2,500 or sometimes 3,000 bricks a week. The boss can complete a kiln load with our output together with the little bit that the other two lazy guys make. That's why the other day I said to the boss: "Look, if you don't pay us more, we're going to work in another brickyard." The boss answered me: "I'll give you a raise. So don't go anywhere."

In the last few lines of Pedro's statement there are signs that the capital-labor relationship regarding the brickyard piece rate is quite different than that posited by Marx and documented in the Rhode Island costume jewelry industry. "Scientific management" of the formalized sort is absent from the brickyards, as it is from other piecework industries in Oaxaca City and in the countryside (Cook 1984a). Piece rates in the brick industry, as in treadle loom weaving, are set by practical knowledge of what the average product of a day´s work is (e.g., the average number of meters of cloth woven per weaver, or the average number of bricks made per **milero**). This production rate is then roughly "lined-up" with the going minimum daily wage rate which is periodically issued by the federal government (6.70 dollars or 150 pesos in 1979).

Oaxaca employers, however, do not engage in "rate busting." On the contrary, in the brick industry employers confront a short supply of steady, reliable, productive workers and the piece rate is subject to periodic demands for increases by **mileros**. Indeed, there has been a constant rise (in money terms, at least) in the piece rate for several decades, and there is no evidence to suggest that the piece rate has ever been lowered (again, in money terms).

Brickyard employers do pay differential piece rates to **mileros** on the basis of skill as measured in the quality of the bricks produced. One drawback to the piece work system, wherever it is in effect, is the difficulty of controlling quality when a premium is placed on productivity (ILO 1951:178). Several brickyard operators felt that the quality of bricks had deteriorated over the decades. **Mileros** are also conscious of the differential quality of bricks produced by different **mileros** in the same yard or in different yards and there seems to be some acceptance of this as a legitimate reason for piece rate differentials. Antonio made the following comments on this problem in the brickyard which he operates:

> **Mileros** are paid according to their work--not by the tasks that they perform but by what they make. In past years work was of better quality. For example, at the present time the **milero** who also stokes for me makes bricks very well. His bricks have a better appearance than those made by my other **mileros,** so I can sell them for a higher price. In other words, one pays particular attention which **mileros** work better; they all perform the same tasks but some of them make better quality

bricks than others. Better quality
bricks command higher prices. My best
milero makes 300 or 400 bricks daily--
sometimes he makes less because his
work is of better quality. Therefore, I
pay him a little bit more. He's the
type of **milero** who deserves raises in
the piece rate. Those **mileros** who do
sloppy work don't get raises. It
doesn't matter if they don't stay
around. On the other hand, if a **milero**
who does quality work leaves my brickyard then it will matter.

Brickyard employers, like Oaxaca City manufactory
operators (Cook 1984a), are not concerned if their
pieceworkers earn more than the official minimum wage
which, in any case, is widely recognized to be well
below the value of labor (i.e., below a level of
income required to clothe, feed, and house a wage
earner's family without some degree of nutritional
stress--Murphy and Selby 1981:250-251). Given Santa
Lucia's proximity to Oaxaca City, it is pertinent to
note that the latter is among the poorest cities of
its size in Mexico; 65% of its households have been
estimated to have a "less than adequate income"
(Murphy and Selby 1981:251). Under such conditions not
even the most hard-pressed, fledgling brickyard capitalist need be concerned with methods for intensifying
the rate of exploitation.

Given this situation, the brickyard employers use
the piece wage as a means to recruit and keep labor,
and to cope with the short supply of productive,
reliable labor. Payment by results is best understood
in the brickyards as a method imposed upon employers
by the conditions of labor, rather than as one con-
sciously applied to systematically exploit labor.This
is what should be expected when dealing with representatives of a fledgling form of peasant industrial
capital rather than of a full-grown form of urban-
industrial capital. Brickyard employers' first
priority is to keep their brickyards in business. This
can be achieved only by making periodic wage conces-
sions (as well as cash advances and loans) to their
mileros. Employers' second priority is to protect,
rather than to expand, their profit levels from the
reductive impact of rising costs of producer's goods
and wage goods. For the most part, they appear to have
achieved this through the years by making compensatory

129

increases in the selling price of bricks.

Pricing and Marketing

There is general agreement among the brickyard operators that there is a going price for bricks but that no individual or group has the power to set it. They refer to this variously as the "going price" (**"precio que está corriendo"**), the "general price" (**"precio general"**), the "standard price" (**"precio estandar"**) or as the "conventional price" (**"precio convencional**)." It is, in other words, viewed by them to be a market price set by the interaction of many buyers and sellers and policed by competition among the sellers. Informants had different ways of expressing this. One asserted that,"One must be subject to the price that the rest have" and further asserted that "I can´t say that I sell bricks at such and such a price." Another, however, seemed to contradict this view by leaving the door open for price movements: "Demand sets the price; there is not a uniform price for bricks." Still another said that he sells his bricks "according to the market. We give them at the price that is, the standard price." Then he referred to the factor of competition: "I can´t raise my price to buyers above the standard price because they will go to another brickyard."

Seasonal and other factors are singled-out as causing price movements and most sellers do go through the formalities of haggling over price with potential buyers. One informant expressed this succinctly:

> There´s a general price that all the brick sellers around here put on their bricks. If I know that so-and-so is selling them for 1,800, then I offer them for 1,800. If I know that he is selling them for more then I will sell them for more. Everything depends on what the buyers are willing to pay. If I see that a client is not willing to buy I´ll lower the price a little bit."

Another informant also expressed the notion of a general price but specified the role of seasonality: "There is a set price. The price is the same at all the kilns. During the rainy season the price of bricks rises and during the dry season it declines because there are too many."

In anticipation of a short supply of bricks during the rainy season, many brickyard operators see it as a desirable strategy to build up as large an inventory as possible toward the end of the dry season. One of the most affluent of them outlined this strategy but denied that he employed it: "There are some who build up brick inventories toward the end of the dry season in order to sell them during the rainy season when the price increases. I don't do it because I lack money." Another admitted to having the idea but said that he had to sell his bricks as soon as possible after they are fired to pay his workers, and added: "Only the brickmakers that have savings to draw on" can hold bricks in inventory until prices increase. Indeed, the **mileros** themselves try to intensify brick production in anticipation of the rainy season when they know that many workdays will be lost due to brickyard flooding.[7]

One factor which favors the buyer in the brick market is the large number of cash-needy sellers--though, admittedly, some are more needy than others. This need factor was introduced by one informant in his description of a typical sales situation:

> I quote a price to him, the going price. If he likes it he pays it, if not he says to me: `Lower the price at least by 100 pesos.´ Here is where my need enters the picture. If I´m really hurting for money I tell him it´s a deal. If not then I keep the bricks and later on another buyer will come along who´ll pay the going price.

This same informant, himself an ex-trucker and brick merchant, related this need factor among the sellers to the strategy of the brick resellers (**revendedores**): "The reseller always earns, he doesn't have to build up inventories. The profits of the resellers go hand in hand with the need of the brickmaker." Brickyard operators who do not own trucks (or those who do but use them only to haul their own bricks) consider the brick market to be controlled by the trucker-resellers. But they are not resentful of the profits earned by the resellers. By and large, they consider the reseller´s profits to be just rewards for investments made, risks taken, and market information controlled.

131

13. Loading a flat-bed truck for a trip to the city

The brickyard operators also recognize their own role in pricing or, more specifically, in increasing their selling prices in response to other price increases over which they have no control. This is the mechanism responsible for the price spiral in the brick market. That such a spiral exists in the brick market is shown by the fact that in Oaxaca City in 1967-68, the price per thousand averaged around 25 dollars, whereas by 1980, it had risen to 90 dollars. One informant explained the role of the sellers in this price spiral in the following terms: "If sawdust prices rise, hauling fees rise, and wages rise, then we have to raise the price of bricks." This viewpoint was echoed by another:

> About six months ago we raised the price of bricks 200 pesos. Sawdust, for example, went up in price to increase our firing costs. Hauling fees also rose. So we had no choice but to increase the price of bricks. In other words, things even out.

A recent tax increase was cited by one disgruntled informant as an underlying cause for price increases. Gilberto, who is still saddled with a balance due on his brickyard and who sells his unfired bricks at a reduced price to his creditor in the process of paying off his debt in kind, summed up the frustration of small dependent producers over their inability to unilaterally raise prices:

> Since the price of sugar just went up we would like to raise the price of bricks but we still have the same price. I haven't said anything to my buyer. I would like to tell him that I have to raise the price of my bricks because the price of sugar went up. But few buyers will be sympathetic and go along with the increase.

Other producers, by contrast, did what Gilberto was unable to do because his debtor relationship to his principal buyer constrained his price-setting capacity. This is clear from the following statement by a young worker-owner who framed the pricing problem in general terms but also cited the rise in the price of sugar as a cause for a compensatory rise in the price of bricks on the "open market":

133

At the same time as food prices rise
one must raise the price of bricks. The
brick price just rose because a short
time ago the price of sugar increased
and the prices of other necesssary
foodstuffs also rose.

In other words, he viewed an increase in the price of
bricks as a normal and necessary response to price
increases in basic wage goods which not only increased
his own cost of subsistence but that of his **mileros** as
well.

Another determinant of the demand for bricks (and
indirectly of their price) is the supply of cement
which is a relatively scarce commodity in Oaxaca. As
one astute informant outlined this relationship:

The price of bricks is pegged to the
production of cement. If there´s no
cement, there are no sales of bricks.
The first thing that architects say is:
Why should we buy bricks if we have no
cement? If there is plenty of cement
you can be sure that there will be a
good demand for bricks. And when there
is a good demand for bricks the price
rises automatically.

This informant, like the one quoted before him, has a
clear insight into the interrelatedness of supply and
demand across sectors in a developing capitalist economy where the distribution of certain basic wage
goods like sugar and of producer´s goods like cement
--both produced in the mechanized state capitalist
sector--has a fundamental impact on the livelihood of
small producers.

Even on the basis of this limited analysis it
should be agreed that there is more to the price of
bricks than meets the eye. It is also clear that on
both the supply and demand sides of the brick market
there are different categories of buyers and sellers,
with the major axis of differentiation being the scale
of their operations. There is a demand derived from
private residential construction where either the
individual owner or the small independent builder
comes directly to the brickyards and shops around for
bricks. More than half of the informants said they
regularly sold bricks to this type of buyer and pre-

134

ferred this kind of direct cash transaction to those involving construction firms, resellers, or the government which usually entail either a great deal of paper work, deferred payment, or both. "I prefer to sell to buyers for own-use," said one informant, "because they pay on the spot." And he added, "There´s a lot of paper work with the construction companies and there´s a longer wait to get paid." Another informant also stated his preference to sell to buyers for own-use and implied that this was based on the fact that he could get a better price for his bricks this way because resellers always drive harder bargains in their attempt to maximize profit.

Both the interview and survey data suggest, nevertheless, that probably about two-thirds of the bricks sold by Santa Lucía producers either circulate through the hands of trucker-resellers or are bought by construction firms or building contractors. At least half of these sales are made by producers and/or resellers who have established, more or less, permanent relationships with clients in the construction industry. The rest occur as open market transactions in which a reseller or a producer either seeks out contracts with buyers by visiting offices or construction sites at random or is contacted at random by buyers. An important role is played in this process by masons (albañiles) who are in charge of specific construction projects. One brickyard operator emphasized the importance of establishing good relationships with masons who "... come to buy bricks for the projects where they are working." This same informant also noted that "The masons to whom one sells recommends one to other masons. That´s how one builds up a clientele."

As the following examples show the brickyards do produce some unorthodox sales practices. One brickyard-owning peasant recalled that when he started his brickyard some twenty-five years ago he unwisely delegated the sale of bricks to the brickmakers he employed who "took bricks and went to Oaxaca City to look around for buyers." He claimed that he lost money on more than one occasion when some of his piece workers who were not native Santa Lucians, absconded with cash received from brick sales and were never seen or heard from again. An especially risky tactic employed by some trucker-resellers is referred to as "al aventón" ("a free ride"). According to this practice, a truck is loaded with bricks, either on

consignment or with a down payment paid to the producers; then the reseller drives around construction
areas, or occasionally to regional marketplaces,
looking for buyers. As one reseller explained this
strategy:

> I leave with a load of bricks without
> knowing where I will deliver them. I go
> with the intention of finding a buyer
> in the city. If I don't find a buyer I
> return to Santa Lucía and lose my car-
> riage expenses. You take a risk because
> you're never sure if you'll make a sale
> or have to return with a full load.

The urban big-buyer market is off limits to the
small and inexperienced seller. Consequently, this
market is controlled by the wealthiest brick merchants
who have both trucks and brickyards with kilns. In the
words of a neophyte reseller who had just purchased a
used truck:

> I don't feel competent to sell to the
> big projects. I don't know how to go
> about it. There are others who have
> more time to make contacts with con-
> struction firms. They help each other
> out. But since I'm just starting out I
> have a lot to learn.

Even Antonio, the ex-Municipal President who was himself successful for a time with a three-truck resell-
ing operation, explained the dynamics of this business
to emphasize the fact that it is off limits to those
with limited contacts and capital:

> In the Oaxaca City business, until you
> deliver bricks to the construction site
> you don't get a down payment. Often
> when you deliver the bricks, they will
> give you a promissory note which tells
> you to come on such and such a day to
> receive payment. Or they will give you
> a check but tell you that you can't
> cash it until some future date. That's
> why the guys with capital around here
> get involved as resellers--because if
> they can wait to get paid they make
> good profits.

136

Take the case of Fernando, he has bought bricks from me often. But he always asks me how many bricks I have and what price I´m asking. I tell him, for example, that I´ll sell them to him for 1,600 so that his profit will be greater. He gives me an advance; he never pays me everything. There´s his advantage. The ones who have money buy for less. On the other hand, I don´t have any money so with the advance he gave me I can pay my **mileros** for the week and have some left over for my household expenses. The reseller earns 200 pesos above the normal price per thousand bricks he pays me, plus what he earns later on. He might sell the bricks he buys from me at 1,600 for 2,500. Just imagine how much he earns!

This happens to us producers because we lack capital. If I had a sum of capital, say around 100,000 or 200,000 pesos, I would become a reseller again. I have a truck. Even if I hired a driver and others to load and unload I would make a profit. But with what capital? Where am I going to get 20,000 bricks? I could go to two or three kilns and tell the operators to save me their bricks. But they won´t put aside any if I can´t give them a down payment in advance. To operate as a reseller you can´t do business with only one architect but with four or five. And you get several orders from these architects, not just one order. To supply these orders, daily the resellers make advance down payments to several kiln operators. So, even 50,000 pesos would not be enough.

At the same time resellers are distributing money they are earning it too. Their earnings are very good. Let´s suppose that an architect places two orders for 10,000 bricks each. To supply those two orders the reseller must go to various brickyards, give the operators their down payments and tell

them that they'll get the rest when the
architects pay the bill. They distrib-
ute money as down payments without
having been paid off by the architect
who put in the order. Immediately they
go to another architect and he puts in
a new order for 5000 bricks. To supply
those 5000 bricks, the reseller goes
right to the brickyards again and makes
the same arrangements. So, if the reseller works with 4 or 5 architects and
each of them puts in 1 or 2 orders
each, the reseller has to pay out money
to the kiln operators to supply those
orders. Fifty thousand pesos is not
enough for this business.

Since I used to work as a reseller I
know how much money it takes. The worst
part is that there are a lot of unscru-
pulous people in the city. They make
orders for bricks and then, when the
construction project is completed, they
still owe balances of 20,000 or 30,000
pesos on the bricks. Sometimes that
money belongs to the resellers; other
times it belongs to the brickyard
owners. The architects sometimes are
not native Oaxacans, and they are the
ones who leave without paying their
bills. But the resellers are natives
and can't get away; they must pay the
producers what they owe them.

I can't get into the business again
because I don't have the money. I don't
want to make commitments to my people
that I can't follow through on. If it
turned out that some architect failed
to pay me off, then I would have to pay
the producers from my own pocket. I
would go down with them. I wouldn't
take the risk because I would lose what
I have and what they have too.

This statement should leave little doubt that the
resellers are the risk takers of the industry. They
are also the most exposed participants in the industry
and, consequently, are vulnerable to government regulation and venality. Since the government classifies

resellers as commercial operators, it taxes them more heavily than it taxes producers.[8]

Class Consciousness and Class Maneuvers:
Struggle for the Fruits of Labor

The preceding analysis of the production, exchange, and distribution of value in the brick industry supports the thesis that there is a definite tendency toward the crystallization and polarization of its class structure. This tendency remains only partially realized but is expressed through constant maneuvering between **mileros** and employers over the piece rate as the prices of bricks or of wage goods rise. It is also true that most of the production units in this industry have crossed the threshold where family labor is the principal source of capital accumulation and have entered a space where wage labor has assumed that role. There are some independent brickyard operators who work alone or with family labor but they comprise only fifteen percent of the units surveyed.

Given the external social origins of a majority of brickyard proletarians, combined with their landless status and marginal position in local society, there is less opportunity for them than there was for **mileros** of previous generations to progress materially through familial cooperation and savings. Today, family labor--rather than a source of capital accumulation for the family itself--has become more important as a reproducer of inferior wage conditions for capitalist brickyards. More specifically, the prevailing piece rate is approximately pegged to the cost of reproduction of the individual **milero**'s labor-power but would fall below this level without the labor contribution by other members of his household.[9]

What are the ideological consequences of this situation within the industry? The most obvious one is the degree to which social relations in the brickyards are conducted within a dichotomized idiom which separates **patrones** from **mileros** or the ones who employ (and pay) from the ones who are employed (and paid). As will be described in the next chapter , the employers attempt to get their employees to join with them in presenting their social relations to the outside world (and especially to representatives of the government) in a non-dichotomized idiom of "family economy." In fact, however, day-to-day social relations in the industry are conducted within a complex structure of familistic, paternalistic, and impersonal market institutions. Even the use of pay advances and emergency loans by the employers to reduce worker turnover and to attempt to assure the loyalty and continuity of the work force, does not prevent opportunistic changes in brickyard employers or aggressive wage-hike demands by **mileros** in their struggle for survival.

Interview data support the thesis that brick industry men tend to view the total community social structure as split into two strata, but that only some of the **mileros** explicitly linked these strata with the fundamental class division in the brick industry. However, when specifically asked whether there are other people who profit from their work or from their products the response was unanimously in the affirmative for all respondents. In further specifying the identity of the profit takers, all of the **mileros** pointed to the employers and to the resellers, whereas all of the employers pointed only to the resellers (the worker-owners either pointed to employers or to resellers).

Some brick industry men, especially the employers, do not view these relations of distribution as exploitative or profits as unearned. As one of the **mileros** put it "what the bosses make with one's work is what they earn." Many of the bosses expressed similar views in defending the right of the resellers to a profit. One of them expressed it this way: "It's fair for the reseller to earn according to his capital because he's made it with thousands of sacrifices; and capital has to earn." Another was less dramatic in expressing the same notion: "The transporters have a right to earn their profits, taking into consideration all the expenses they have."

Support for the thesis that relations between **mileros** and employers are not antagonistic is found in their responses to a question asking them to identify major problems they have encountered in the industry. Only two employers raised the issue of irregular work patterns by their **mileros** in their responses to this question, whereas only one **milero** felt that his relation to his employer was the most difficult problem he had to confront. Since his statement deals with a problem which is of concern to all of the brickyard operators, namely, that of opportunistic "brickyard shifting" by the **mileros,** it is worth quoting here at length:

> My boss used to get mad at times when I went to work in another brickyard. He'd come and give me a dressing down and I didn't like to respond to him. We used to have arguments but we never got into a fight. I think it was last May when I went to work for a few days with another boss. My regular boss told me that I was working for him and not for another boss. I told him that maybe it would be better for me to change bosses, and that if I owed him money I would pay it to him--but little by little with installments of 500 pesos. It's true that I owed him 2,500 pesos.

This same **milero** elaborated further on the nature of the relationship that had developed between him and his boss:

> Six years ago when I began to work for him, I'd ask him for loans of 200, 300, 500 or 1000 pesos to buy necessities. He gave them to me. Afterwards, he stopped doing it. So we came to an agreement that when I needed extra cash I had a right to moonlight for another boss.
>
> One time my infant son got sick. We had rabbits and a hog and we sold them but I still needed more cash for the medical expenses. My son got worse so the boss paid 4,500 pesos to cure him. My son was saved because we took him to a good doctor. My boss treated me well then but lately he's changed and he won't loan me money. "

This is neither an isolated case of **milero** opportunism and disloyalty, nor of cynical paternalism by one employer to place a **milero** in a situation of quasi-debt bondage. Rather it exposes a basic dilemma of an industry which is outside the modern industrial capitalist system where government regulation and formal organization of capital-labor relations prevail. The brickyard proletariat, severed as it is from

141

traditional social supports, must survive through the labor market and petty trade, whereas brickyard operators efforts to maintain a viable work force oblige them to extend cash advances and to provide for emergency needs of their employees. This personalistic form of paternalism may be anachronistic in the broader context of the evolving institutional structure of the corporatist Mexican State but is not necessarily so in the provincial context.

Most of the **mileros** would like to earn more but not all of them feel that they are being underpaid for their work. A commonly expressed view is that "the work is hard and heavy and we don´t earn what we deserve." A contrasting view was expressed by one **milero** who said that he would like to earn more but "the bosses base their pay scale on their expenses." Another stated, in the same vein, that the bosses "pay what the work is worth." A third **milero** cited the scarcity of jobs and wondered what his job alternatives would be if he left the brickyards in search of higher pay.

Another **milero** also complained about the lack of generosity on the part of the bosses:

> The boss never tells us, `Look you have a lot of years with me so here´s a bonus of 100 pesos.´ The bosses never do that. Not even a fiesta, not even a free meal for their employees. They never show they are pleased to help us. Everything goes right into their pockets. If one asks them for a loan, yes, but a bonus offered voluntarily, never![10]

Coming as he does from a closed, corporate peasant community in an outlying region, this **milero** reacted negatively to the higher degree of market penetration and weakness of redistributive mechanisms he encountered in Santa Lucia. However, his complaint about the absence of the end-of-year bonus in the brick industry suggests a modern proletarian, rather than a traditional peasant, orientation.

Just as there is a difference of opinion as to the equity of their wage, so is there a lack of consensus among the **mileros** about whether the earnings of their bosses are excessive (or unjustified on the

142

grounds that the bosses do not perform manual labor in the brickyards). A tight-lipped, serious **milero** of peasant-indian background in a remote mountain village, made the following forthright and articulate statement which many of his colleagues would echo:

> One should earn more. They ought to pay us more for our work. The bosses right now are selling bricks for 2200 pesos per thousand and they pay us only 600 pesos. So the biggest share is for them and we´re the ones who screw ourselves doing the work. They simply pick up the bricks from the patio, take them to the kiln, sell them, and earn a lot. We prepare the clay, mold the bricks, scrape them, stack them in the storage shed, and earn very little.

Another **milero** expressed this same sentiment but added the factor of inflation in wage goods which is a principal nemesis in the **mileros´** struggle for sub-sistence:

> The boss pays me cheap but he doesn´t sell the bricks I make cheap; he sells them for double what he pays me. I am losing. The bosses pay us cheap and we go to buy in the city where prices are expensive--starting with corn, beans, clothing--everything is expensive. Yet one works for the same piece rate.

These and other **milero** statements imply their understanding that the distribution relations between them and their bosses are exploitative. More specifi-cally, they seem to be expressing implicitly the view that, as a class and by virtue of their relationship to employers, they are being deprived of value to which their labor entitles them. In other words, **mile-ros** seem to resent the fact that their employers´ shares of the brickyard product are, for the most part, unearned in terms of labor performed. This view is, however, subordinate to the **mileros´** sense of frustration over the fact that their purchasing power is constantly eroding as the prices of wage goods rise.[11]

There is a consensus among **mileros** that when brick prices rise compensatory wage increases should follow. Furthermore, and even more crucial for employer-employee relations in the industry, **mileros** are unanimous in their belief that their employers are obliged to grant wage increases to compensate for increases in the prices of wage goods. That this posture regarding the obligations of brickyard employers, together with the workers´ strategy for assuring that it is met, has been present for several decades is clear from an elderly **milero**´s account of a situation which he recalled from around 1950:

> The bosses began to sell bricks more expensive and we, the ones who made them, agreed that we should be paid more. They paid us ten pesos per thousand before and afterwards they paid us fifteen pesos. We saw that the bosses were selling at a higher price and they weren´t raising ourpiece rate. That´s why we made an agreement among ourselves that the bosses should pay us a little more. We were a group of **mileros** who worked together for the same boss. There were six of us. Between us we made an agreement to tell the boss to give us a raise. We spoke to him together and he agreed to give us the raise. That´s how we began earning fifteen pesos per thousand."

To this day, any brickyard employer can expect to be petitioned by his workers for a piece rate increase if the market price of bricks is increased, if the prices of basic wage goods increase, or if other employers grant piece rate increases higher than the one he is paying. Information about brick prices (and piece rates) travels quickly between brickyards, given the circulation of personnel and, especially, of the truckers and their helpers who are constantly moving from brickyard to brickyard. Higher prices for bricks or piece rate hikes by particular brickyard operators quickly become common knowledge and provide ammunition for the **mileros** in their persistent struggle for higher incomes.

Another series of statements by different **mileros** describes the conditions surrounding their last request for a piece rate hike prior to the time that they were interviewed (the mean period of time that had elapsed since their last wage hike was 3-1/2 months). As the following quote illustrates, these statements confirm the importance of price increases in wage goods and of piece rate increases by other brickyard employers (knowledge of which is quickly disseminated throughout the brickyards by word of mouth) in triggering new wage demands by **mileros**:

> He was paying us 650 pesos and we asked him to give us a raise of fifty pesos. We asked because when we take five hundred pesos to the market we can buy very little. Also, bricks were selling at high prices. For these reasons it occurred to us to ask for a raise. We had to speak to the boss to find out what his thinking was. He knows what our work is worth so we can ask him for a raise. If he doesn't want to pay what we ask, no problem.

Mileros employ the threat of changing brickyards (i.e., of playing the bosses off against each other) as an ultimate bargaining tactic in their effort to maintain their share of the industry's earnings (and to keep their purchasing power from eroding to a level which threatens their survival). This strategy of brickyard shifting was clearly expressed by another informant as follows:

> Right now I'm being paid 600. If I knew of some boss who would pay me 700 I'd go with him. One always looks for the best deal. One lets the boss know that so-and-so is paying a better piece rate, and if he says that he'll meet it well one stays on. There are no ill-feelings. If he refuses to give a raise, I'll go to another brickyard where the pay is better.

Two aspects of the wage-price dialectic in the brick industry should be clarified at this point. First, **patrón/milero** relations are restricted to individual brickyard operators and their employees; there is no formal organization of either group which plays a collective bargaining role although there is some talk among both groups of the possibility of establishing such organizations. Second, conditions in the industry favor a policy of accomodation by the employers to the wage demands of their employees since the alternative entails the real possibility of worker turnover and temporary interruptions in brickyard output.

Not a single instance was found where a substantiated request for a cost of living increase in the piece rate was not duly conceded. These two aspects are, of course, related. So long as employers concede wage hikes periodically on an informal basis there is much less incentive for **mileros** to attempt to unionize. Moreover, disgruntled workers have the option under the present system of changing employers to take advantage of piece rate differentials or differences in the way employers deal with cash advances and housing.

Responding to a question regarding the possibility of unionization, one **milero** expressed his opinion that, "There hasn´t been an organization of that kind because the bosses always give us the salary that we ask for." Another factor which has operated to discourage unionization has been the feeling among some **mileros** that, in the words of one of them, "the boss could get mad and refuse to give us work." Even though they feel entitled to a larger share of their employers´ profits, they recognize that a radical tactic like a strike would be punishing for them since they have no financial resources to fall back on. The following appraisal made by a **milero** expresses this clearly:

> The bosses benefit from us because they pay us cheap and the profit is for them. We can never resolve this because all of us need to work. All of us have that need and we´ve never had a strike. For example, I´m without money and the boss tells us to load the kiln tomorrow. Well we will load it because we need to. The boss won´t show up but I will because I don´t have any money and I need whatever the boss pays me. Around here people aren´t on an equal footing.

Some **mileros** agree with the concept of unionization. "A union is needed to give us more guarantees," said one, "because as it is now it´s up to the boss whether or not he wants to help us." As will be discussed in the next chapter, this issue was introduced into the

146

brickyards by government functionaries in association with the issue of social security.

Below are some statements by employers which indicate their positions on the issue of piece rate increases and general relations with **mileros**:

(1) If the standard price of bricks goes up then one should raise the **mileros´** salary accordingly. But if by chance I sell a thousand bricks for 3000 pesos because the clients liked them and were willing to pay that price, well in that case I don´t have to raise the **mileros** piece rate. On the other hand, if there is a price increase in all the brickyards, of course, I have to raise the piece rate. One has to ´get along´ (**convivir**) with the **mileros**; one shouldn´t bother them or coerce them. One should treat them as members of one´s family and help them with their problems. That way they will be content, they will work quietly and do a good job.

(2) If they make bricks well, the **mileros** have a right to ask for an increase in the piece rate if the price of bricks rises.

(3) I agree that if the price of bricks rises and that if the boss is conscientious and has been a man who has suffered in work, he will increase the **mileros´** wages so that they will work more contentedly. But, if he´s a weak boss who doesn´t want to ´get along´ (**convivir**) with his workers he´s in trouble. The **mileros** will threaten to leave him and go to work for another if he doesn´t increase their wages. If the **mileros** are making good quality bricks that are selling well, they have every right to expect a raise.

(4) The **mileros** are always on top of you. If they hear that you sold bricks for more than the going price they ask for a 50 peso raise. But they forget

147

that sometimes sales are sluggish. If that happens one sells below the going price in order to do business and to be able to pay his **mileros**. They never take reductions in the piece rate. They only take increases. But when the boss sees that he has a big inventory of bricks on hand, to get money to pay his **mileros** he has to lower the price of his bricks.

(5) The **mileros** say that what they earn is not enough. Right now they´re making a big fuss because some of the other bosses raised the piece rate 50 pesos since the price of sugar went up.

Several points made in these statements provide the basis for concluding this discussion. Two employers emphasized the need to "**convivir**" ("get along") with the **mileros**, which is another way of saying that the employer should interact with them in an egalitarian way. The first statement goes even further in advocating a policy of paternalism, to treat **mileros** as members of one´s own family and to help them with their problems. We have already seen that this is by no means an isolated approach to employer/employee relations and clearly is a main strategy for assuring continuity and loyalty in the labor force, thereby, reducing the risk of disruptions in brickyard output. On the other hand, there is a clear tendency on the part of most of these employers to not accede to wage demands on the basis of temporary, capricious or isolated fluctuations in prices of bricks or of wage goods.

Nevertheless, they would all agree that intransigence in the face of persistent demands for a piece rate increase is counterproductive. This is especially true with regard to demands from **mileros** who work steadily and produce good quality bricks. The bottom line is that experienced and reliable **mileros** are in short supply and, consequently, are a focus of competition among the brickyard operators.

[1] Gudeman engages in a tortured qualification of his "labour as the ultimate factor of production" thesis as illustrated by the following statement: "After all, even in the completely planned economy, the labourer does not receive the total output of his efforts. Some portion of the product must be taken to provide for accumulation" (1978:6-7). The implication is that Marx's labor theory of value implies that the individual worker has a right to his entire surplus product. This misconception is cleared up by reading Marx's **Critique of the Gotha Programme** in which he delineated the economically necessary deductions (above and beyond the provision of the means of production) from the total social product which are made in every society (Hindess and Hirst 1975:26; Cook 1977:372).

[2] In his comprehensive review Raymond Firth, the premier marginalist in economic anthropology, concludes ambivalently that Marx's "law of value" and the labor cost theory of value "express important truths but only part of the truth" and that they are "very fertile for theoretical development" (1979:201-202). By contrast Harold Schneider, a staunch marginalist, cavalierly dismisses the labor theory of value on grounds that "Marx was intruding normative considerations...by saying that low wages for workers are unfair and should be raised on moral grounds" (1974:205-206)--an interpretation which even a leading marginalist textbook rejects (Baumol and Blinder 1982:774). George Dalton, the leading substantivist, has attacked the concept of exploitation on various grounds in a series of polemical articles (1974; 1975; 1976; 1977). Littlefield (1978), in refutation, has shown how the concept can be operationalized and fruitfully applied in economic anthropological analysis.

[3] The 560,000 peso estimate of the potential market value of Santa Lucía's brick output is based on the average 1980 brickyard price of 70 dollars (1600 pesos) for 1000 bricks. This estimate increases to 373,474 dollars (8,589,000 pesos) when the average price of bricks delivered to Oaxaca City construction sites (90 dollars or 2045 pesos per thousand) is used.

For five days in March and April, 1980 a survey of construction sites in Oaxaca City was conducted by the project (using a list compiled from official building permits) to collect data about the provenience, quantity, and purchase price of bricks used at each site. A total of thirty-three sites was surveyed in all sections of the city representing both single- and multiple-dwelling residential projects as well as commercial building projects. Some 63% of the 1,157,500 bricks in use at these sites came from Santa Lucía, with the remainder allocated among four other production centers. This was surprising given the prolific growth of the Yatareni industry which is widely believed to have displaced Santa Lucia as the major brick producing center. However, a 1980 government study of ninety brickyards in Yatareni shows that these are mostly small-scale family operations, a majority of which fire bricks only six times a year in the dry season with outputs per firing ranging between 4,500 and 8,000 bricks. In other words, Santa Lucía has fewer but more productive brickyards than Yatareni and, consequently, continues to dominate the brick traffic to Oaxaca City.

[4] A rigorous marxist analysis of the economics of the brickyards would probably require a consideration of the factor of differential rent (Mandel 1970:276-8). Like the poorest peasants in agriculture, who work marginal lands of bad quality, the poorest brick producers who work brickyards with bad quality clay, pay a differential rent to the rest of the brickyard operators as a consequence of the lesser productivity of their yards (cf. Stavenhagen 1978:32).

The problem of how to deal with land values in the brick industry can be neatly resolved for purposes of formal cost accounting. The 1980 going brickyard price of in-ground clay was 6.70 dollars (150 pesos) per thousand bricks; this was the price paid by those brickmakers who are neither **mileros** nor owners and who "buy clay" from brickyard owners. In other words, for every 10,000 bricks fired, a clay cost of 60 dollars (1500 pesos) could be assigned. This would reduce the average profit per firing (Table 8) of 309 dollars (6944 pesos) by 22%. I have chosen not to do this simply because the brickyard operators do not include it in their own cost and profit calculations--unless they are actually making payments on their brickyard or are selling clay from their brickyard to others.

5 The flatbed truck is the only factory-made capital good of substantial cost which has become essential to the mass production of bricks in the Santa Lucía industry; still, the realization of its use value (e.g., driving, loading and unloading) depends upon a continuous supply of local human labor power to realize its use value (i.e., driving, loading and unloading, etc.). The same can be said for all of the factory-made tools which are used to produce bricks.

6 An important difference between the piece and the time wage was emphasized in a comprehensive study by the International Labor Office (1951) as follows: "The chief characteristic of systems of payment by results under which the worker's reward varies in the same proportion as his output is that any gains or losses resulting directly from changes in his output accrue to him (leaving to the employer any gains or losses in overhead costs per unit of output). In contrast, when the worker is paid by the hour or by the day all gains or losses resulting from changes in his output accrue to the employer" (1951:7).

It is significant that three of the principal advantages of piece wage systems listed in the ILO study (1951:178) are compatible with Marx's analysis, namely: (1) "They can make a substantial contribution to the raising of productivity, to lower costs of production and to increased earnings for the workers" (here Marx would say "temporarily by some workers"); (2) "In general, less direct supervision is required to maintain reasonable levels of output than under payment by time..."; and (3) "Workers are encouraged to pay more attention to reducing lost time and to make more effective use of their equipment..." The same study also notes that one of the principal disadvantages of piece work is that "wide differences in the ability or capacity of workers working in close proximity may lead to large differences in earnings and to ill-feeling between workers" (1951:178-9).

Concerning the last point, this chapter has shown that differences in worker ability or capacity is less an issue than differences in piece rates between brickyards; and that these differences may lead to conflict between brickyard operators and their pieceworkers. The ILO study does acknowledge that, "One of the greatest difficulties with systems of payment by results is in the setting of piece...rates" (1951).

151

[7] The market structure in the metate industry is diametrically opposed to that described here. Metate prices decline during the rainy season when, for various reasons, the supply of metates dwindles. In the post-harvest dry season both metate prices and the supply of metates increase. Perhaps the main reason for this difference lies in the contrasting conditions of labor, and in the structure of demand, in the two industries. The **metateros** are mostly peasants who are still involved in agriculture whereas the brickmakers are more heavily proletarianized and depeasantized. Likewise, metate buyers are other peasants and artisans who are bound up with the agricultural cycle whereas brick buyers are mostly urbanites who are totally disengaged from agriculture and the rural economy (see Cook 1982a: Ch. 6).

[8] Although the tax code was undergoing major revisions during the period of our study, the resellers were paying at least three sets of taxes: the major one was a gross sales revenue tax which was paid every two months, another was paid to federal transit authorities for the truck (13 dollars or 300 pesos every 6 months), and the third was levied by the city of Oaxaca. One of the largest resellers showed me a tax receipt from the state treasurer´s office for 60 dollars (1,400 pesos) which he paid every two months (government auditors established the rate in negotiations with all of the resellers). This informant told me that he sold bricks only to clients in the city and did not attempt to transport them elsewhere to avoid difficulties with federal highway police and with the **Casetas Fiscales.** The latter, which are strategically positioned outside the city limits on all main highways, levy a fee of 1.30 dollars (30 pesos) per thousand bricks if the trucker fails to present valid documentation of exemption.

[9] The concept of "reproduction of labor" is to be distinguished from that of "social reproduction" but is also fraught with ambiguities (cf.Harris and Young 1981:123-132). The focus of this chapter (and throughout the monograph) is the "material dimension of the reproduction of labor, that is, the day-to-day maintenance of people adequately nourished, clothed, and ´recreated´ ... to work for capital" or the "material reproduction of labor" (Harris and Young 1981:124). The latter notion is closely related to that of "nec-

152

essary labor" or "necessary product"--food, clothing, dwelling, and a "more or less stable stock of tools serving to produce these...things" (Mandel 1970:25). In other words, "surplus labor" or "surplus product" must be defined as that which is above and beyond the level of these things identified as necessary in the reproductive sense (cf. Hindess and Hirst 1975:27; Cook 1977:371-72).

[10] The bonus or **aguinaldo** is widely practiced by government agencies and urban private firms but not practiced in rural small industries.

[11] One automatically tends to associate inflation with the Mexican economy. However, it is a relatively recent problem in modern Mexico. During the 1950s the inflation rate was a comparatively low 11.2%. Since then there have been wide fluctuations in the annual rate of price increases. By 1976 the rate had climbed to 4% per month (Barkin and Esteva 1979). The galloping inflation of the late 1970s and early 1980s, with annual rates soaring near 100% are unprecedented in recent decades. Unfortunately, there are no studies of the impact of inflation on the village economies of the Oaxaca valley. It is clear that the buffer advantage of household production of foodstuffs for own-use has had a special significance in rural Oaxaca and elsewhere in Mexico for about a decade. I have documented how sellers in the metate industry adjust the prices of their products upward in an effort to match price increases in products they must buy (Cook 1982a:63-64, 176-77, 321-24).

14. Peasant plows near a brickyard

CHAPTER 5

THE IDEOLOGICAL MATRIX OF BRICKYARD
PIECE WORK RELATIONS

There is little outward reason for the casual visitor to be skeptical when assured by informants in the brickyards that, as one of them expressed it, "We are all family here. There are no employers and employees, no capitalist. Brickmaking is just one way we make a living when we´re not doing agricultural work. It´s not a business." This kind of statement, as the material presented in previous chapters shows, is inaccurate. However, it must be understood as embodying an ideology which has been devised and nurtured by local empl'yers to camouflage the real nature of their role in the brick industry and of their relationship to the mileros. This kind of statement does partially correspond to social reality; and its deceptive content can be justified in terms of the political economic matrix in which the industry operates.

For example, it has been shown that some brickyard operators are, indeed, heads of domestic enterprises which are seasonally bifurcated between agriculture and brickmaking, and do not regularly employ wage labor. On the other hand, many others operate enterprises which exclusively employ wage labor. Most importantly, as will be described below, both groups of brickyard operators attempt to shield themselves from government tax collectors and representatives of government programs like social security which they view as prejudicial to their economic interests. It is here that the strategy of cloaking their employer status and their year-round involvement in brickmaking behind the ideology of family subsistence agriculture comes into play.

Brickmaking and Agriculture

It has been established that most of the brickyard operators came from peasant family backgrounds; that most of them continue to cultivate the land to supplement brick production; and that, in both the past and present, earnings from the sale of crops and animal products have contributed to both fixed and circulating capital expenditures in their brick making operations. What are some ideological aspects of the relationship between brickmaking and agriculture? What are some ideological implications of agriculture´s

155

declining importance in the brickyard economy?

A twenty-nine year old informant who is co-owner of a brickyard with his two brothers, all of whom were born and raised in Rancho Nuevo, admitted in a pensive moment: "My job is in the brickyards but my heart is in the fields" ("**Mi oficio es el ladrillo pero mi amor es el campo**"). Aside from being a statement of work preference, his words can be interpreted as having two deeper meanings. First, they are diagnostic of an underlying process of depeasantization and expropriation which has been occurring in Santa Lucía (and in Yatareni) for at least two decades as a concomitant of the expansion of the city. Second, they identify an ambivalent occupational involvement which is shared by many Santa Lucians, namely, that their principal mode of livelihood entails extracting the soil as a raw material and transforming it into bricks, whereas their agrarian upbringing has instilled in them the notion that they should be cultivating it.

Peasant brickyard operators realize that they can make more money from seasonal land by converting it to brick production. But they also realize that, to do this, entails foregoing the production of subsistence crops which would have provided them with an important buffer against the rising price of foodstuffs in a continuously inflationary economy. The informant referred to in the preceding paragraph has set for himself a goal of acquiring additional land for cultivation as an alternative to investing further in his jointly owned brickyard (in contrast to his brother who recently acquired a flatbed truck). Only one third of the informants expressed such an investment goal; the majority indicated that they would invest in expanding their brickyard operations. On the other hand, all of them extolled the benefits of agricultural production for own-use, even though some of them no longer practice it and have no future plans of doing so.

In Chapter 2 the role of agriculture in the case of two brickyard operators, Gilberto and Porfirio, was discussed. Gilberto liquidated his agricultural holdings to buy a brickyard, whereas Porfirio continued to work the land to grow subsistence crops but preferred brickmaking as a business. While many of the brickyard operators like Gilberto, have liquidated agricultural assets to raise sufficient capital for acquiring brickyards, none of the others has completely with-

156

drawn from agriculture as he did. Porfirio's strategy seems to be representative of the majority although some grow only fodder, either for their own animals or as a cash crop, rather than corn or other subsistence crops. Whereas agriculture served as a source of capital to facilitate the initial acquisition of brickyards by several established peasant brickyard operators, it has come to play a subordinate role in their operations. Indeed, in many cases its continued practice is often sustained by income from brick sales.[1]

The Brickmaking Craft: Views from Within

Neither the operators nor the **mileros** are enthusiastic about their involvement in the brick industry, but it is fair to say that a majority of them agree that it represents the best mode of livelihood, or business opportunity, available to them. Most of the operators indicated that they were considering withdrawing from the brick industry but only one of them had a clear idea of an occupational alternative, namely, to open a small variety and food store. Some responses to a question asking whether they were considering an occupational change are as follows:

> (1) Day and night I consider leaving it. I work hard and I earn very little. I'm in the brickyard from 6 a.m. to 6 p.m. working hard. There are lots of jobs that aren't so physically demanding: you put in your eight hours and you're ready for your salary.

> (2) It's very heavy work. It tires you out. Maybe the money one earns makes it worthwhile but it exhausts you.

> (3) I'm thinking of selling the brickyard. I'm tired. My family is large. Bricks aren't selling well. There isn't much demand.

The first two statements are by worker-owners; one of them works alone and the other employs **mileros** on a part-time basis but is himself responsible for the bulk of his output. This latter individual presents an interesting case. He is the youngest of the brickyard operators and has a kiln. He did a tour of duty in the army and, following his discharge, invested all of his savings in opening a brickyard. Not a

157

native of Santa Lucia, he had only minimal experience with brickmaking and found this to be quite a handicap-- especially with regard to firing where he has had very low yields of first class bricks. Moreover, his brothers have proven to be less cooperative in assisting him than he had anticipated when he opened the brickyard; this has forced him to hire **mileros** more often than he would like. This combination of factors caused him to abandon his brickyard for about ten days during the fieldwork period in a vain attempt to get across the U.S. border to work and earn dollars.

The third statement is probably a situational response to a temporary slowdown in brick sales because the individual who made it was a reasonably successful brickyard operator. His complaints about the low profitability of his business were belied by the fact that he lived in a large, new, brick house, employed several full-time **mileros,** and no longer made bricks himself. In any case, his was a minority position among the brickyard operators.

Of the **mileros** interviewed only three indicated that they preferred another occupation to brickmaking; and in all three cases the preferred occupation was peasant cultivator. One of them, who is from the Mixtec highlands where he still owns land, considered brickmaking to be more physically punishing than agriculture. He hopes to retire from brickmaking and return to his village when his teen-age sons finish their schooling and become independent. The second **milero** cited the same reasons for disliking the occupation ("One gets tired, one gets disgusted in this job") and said that he preferred working in agriculture because of the advantage of being able to produce his own food. However, since he is from the neighboring brickmaking community of Yatareni which , like Santa Lucía has seen its land base dwindle over the years as the city expanded, it is unlikely that he will be able to realize his aspirations. The third **milero**, who is from a peasant community in the district of Sola de Vega where he has one hectare of arable, stated that his goal was to "save money" to enable him to "buy an ox team to plant corn and beans," but he admitted that "one can earn as much in bricks as one can in agriculture" so his occupational future is ambivalent.

When asked to select the best occupation in the local division of labor, most **mileros** selected brick-making over agriculture. The majority response emphasized higher cash earnings for brickmaking as the principal reason for their preference ("The only job that provides a livelihood" or "The job that brings in the most money"). The minority response emphasized the economic security asssociated with agriculture ("If it rains well one need not worry about anything" or "Those that earn more money and produce more are the peasants") as the principal reason for their preference.

Responses to a general question asking the respondent to characterize differences he perceived between brickmakers, conveyed a variety of attitudes about different dimensions of the industry. One half of the respondents emphasized differences in levels of remuneration, whereas the other half emphasized differences in work habits, assets, or productivity. The **mileros,** the self-employed and the worker-owners tended to alternate between these two types of responses, whereas the responses of the employer-managers fell exclusively into the second type with an emphasis on assets. It proves most instructive to examine these responses more closely from the perspective of each category.

A representative response from an "employer" is as follows:

> Here we are almost equal. We all have the same problems. Only a few of us have a large-scale production and a flatbed truck. Those are the ones who have more land or other assets that favor them, or their parents were wealthy and left it to them.

It is clear from responses like this that even within the industry´s most privileged stratum there is a focus on intra-stratum differences rather than on differences between strata. Finally, the sources of differentiation mentioned--amount of land owned for brickyards, ownership of trucks, and kiln-firing interval--have already been shown to be crucial.

A representative response from the "working" brickyard operators is as follows:

159

> Some are already capitalists. We
> aren't. We're still small. They have
> had lots of good orders and that's how
> they've developed. Those who deliver to
> the city earn more than those who sell
> in the brickyards.

What is most interesting about the responses from this
group, when compared with the employers' responses,
is the fact that most of them imply a self-categoriza-
tion on the part of the respondent as either an operator of an enterprise or as a brickmaker. Those who
categorize themselves as brickyard operators emphasize
differences in terms of fixed or operating capital or
profits, whereas those who see themselves simply as
"brickmakers" focus on differences in work habits.
Only one of these respondents specified the difference
between "working" operators like himself and those who
are capitalists ("the bosses who don't work with their
hands"). It is clear that the respondents have a
fairly sophisticated understanding of the significant
differences within their half of the industry and,
more specifically, of the material bases of differential rates of profit and of different scales of operation.

The **mileros'** responses emphasize work habits and
earnings which is what we might expect from piece
workers. Once again, these respondents assert generally and subjectively what the observational study demonstrated specifically and objectively regarding differential worker productivity. For example, one **milero**
said that, "Not all of us have the same hand movements; some of us work faster than others." Also of
interest is the "craftsmanship" factor mentioned in
some of the responses. Although not as prevalent as in
the more aesthetically oriented craft industries
(e.g., weaving, embroidery, woodcarving), it may seem
odd that product quality is of concern at all in an
industry which mass produces the most utilitarian and
esthetically simple of commodities. However, as was
pointed out in the previous chapter, brick quality is
a determinant of brick prices, and the latter are of
concern to **mileros** and employers alike.

Finally, it is appropriate to examine **milero**
responses to a question asking them whether they in-
tended or expected to become independent operators of
brickyards in the future. Less than half of the respondents indicated that they had intentions or hopes

of becoming independent operators. One of the younger **mileros**, who still might have a chance of realizing his aspirations, stated them as follows:

> I'm thinking of going independent as soon as I save enough cash to support the move. I need about 4,000 pesos to buy a piece of land for a brickyard. It's better to buy a piece of land because the way we are now it's only the boss who benefits from our work.

Another young informant said:

> My thinking is to continue as a **milero** for another three or four years to save some money, since I understand this work. Then I'll see if I can come out ahead by buying clay to make bricks on my own account and rent a kiln. That way I'll be making my own bricks and I won't have to spend money on **mileros**. I'll make bricks and money out of my own sweat. After that I'll buy a piece of land for a brickyard.

It is noteworthy that both of these statements imply a trajectory of brickyard development which was described in Chapter 2 as representing the typical stepwise pattern experienced by many contemporary operators. The first statement also implies that a desire to escape exploitation motivates some **mileros** to seek independent status, whereas the second--emphasizing the cost of labor--traces a trajectory involving capital accumulation as a result of own and family labor.

The majority of **milero** informants, however, either seemed resigned to their condition as pieceworkers ("It's better for me to work for the bosses because they supply the materials and the tools") or cited extenuating circumstances which precluded the possibility of becoming independent. One of them said regretfully that "I can't do anything on my own account...with my children being so small," implying that when they are older he might be able to think in terms of that strategy. This same informant also noted that in his circumstances "it's not possible to save." Another, who was even more discouraged, said simply "we don't have any hope yet" of acquiring a brickyard.

161

Inequality, Capital Accumulation, and Ideology

The unequal distribution of wealth among brick industry households has been documented above. Therefore, the objective framework is in place to facilitate an exploration in this section of some of the subjective dimensions of inequality, as expressed in interviews with brickyard men. The process of capital accumulation which occurs in many of the brick production units will also be examined to expose and explain how some factors promote or constrain it.

All informants expressed a dichotomic conception of the community social structure, that is, they viewed it as being essentially split into two strata referred to variously as backward (**"atrasados"**) and better-off (**"adelantados"**), poor (**"pobres"**) (poor) and rich (**"ricos"**), or humble people (**"gente humilde"**) and wealthy people (**"gente rica"**). Interestingly enough, only a few informants--all **mileros**--explicitly associated these dichotomous strata with workers and employers. In the words of one of them: "The bosses earn, they have the wherewithal, while the poor worker gets only his salary. The bosses own the brickyards. They are the ones who really earn." This minority of informants considered the local population to be split along lines of ownership of means of production (especially land for brickyards and for cultivation), income, standard of living, and patterns of allocation of labor-time.

Below is a representative sampling of views regarding social inequality, expressed with about equal frequency among all groups within the industry:

> Some live better and others live worse because of drunkenness. They don´t bring money home so their wives and children have nothing to eat. Not all of us enjoy life like some do. The employers enjoy it one way, and we **mileros** enjoy it in another way. We accomodate ourselves to the income that we make. We do what we can with our salary: we buy a little clothing, we buy our shoes and with what´s left over we see what else we can buy--a radio, a watch, a writing tablet, a few laminated sheets for our house. That´s the situation of us workers. The bosses

162

enjoy life in another way because they
get all of the money from our work.
It´s the boss who always comes out
earning.

Separate questions were asked to elicit responses
from the respondents explaining their understanding of
the causes of perceived social inequality in Santa
Lucia. The following statement by an employer is representative:

There are poor families because they
don´t want to work. There´s work but
they don´t want to do it. The ones who
want to earn get up early and get to
work. Others, at 7:00 or 8:00 in the
morning are still at home. What money
are they going to earn? Those who are
rich work, save, and don´t drink.

With few exceptions, the **mileros´** responses to
general questions about inequality failed to systematically associate the accumulation of wealth with the
existence of poverty. They viewed poverty as a condition of a paucity of property and income, and with a
low standard of living but they considered it to be a
consequence of behavioral deficencies in the poor
(e.g., having too many offspring, not working hard
enough or with enough regularity, squandering earnings on liquor). There was, in fact, no discernible
difference between their general views on the causes
of wealth and poverty and those expressed by the
worker-operators and the employers. This seems to
reflect the fact that the **mileros** share with these
other groups an ideology which extolls the benefits
and ignores the costs of capitalist accumulation.

Several informants cited inheritance as a principal source of wealth in contemporary families. This is
a factor which certainly has been operative in many
cases and which would appear to partially contradict
the emphasis on hard work, clean living, and thrifti-
ness as sources of wealth. Obviously, these factors
are not mutually exclusive. Again, what is most striking about such statements is the absence of any conceptual linkage between the dynamics of wealth accumulation and poverty.

Another question designed to elicit statements
relevant to this topic was "Do you think that a poor

163

family can become rich?" The range of responses here is quite consistent with what would be expected on the basis of the material presented above: there is a marked tendency to give a qualified positive response which emphasizes hard work and frugality, but which doesn't ignore intervening variables that may operate to hinder or to facilitate upward mobility or capital accumulation. Moreover, as before, the content of these responses tends to cross cut industrial role categories, except that employers cite "laziness" as a constraint on upward mobility more often than other respondents. This is illustrated in the the following three statements:

> (1) It can be done if one struggles in his work. But with some basis in money because that is important. For example, to pay for a firing one needs 10,000 pesos to pay for the work, to eat, and to buy sawdust. That's one way to get rich. Another way that we've seen is with a store. If you have 20,000 pesos saved up and are looking for a way to invest it, well all you have to do is construct a simple little building with laminated sheets and start up a store-- with tomatoes, sugar, chile peppers, beans, soft drinks, everything people buy daily. Then you would go little by little; you would live off some of the earnings and keep the business going with the rest. That's how poor people get rich around here.

> (2) If one has a big household to support he won't be able to become richer. I won't be able to get out from where I am now, though I still have some hope. But to say that I am going to become rich is nothing more than a hope.

> (3) One can become richer if he has a good intention of working, of progressing. Money won't come to one who is lying down or sleeping. One must look for it. One must work and save.

The first of these responses is a **milero**'s, the second is a worker-owner's, and the third is an employer's.

Whatever their source, the prescriptions for family material progress that recur throughout the statements of brickyard personnel--embodying precepts like hard work, deferral of gratification, frugality, and abstinence--are precisely those emphasized in the Weberian and in the "achievement motivation" approach to capitalist development (Higgins 1959:219-23, 295-301). It is impossible to say, in specific cases, whether such precepts preceded or were products of successful familial careers in the brick industry. Clearly, in the case of informants who have achieved upward mobility, the precepts in question may conceivably have served as ideological catalysts to material achievement. However, in the case of informants who have not done so, such precepts and other expressions of optimism about the future rewards of hard work and economizing express unrealized aspirations, and help to reproduce ideologically the very relations of production which hinder substantial improvements in their material conditions of life.

The following uniquely autobiographical response to the question just examined provides a way to bridge the discussion of social inequality and economic progress with the analysis of productivity and output in Chapter 3, and with the case studies of the development of family enterprises in Chapter 2. It also serves as a point of entry into a discussion of capital accumulation:

> The poor family can't become richer. Do you know why? Because the household head doesn't take great pains in his work. I was poor once; I arrived here and I began to work like a man. Just like the saying: `If you work, you have; if you work, you eat. If you don't work, you don't have; if you don't work, you don't eat.' It might only happen in those cases of poverty where the sons grow up and tell their father: `Let's make bricks and fire them even if we do so by shares.' Then the sons help to pull their father out of poverty; the father is working and his sons are helping out. That happened in my case. But sons might also take on bad habits of their father. They might see that their father is drinking and work less. When they earn money they

might give some to help out their
father but spend the rest in a bar, the
movies, or wherever they please. When
are they going to progress? Never.

Let´s suppose that the father of this
guy left him an inheritance. He´s worse
off then because he says to himself,
why should I work? He sells or leases
his land. Why? Because he doesn´t realize how much it cost. One must take
products out of the land. One must work
in order to have more. Not all of us
think that way; there are those who
squander their wealth, who squander
their money. For example, a guy grabs
500 pesos, some friends come up, and he
goes with them to the bar. They blow
all the money. The next day the same
guy goes around asking for a loan to
load his kiln or to pay for molding
some bricks. When is a man like that
going to progress?

This semi-autobiographical statement was by Porfirio
(see Chapter 2) who moved to Santa Lucía more than
twenty years ago as a basketmaker and butcher; due to
the encouragement of his sons, he became involved in
the brickyards as a **milero**. Subsequently, through a
combination of hard work by his sons and himself--and
his accumulation of capital by saving and by obtaining
bank loans--Porfirio was able to develop a successful
brickyard with a kiln, a flatbed truck, and several
mileros.

The development of Porfirio´s brickyard over the
years depended heavily on the contribution of his own
and his sons´ labor--whatever capital was accumulated
prior to his initial bank loan derived from that
source by reducing the wage bill. After Porfirio´s
brickyard was established, and as his son´s grew up
and left the village, wage labor gradually replaced
household labor in his operation. In other words,
Porfirio´s brickyard passed through the stage of
"endofamilial" accumulation and entered a stage of
simple capitalist accumulation where the source of
profit became the labor-power purchased from **mileros**.
This transition does not mean that family labor ceased
to be important to the viability of Porfirio´s brickyard. It simply meant that the source of that contri-

166

bution no longer came from his own household but from the households of his **mileros**. With few exceptions, capitalist brickyard enterprises in Santa Lucia developed via the route of "endofamilial" accumulation.[2]

The existence and viability of capitalist enterprises in the brick industry depends upon the availability of workers who can be hired for a low piece rate because of the regular contribution of their family members to the labor process. Without this in-kind contribution to productivity, which increases the household´s earnings from brick production as well as the employer´s profits, the surplus labor/necessary labor ratio in the brick industry would fall below the survival minimum. This would force the employers to raise the piece rate with the twin effects of increasing their wage bill and lowering their profits to the extent that compensatory brick price increases could not be made.

Here lies a principal reason why requests for increases in piece rates by **mileros** are usually conceded in due course by their employers, and also why they, in turn, make compensatory increases in the price of bricks. Thus, the viability of the capitalist brickyard enterprise resides in its ability to engage several workers for the price of one. It is this intimately exploitative relationship with the domestic economy--and specifically with teen-age males and adult females of the household--that separates the small-scale, labor-intensive enterprise from the larger, capital-intensive variety.[3]

Brickyard Women

The empirical record of participation by women in the labor process of brick production showed that their contribution is most important in the finishing stages of trimming and stacking bricks but that some of them also assist in clay preparation. In this section additional data on the the role of women in the brickyards is presented and analyzed, together with women´s and men´s views of that role.[4]

The mean age of the eight women interviewed was 34 (youngest 25, oldest 50). None of them was born in Santa Lucia and only two of them were born in the Oaxaca Valley. The majority were born and raised in rural communities in other regions of the state. Most

167

of their fathers were peasants and their mothers divided their time between household duties, agricultural work and/or the production and sale of **tortillas**. Only two of these women had relatively uneventful childhoods in which they performed mainly household duties assisting their mothers. The others, by the time they reached the age of ten were involved in some form of paid work, either as domestic servants in Oaxaca City or in Mexico City, as artisans, as helpers in small businesses, or as agricultural workers.

The relatively sheltered upbringing of one woman ended abruptly after her marriage when she spent several months in Mexico City as a seamstress, a newspaper vendor, and a general purpose helper in a restaurant. Later she ended up in the brickyards as the only woman in the sample who regularly performs all the tasks in brick production to support her alcoholic husband and their four children. The mean age at which these women were first married is sixteen (two of them have been divorced and remarried). They have an average of 3.5 children each and have lived in the brickyards for an average of six years (range from six months to fifteen years).

When asked to compare the quality of their lives in the brickyards with that of their childhoods, half of them felt that it was better now--principally because of the proximity to the city and a somewhat better standard of living. Only one respondent, Marcela, who supports her alcoholic husband through her work in the brickyards said that she was worse off now than she was before her marriage. This is understandable since her living conditions at the time she was interviewed were as poor as any that can be found in rural Oaxaca.

With only one exception, these women had no prior experience in the brick industry before moving to Santa Lucia. They all maintain that their contribution to brick production is voluntary and does not reflect their husbands´ coercion or suggestion, yet this disclaimer becomes academic given the constant economic crisis which their households confront and their effort to overcome it through work. The following statement by Marcela describes how she replaced her husband as the full-time **milero** in their employer´s brickyard:

> I worked with my husband for a week
> and, after that I started working

alone. The boss showed up one day when I was in the pit with my neighbor Lola who also wanted to learn the work. The boss wouldn't accept her bricks because they were too badly made but he said that mine were okay and he paid me for them. That's how I began. I make bricks because I want to. Sometimes my husband gets mad about it. But I tell him that there's no other way for us to make it. The boss is now in the habit of giving me loans when my husband isn't working, since he knows that I can deliver. But when my husband goes to see him he won't give him money because he knows that he'll waste it on **mezcal**.

Incidentally, Marcela at the time she was interviewed (only a few days after she had given birth to her fourth child in her shanty, assisted by a local midwife) had been molding bricks for two years following the successful tryout with her boss. A similar tryout was failed by her neighbor Lola who assists her husband in the brickyard but does not mold bricks.

Marcela was the only female informant who talked about her brickyard activities as "work" ("**trabajo**") and who is paid directly for them. All of the others adhered to the ideology of male dominance which classifies men's activities as "work" and women's activities as "helping out"("**ayuda**"). None of them received any direct payment, a fact which did not seem to bother most of them. As one woman succinctly expressed it: "I help out and my husband gets paid." One informant admitted that she would like to be paid but felt that it was up to the boss to make a decision to do so, and that meanwhile her work was tied to her husband's.[5]

It is clear from the interview data that brickyard women are confronted with conflicts in the scheduling of their labor-time between household duties and brickyard tasks. Marcela, for example, continued to prepare **tortillas** while making bricks but found the schedule too demanding. She subsequently reached an accord with her husband that it would be better to buy ready-made **tortillas** so that she could devote more time to brick production. As she explained it:

> I got up early to make **tortillas**; then
> I went to the patio, molded, laid out
> some bricks, and then came back to the
> house to finish making my **tortillas**. I
> bought corn to make dough from scratch.
> I did it that way for a while but
> afterwards I realized it was better to
> buy **tortillas** because, as I told my
> husband, it was too much of a hassle to
> mold bricks and then make **tortillas**
> from scratch.

Women follow various strategies to enable them to combine household chores with brickyard work. Some women postpone or reschedule domestic chores or leave one block of time for brickyard work. Typically this entails getting an earlier than usual start in the morning on chores. Other women prefer to alternate between domestic chores and brickyard tasks throughout the day.

Most of the informants said that they preferred housework to brickyard work; they also considered it to be more important, as well as the most appropriate activity for women. However, several women said they did not mind doing brickyard work; they noted that their contribution increased their husband´s daily brick output and the household´s weekly cash income. As one woman expressed it: "It´s worthwhile to help him in the brickyard because it earns us more money for our expenses. But domestic chores are more important because I feed and care for the children."

Even though women regularly perform many brickyard tasks which obviously increase daily brick output, most of their men expressed views which seemed to ignore this. The men´s views strongly supported a traditional conception of the sexual division of labor stereotyping women as the weaker sex whose proper role is housework. "A woman," said one **milero**, "was not made to work in the brickyard. She´s made to be in the home, to do domestic chores. She should always be there at lunchtime, at suppertime, to wash clothes, and so on." Another said: "Women are weaker than men. They help us with our work the little that they can." The last statement is especially ironic since it was made by none other than the husband of Marcela who had displaced him in the eyes of the employer as the **milero** of their household. Only two **mileros** acknowledged their wives´ contributions to brickyard income;

and only one considered his wife's housework to be as important and demanding as his work in the brickyard.

Every female informant expressed the view that men work more and that a woman's place is in the home. A typical statement was: "Men do the brickyard work and women do housework. Men work more. Men earn more than women. Women do nothing more than make some **tortillas** to sell to make a little cash to help out the men." What is ironic about these women's situation is not so much their contention that work done by men is physically more demanding and more remunerative than that done by women, which is generally true of the brickyards, but that they all (except Marcela) implicitly accept a rigid sexual division of labor between housework and brickyard work, even though all of them perform several tasks in the brickyard daily.

How did views expressed by the **mileros'** wives compare with their husband's views on other issues? With regard to their responses to a question about how they would spend a windfall of several thousand pesos, the wives were uniform in saying they would buy a lot and build a house, whereas half of their husbands said they would buy a brickyard. This is a difference in priorities which may reflect men's and women's differing degrees of involvement in the brick industry. It can also be viewed as representing a stronger internalization of the ideology of domesticity among the women. Perhaps as a partial reflection of this same factor, the women were for the most part less assertive than the men on the issue of whether poor households could become more affluent. Two of them responded negatively and the rest (with one exception) felt that this could be achieved through work and saving. None of them specified any plausible strategies related to their concrete circumstances for achieving this, as some of the men did.

Regarding household budget management, there was a consensus among husbands and wives that all earnings should be pooled and either administered by the husband or jointly. This is quite compatible with the cooperative nature of the labor process of brick production. Nevertheless, the fact that men are the payees makes it relatively easy for them to divert earnings from the family pool (e.g., for purchase of mezcal in the local cantinas).

Finally, with regard to the issue of social inequality and employer-worker relations, the women's
views were compatible with the men's but were
expressed with less clarity. Most of them recognized
that there was inequality between households in their
community but only two of them related it, in very
general terms, to differential control over means of
production. The majority simply said that some people
had better jobs or higher incomes than others. A few
associated the condition of wage labor with poverty
(e.g.,"We are among the poor because we work for a
wage") and one attributed it to the fact that they
cannot sell the bricks they produce. Several linked
wealth to the ownership of land but only a handful
specified this in the context of the brick industry.
Their position was that wealth was associated there
with the ownership of brickyards, trucks, or kilns
(e.g., "There are families that are a little bit
better off due to the fact that they have brick kilns"
or "The rich have their own brickyards; they have
better houses, they have animals, they have trucks").

Contradictions of Women's Indirect, Partial Proletarianization

What has been documented in this section are some
of the contradictory ideological consequences of piece
work capitalism's peculiar form of intervention in the
brickyard domestic economy. This has imposed a special
burden on the **milero** housewife since it requires her
participation in both household and brickyard production which are both essential to the short-term reproduction of labor-power; and in child-bearing and -care
which are essential to the long-run reproduction of
labor-power (cf. Benería and Sen 1981:291-293; Young
1978).

To the extent that womens' work is restricted to
the domestic sphere of own-use production and mothe-
ring among the Oaxaca valley peasantry, it tends to be
ideologically separated from and subordinated to mens'
work (to the degree that the latter is more directly
engaged in commodity production). As peasant households, whose women were previously uninvolved in commodity production, become involved in the brick industry, their women are obliged to participate more directly in commodity production--in most cases performing tasks which are accessory to those performed by
men but which are, nonetheless, instrumental to increasing household productivity and income.

172

This increasing involvement in commodity production creates scheduling conflicts in the household's allocation of labor for domestic own-use production and, thereby, highlights the importance of that sphere--especially because of its role in the short- and long-term reproduction of the commodity labor-power. This has both practical and ideological repercussions. It begins to subvert the rigid stereotyping of sex roles in the division of labor by dramatically demonstrating women's capacity for hard work in the sphere of commodity production on a level commensurate with that of men, and also by highlighting the importance of womens' role in the reproduction of family labor-power. In essence, brickyard women are experiencing indirect, partial proletarianization, and their own as well as their men's understanding of this process reflect the contradictions of evolving piecework capitalism.

When a woman becomes a full-time brickyard pieceworker, as Marcela did, then a significant portion of her labor-power enters the direct remuneration circuit. Although this involvement in wage labor may be temporary, it may still have an impact on her status in the household. In Marcela's case, it did appear to generate a higher degree of class consciousness than was manifested by brickyard women who were not pieceworkers. However, this new involvement was accompanied by the strain and conflict of the "double day" (Young 1978:146).[6]

On the Role of Government

The activities of government functionaries in Santa Lucia and other brick-producing communities in recent years has provoked much controversy and antagonism, and has raised the level of discourse surrounding relations between **mileros** and **patrones**. As might be expected the principal area of government concern has been with taxation or, more specifically, to devise a more effective and equitable tax policy for the brick industry. But there has also been periodic interest in the possibility of bringing the industry into the federal social security system, which means that employers would have to pay regular premiums for each employee. Also, there has been some discussion about organizing producers' cooperatives, unionizing the workers and enforcing work-safety and other components of the Federal Labor Law , and even about modernizing and reorganizing the industry.

173

During the latter part of 1979 the Economic Development Office (**Dirección General de Desarrollo Económico**) of the state government conducted a socioeconomic study of the industry in collaboration with another government agency, CIATO (**Centro de Investigaciones y Asistencia Tecnológica de Oaxaca**), which had as its primary purpose a revision of brick industry taxes, but was also designed to encompass all of the other areas mentioned above. The study was undertaken as a response to an organized protest in the fall of 1979 by the brickmakers of San Agustín Yatareni, operating through their **ejido** organization and with the support of their elected representative in the state legislature, of an arbitrarily imposed new tax of 33 dollars (740 pesos) per month per brickyard operator (presumably assessed a flat rate of 10% of mean monthly brick sales for all production units).

For many years prior to the imposition of this new tax the brickyard operators had been paying a tax of only 2.25 dollars (50 pesos) per month (assessed on the basis of an assumption that each brickyard operator fired his kiln once a month). In the aftermath of the tax protest--and until the study provided a basis for revising the tax--the federal tax office (**Impuestos Mercantiles Coordinados**) in Oaxaca City lowered the flat rate for the brick producers to four percent.

One of the two CIATO officials in charge of the study (which was initiated in November 1979 and completed in January 1980) explained its purpose succinctly as "establishing categories from which to determine 1) the percentage of their gross monthly income that the brickyard operators will have to pay, and 2) the number of categories that will apply to this industry." Three criteria were selected as a basis for classifying the brick producers: kiln capacity, frequency of firing, and monthly income. The study divided the brick producers of Yatareni into four groups whose gross monthly incomes ranged between 180 dollars and 280 dollars, with a low of six and a high of nine kiln firings per year.

The government functionary responsible for the study, and for instituting corresponding changes in the tax system, explained its rationale and scope in comprehensive terms as follows:

The study was undertaken not only to establish an equitable or adequate proportional quota but to deal with issues of wider scope as well. To see about the future possibility, not of converting it into a large industry, but at least into a medium industry because it is a source of employment that should be fostered--not to mention the fact that the city derives benefits from it. We have thought about organizing the brick producers but it has not yet been determined if a cooperative would be appropriate given the origin of these people. Perhaps it would be best to create another "legal entity" at the **ejido** level since they are in **ejidos.** Then a union or some other organism that brings together **ejidatarios** could be considered. This would be beneficial for them.

First we have to educate them because they don´t have an exact idea of what this would be. It´s sad and it grieves me to say it but it´s the truth: many of them are illiterate. With persons of that kind one can do very little. When the investigation was being conducted, I went to hold meetings with them and on those occasions the possibility of organizing them was announced--to control prices, to offer them the possibility of buying materials and tools at group discounts. But I don´t think they were interested. To this day not one of them has responded favorably to the possibility of organizing.

I believe that the independent character that all of us Mexicans have is evident here because the only thing that interested them was "my quota", "my tax" in a very personal way. We told them that if they were interested we wouldn´t organize at the level of all three villages but that we would go to each village to work with them. To this day we have had no communication from them. When we spoke to them in

> each community our proposals didn't
> interest them; they talked about this
> compadre and the wife of that neighbor,
> so that they were unable to get their
> act together. It's a pity because two
> months have now passed in this year and
> they have forgotten about the matter. A
> year will probably pass and we won't be
> able to create a "legal entity" that
> would benefit them.

After reading this well-intentioned (if pedantic, patronizing, and ingenuous) statement, it can be understood why our study, which was coincidentally initiated on the heels of the government study, was not initially received with great enthusiasm in the brickyards. Nevertheless, in retrospect, this unfortunate coincidence turned out to be an advantage since it provided an opportunity to analyze aspects of the relationship between government and small industry which otherwise might have been missed.

The principal concern of the brickyard operators was, of course, the potential impact of the government study upon their income. Those producers who had already been assessed at the 33 dollars per month rate generally cooperated with the government investigators in the hope of getting their rate reduced, whereas the producers who remained untaxed (or taxed at the old rate of fifty pesos per month) were generally hostile and uncooperative. According to a spokesperson for the federal tax office, seventy percent of the revenues derived from the new tax were earmarked for the federal treasury and thirty percent for the state treasury.

One producer who had the misfortune to be involved in the arbitrary tax increase which prompted the study (he was one of only three brickyard operators in Santa Lucía who were on the tax rolls in 1979 as opposed to seventy-one from San Agustín Yatareni), was told by a government auditor that his tax would be increased from 3.75 dollars monthly to 35.50 dollars monthly under the new system. He protested this so vigorously (and was able to pull enough strings in Oaxaca City since he is a former Municipal President and member of a prominent family) that he was able to have the application of the new tax suspended and to continue paying at the pre-1980 rate.

The following statement by an astute brickyard employer presents one view of the tax problem together with his proposal for how the government could play a potentially constructive role in the industry:

> If the government raises taxes, it will also have to raise brick prices and, then, raise **milero** piece rates. It would be a complicated affair. The big industrialist never loses when the government raises taxes; he compensates by increasing prices on the products he sells. Now, when we small fries go to buy a tool or another product that we need, we pay higher prices because of the new "value added" tax. The large businessman or industrialist doesn't feel the pinch but we small fries feel it a lot. If the government raises taxes on us brick producers, who are after all small industrialists, we won't be able to absorb it or pass it on. It will be better for us to get out of this line of work and find something else to do. We won't be able to pay our **mileros** because we will have to pay higher taxes without necessarily being able to raise brick prices.
>
> If the government were to establish a program for credit assistance to the brick industry, we could produce more bricks since we could employ more people who need the work. But I don't think the big producers would go along with such a program. Only small producers like me would benefit from it.

Most brick producers who do not own trucks have, over the years, managed to stay off the tax roster and, consequently, have paid only a municipal tax of one dollar monthly. More than half of the producers interviewed were in this category. The only conclusion one can draw from these data is that the tax system is both inefficient and inequitable. It is clear that the principal goal of the tax reform was to make the system more efficient and equitable with regard to mercantile incomes. This means that, by government choice in the case of the brick industry, the focus was on commercial operators (**comerciantes**) rather than producers. To my knowledge, the government's study was never completed in Santa Lucía and the provisional findings and recommendations for reform had not been enacted in 1982 at the end of the López Portillo administration.

Another dimension of the government's periodic interest in the brick industry has been directed specifically at the producers; it revolves around the applicability of the the Federal Labor Law (**Ley Federal del Trabajo**) and the Federal Social Security Law (**Ley Federal del Seguro Social**) to the brick industry. A government spokesperson made the following comments regarding this dimension:

> If they produce and have personnel at their service, according to the law they would constitute true employers and in that case they supposedly would be subject to the Federal Labor Law as well as the Social Security Law. I believe that in our environment this won't become a reality for one reason. Don't forget that in family production units wage labor is rarely employed.
>
> Regarding the producers, their economic potential is so weak that even when there is an employer-employee relationship between them, there isn't sufficient economic capacity to enable the worker to claim benefits under either one of the two Laws. Having observed their low economic capacity, I think that it would not be possible for the employers to comply with either of the two Laws. On the other hand, Social Security has forgotten them, nothing has been legislated to apply to them. I don't understand why when laws do exist pertaining to domestic workers. After all, brickyard workers are just as necessary since they materially supply the urban construction industry.
>
> Perhaps the matter has never been introduced because if a new charge were levied on the employers there would have to be a compensatory increase in the price of bricks. But I think it is

178

necessary to introduce social security to the industry because the working day is hard, it exhausts the workers--not to speak of the firing process which is enormously risky. The truth is that they don´t pay social security quotas because to do so they must be paid a minimum salary that is presently 105 pesos daily. Starting right there they would not have to have salary withheld; they would have to present monthly statements even if their withholding contributions were zeros.

The employer would be obliged to pay a contribution of 1% of each worker´s salary. In other words, there would be various special economic problems and the system would require a knowledge of fiscal matters that our people don´t have. I reiterate, however, that we don´t take the employer-employee relation into account even when we know it exists in this industry because, as I insist, they are family production units which only occasionally hire the labor of third parties.

Aside from the fact that the extent of capitalist relations in the brick industry is underemphasized (to some degree a measure of the success of the employer-sponsored campaign of deception), this is a careful statement of a complex issue. The government spokesperson was essentially correct to judge that the social security law might do more harm than good if imposed on the brick industry. This is especially true given the prevailing marketing structure which makes many of the brickyard employers dependent on the trucker-intermediaries, even though the need of the workers for its benefits is undeniable. Employers are quick to point out, however, that they could not in all fairness be forced to pay social security quotas since "**mileros** are temporary workers who work for a time and then go away."

Antonio, one of the ex-municipal presidents among the brickyard employers whose career trajectory was examined in Chapter 2, described the scenario that he and his colleagues envisage would result from the enforcement of the social security law:

179

The day that social security comes to
this industry we will all stop working
and those who will be hurt most are the
workers, not us. What I would do per-
sonally is get rid of all my bricks
cheap and start another business. I am
not going to pay insurance for someone
who is going to work for me for one or
two weeks--and do bad work on top of
it--that's not going to make enough for
me to pay the cost of the insurance!
That would be money badly invested.

One complicating factor is that many brickyard
employers seem to pay out at least as much in loans to
workers as they would pay in quotas to the social
security system. Of course, loans, unlike social security quotas, are either repayable with interest or are
deductible from wages and, consequently, do not represent an unrecoverble deficit; my impression is that
relatively few loans go unpaid. In any case, the
employer is able to informally bind workers to his
brickyard by being "generous" with emergency loans or
cash advances, whereas direct payments to social security would not have that effect. In short, nothing
less than a reorganization of the industry might be
required to bring it into compliance with the federal
social security and labor laws.

The issue of the applicability of these federal
laws was independently raised by a group of **mileros**
who did so as a result of a radio program which discussed the benefits to workers of their participation
in the social security system. One of the involved
mileros described the event as follows:

We heard over the radio that many workers have social security and that when
they are sick the insurance meets their
needs. And since we don't have insurance, well, when we get sick it comes
out of our hides. It's true that they
would deduct from our pay, but at least
one would be insured. Ten of us workers
spoke to a boss about the matter since
we believe that it would be beneficial
to us to get it. He didn't want any
part of it. Once we saw that the boss
was against it well we didn't do anything more about it. It's that one

180

needs a lot of effort to get through to
him. Here the work is very dangerous.
It's worse during the rainy season, the
walls of the clay pits loosen up and
can cave-in on you and break an arm or
a leg; then you don't work. With insurance or with a union, well one gets
some compensation. The bosses have to
respect the law. The government should
make them respect the law because there
is no other way.

This statement suggests that brick industry workers do not need government functionaries to tell them
what their interests are, but that they do require
government intervention and support to apply and en-
force the provisions of federal laws since employers
will be slow to voluntarily comply with them. This
reluctance is illustrated by a "cover-up" strategy
which is regularly employed in encounters between
brickyard personnel and outsiders.

In the face of what they perceived to be an on-
slaught of zealous tax agents and assorted meddling
functionaries who were ignorant of conditions in the
brick industry, many of the brickyard employers during
1978-1979 instructed their workers to be uncooperative
with interlopers who might come to the brickyards
asking questions. The principal instruction was to
deny that they had employers and to insist that the
brickyards were run as family operations where everyone was equal. One of the workers presents his own
views of the government's role in the brick industry
and specifically describes the instructions from his
employer concerning how he should respond to questions
by interlopers:

The government wants to screw us because all it does is find out how much
we earn. It comes, makes an investigation of all that and puts the screws to
all the bosses. Then, they are going to
increase taxes, they are going to impose a hard tax. They have been wanting
to do it. But these bastards, the
bosses, don't let them. That's politics
for you! Oh what the hell, what can we
do? It's a question of the government,
because the government is what it's all
about for us. The government has to

defend us. Right? For example, the previous governments--those of Juárez, of Porfirio Díaz--those were good governments. In those days they didn´t have things like we have today. Our government knows how much we earn here. It´s going to screw us all, but the bosses worst of all because it will make them poor like us.

The government should keep its nose out of our business. They send employees here to poke around. The employees ask questions about how one makes bricks, if one is unionized or is in social security, all that. Then **the bosses here fool** (my emphasis) the "little employees" (**empleaditos**) by telling them, "Here we all work together, there are no bosses. Here we are all united, we are a cooperative." That´s how the bosses get the "little employees" off their backs. The employees came here. They asked me: Who is your boss? But the bosses were already informed about this--I don´t know how they got their information.

The employees asked me that question and I answered, "I don´t have a boss." And they said to me: "What do you mean that you don´t have a boss?" "How do you work?" I told them that we work together, in a cooperative, like a society where everyone works together as partners. Here, I said, we all earn the same, we work as one. "Is that so?" they asked."That´s the way it is" I responded. "This work is not of the kind that has bosses" I told them.

We had been advised what to say beforehand (emphasis added) because they wanted to impose social security and from that they were going to learn about everything and make the bosses pay compensations for injuries or deaths of workers. But the bosses aren´t fools. They said, damn it, one of those bastard **mileros** dies and it´s

182

going to cost us. It's better if they
don't have insurance. **The bosses told
us** (emphasis added): tell the government employees that we are all working
together, that there are no bosses, and
that's that. That's how they got them
off their backs.

This **milero** was by no means alone in cooperating
to "cover up" the capitalist identity of relations of
production in the brickyards. Many **mileros**, in fact,
participated in this campaign to deceive the **"empleaditos"** from the city (who are for the most part are
viewed with a mixture of envy and contempt by rural
workers in Oaxaca) with a genuine feeling of gratification. So the **mileros** are in a real bind when it
comes down to deciding how best to serve their own
material interests. On the one hand, they clearly
recognize that their interests and those of their
bosses are ultimately at odds over income distribution
but, on the other, as members of an immigrant proletariat they are dependent on the "good will" of their
bosses for their "social security" needs.

Other **mileros** explicitly expressed the view (implicit in the above quote) that problems between themselves and their bosses should be resolved in the
brickyards and that decisions regarding programs like
social security, as one of them put it, "ought to be
voluntary on the part of the boss." Another expressed
the same notion in a different way: "The government
can't help. Here everything is fixed by the boss." And
still another expressed the common view that the
government cannot be trusted: "Everyone says that
instead of helping us the government exploits us. I
don't think the government can do anything." This view
was echoed succinctly by one **milero** who said: "All
the government employees do is a lot of talking."

In short, the **mileros** as a class understand where
their interests coincide with and diverge from those
of their employers. They prefer to work out their
problems in the brickyards without outside intervention simply because they dislike having to deal with
patronizing government functionaries whom they dis-
trust. They believe that the government should be
serving their interests but recognize through experience that it rarely does so, except in its slogans and
in the rhetoric of the politicians. A worker-owner who
has one foot in the camp of the **mileros** and another in

that of the employers put it this way:

> The government is useless. When the
> candidates are campaigning they go
> around promising a lot but, when all is
> said and done, they don't accomplish
> anything. Governments promise a lot but
> deliver nothing.

During Antonio's period of tenure as municipal
president the government instituted a tax on business
income which was collected from truck drivers on each
truckload of bricks at the toll houses (**casetas fiscales** on the highways. Antonio explained what tran-
spired:

> They came to see me with a receipt for
> a tax surcharge which they had been
> obliged to pay at the toll house on the
> highway and asked what could be done.
> Others from Yatareni also showed up
> with the same problem. I told them that
> what we have to do is talk to the
> governor. They had never charged us a
> tax before because we were considered
> to be artisans; and if they were going
> to charge it was supposed to be mini-
> mal. We were then and are now ready to
> pay a tax so long as it is minimal. We
> won't refuse to pay our fair share
> because the government has its ex-
> penses, but we won't pay as much they
> wanted us to pay. They wanted to charge
> us 50 pesos for every truckload and, at
> that time, not even the truck owner
> earned that much; he earned 30 pesos
> per load! On what basis were they going
> to charge us 50 pesos? That was when we
> all united. The protesters came of
> their own accord; I didn't organize
> them. And just as they came then, so
> they will come again in the future to
> resolve other problems like social
> security.

Antonio went on to emphasize why no formal organization of brick producers was established:

> An organization wasn't formed because
> it would be prejudicial to the inter-
> ests of the brickyard operators. Upon

forming an organization or united front of brickyard operators, the first thing that would come down on top of us would be social security for the workers. Immediately they would force us to open an office, have secretaries, and all that. Not all of us would be able to meet the expenses of such an operation. What we did was to agree among all the village authorities that when any problem of common concern to the brickyard operators arose that we should unite as if we were one person to deal with it. That's the agreement we have.

With a unique blend of pragmatism and libertarianism, the brickyard operators have devised an acephalous, ad hoc institutional vehicle for protecting their interests from the meddling government bureaucracy.

Some of the brickyard operators emphasize the "envy" (**"envidia"**) and "egoism" (**"egoismo"**) as a barrier to formal organization. However, the bottom line seems to be a laissez faire form of individualism which fundamentally distrusts formal organizations. "Here we are all free," emphasized one brickyard operator. "No one is going to want an association. There is talk of working together in a society but we don't want to, it's not worthwhile." This same current of thought but with a more specific accent on upward mobility was expressed by another: "It's all right being independent like we are. A person who wants to get ahead has to work hard. The government would come here to impose upon us and that wouldn't be acceptable to us." In short, functionaries in the government offices of Oaxaca City will continue to try to impose their corporatist ideology which would transform the brick industry into a manipulable, taxable, and regulable entity within the corporate state. Barring a major social upheaval, however, several more government administrations will come and go before that goal is achieved.

This review of the role of the government in the brick industry leads to one inescapable conclusion: the relationship to date has been one-sided, with the brick industry being considered almost exclusively as a source of tax revenues for the public treasury. The tax policies themselves are either ambiguous or inconsistent, and the tax burden appears to be inequitably

185

and capriciously distributed among the brickyard and commercial operators. Consequently, in many areas where the government could and should be playing a role (e.g., health and medical care, work safety and workman´s compensation, credit, technical and marketing assistance) it is not, and in the one area where it is playing a role (i.e., taxation), it has sown a legacy of mistrust, hostility, and cynicism.

The fact remains, however, that substantial constituencies in the industry could benefit from enlightened and even-handed government intervention in many of the areas mentioned above. There would be significant, if not unanimous, support for this. Yet, if such intervention is to get past the planning stage and have lasting beneficial effects, it should come only at the request of a specific industry-wide constituency that includes both employers and workers. At the very least, there should be no government intervention without careful preliminary research on need and impact upon the different groups and classes that comprise the industry.

NOTES

[1] This is evident from the following statements by other brickyard owners comparing agriculture and brickmaking: (1) "Brickmaking is preferable to agricultural work. One gets money more quickly in bricks. In agriculture one gets money once a year." (2) "Agriculture also has benefits. When the harvest comes, one doesn't have to buy corn for six or eight months. That's a savings for the household. That's why I haven't stopped working in agriculture. I have a few milk cows that also help out with the budget." (3) "The produce of the fields is not sufficient to meet household needs. That's why we alternate brickwork with agricultural work. Brickwork sustains us while we work in the fields."

[2] Some readers may wonder why I have coined the term "endofamilial" accumulation for what they may associate with a notion which Chayanov (1966) labelled "self-exploitation." There are three reasons why I have done so: first, it is not so much "self-exploitation" as it is the systematic use of the labor-power of others in the worker-proprietor's household (especially teen-age sons in the case of the brick industry but wife and daughters in the treadle loom industry) which needs to be emphasized; second, exploitation is a term which I prefer to restrict to the relationship between capital and labor that is mediated by a wage payment; and third, to emphasize that the family labor-power expended may result in capital accumulation and not just in simple reproduction as Chayanov emphasized.

[3] Carmen Diana Deere has made the following argument: "...the division of labor by sex characterized by female production of subsistence foodstuffs and male semi-proletarianization allows the payment by capital of a male wage rate insufficient for familial maintenance and reproduction ... the familial division of labor by sex, thus allows the wage to be less than the cost of production and reproduction of labor power. This inequality is then reflected in a low value of labor power within the periphery, which either enhances peripheral capital accumulation or is transferred to the center..." 1979:133-134).

The brick industry situation demonstrates that females need not be involved in the production of subsistence foodstuffs to have these positive effects on capital accumulation. The same effects can be achieved either through unremunerated participation in the male household head's piece wage job or by direct, underremunerated participation in industrial commodity production like basketry, weaving, and embroidery. This was precisely the situation in late 19th century France where among the linen handloom weavers of the Cambrèsis Tilly concludes: "Without the unpaid labor of his wife and the wages of his children, it would have been impossible for the male weaver to support a family" (1981:406).

[4] It is informative to compare the situation of women in the Oaxaca valley brickyards with that of women in the brickyards of Kerala, India. The main difference is that in Kerala women participate full-time exclusively as brick haulers on a piece rate basis; men and boys perform all other tasks. Brick hauling is classified as unskilled work, whereas tasks performed by boys and men are classified as semi-skilled and skilled respectively. Women's daily earnings average out to about one-half those of boys and men--which reflects the lower piece rates assigned to unskilled labor rather than actual number of hours worked (Gulati 1982).

[5] Deere and León de Leal (1981) make a similar observation regarding attitudes toward women's tasks in the Peruvian Andes, as follows: "A typical aspect of this technical division of labor is that both men and women consider the tasks carried out by women to be much less important than the tasks carried out by men. This is reflected in the way that both sexes often refer to women's participation in agricultural production as simply "helping out." But women's tasks in such a technical division of labor are certainly important to the production process. If these weren't carried out by women, they would have to be carried out by men, and often are" (1981:349).

[6] Kate Young (1978) has analyzed the complexities of women's economic roles and social status over a century of changing political economic conditions in two mountain villages of the northern Oaxaca **sierra**.

Among her important findings is that the growth of coffee production and the decline of weaving (both of which occurred via external forces) caused a shift in the status of women from secure skilled laborers to insecure non-skilled manual laborers. In her words: "As weavers they controlled not only the labor process but also the proceeds of their work; as coffee pickers on the household plot their labor was unremunerated. Women who once enjoyed the status of skilled craftsmen fell to the insecure status of non-skilled rural laborers" (1978:149).

In the valley of Oaxaca and its immediate mountain hinterland the transition from self-provisioning local economies to local economies controlled by merchant capital, and then to local economies controlled by commercial capital, has not evolved in the way described by Young for the northern **sierra**, nor has capitalist development had many of the same effects. Commercial capital has, indeed, become dominant but has not completely displaced merchant capital nor has it destroyed rural industrial commodity production. In many instances, it supplies the latter with tools or raw materials. Indigenous merchant capital has expanded in industries like embroidery and other tourist-related crafts, and rural industrial commodity production has expanded or has held its own in many industries where women are skilled artisans (e.g., back-strap loom weaving, palm-plaiting, embroidery). Moreover, in the Oaxaca valley, as the brick industry exemplifies, indigenous industrial capital has developed from a peasant simple commodity base, and must be taken seriously in the capitalist arena along with commercial, financial, and merchant capital.

15. Milero, wife, and 3 year old daughter
    perform complementary brickyard tasks

190

CHAPTER 6

CONCLUSIONS: PEASANT INDUSTRY, PIECE WORK, AND PROVINCIAL CAPITALIST DEVELOPMENT

Small industrial commodity production in today's Third World economies incorporates noncapitalist elements but is within capitalism. The two-sided nature of small-scale household industry complicates its role in the development of native capital. In essence, it may provide either a seed bed or a sick bed for such development.

On the one hand, in certain branches of production dominated internationally by capital-intensive enterprises operating with economies of scale, it is arguable that a trend toward labor-intensification in particular industries bodes ill for long-term national economic development. For example, Alonso (1983) has argued that such a process in the Mexican clothing industry is a short-sighted response by national capitalists to increased competition from intruding U.S. monopoly capital. Mexican industrialists, according to him,"are not interested in the technological renovations of their factories..."; instead "their answer to the problems created by industrial competition relies on finding and superexploiting the unorganized labor force" (1983:167). Consequently, argues Alonso, the "participation of domestic seamstresses (who are "semi-independent producers") ...contributes to the stagnation of the Mexican clothing industry and not to its development and modernization" (1983:171).

The other side of the coin, which Alonso ignores, is that the reorganization of an industry from congregated manufactories to dispersed household workshops may, in fact, enable it to survive competitively; and also create a situation in which un- or under-employed labor is employed, and in which small-scale capital accumulation is promoted. Thus, Alonso notes that the Mexico City seamstresses "dream of having their own workshop, their own small business that will grow with the years" (1983:171). To some extent such dreams are apparently being realized (though Alonso does not admit this) when "unipersonal" workshops become "multipersonal" as more household members or hired employees are absorbed into the production unit (1983:163-164). In other words, to the degree that household production units move from endofamilial accumulation (i.e., capital generated by family labor)

191

to simple capitalist accumulation (i.e., capital generated by hired labor with or without family labor), Alonso fails to recognize that the reorganization of the Mexico City clothing industry (as a strategy to protect the short-term interests of national medium-sized capital) has the unintended consequences of stimulating the growth of small capital and of providing jobs for the un- and under-employed.

Small rural industry, like its urban counterpart, also relies upon the use of unpaid family labor and displays minimal technological innovation because of resistance to the replacement of labor inputs by capital inputs (see Kahn 1980: esp. chs. 5,7, & 9). However, this tendency should not be emphasized to the extent of overlooking the possibility that unpaid family labor can be replaced by hired labor in rural production units, and that capital may be invested in acquiring means of production which are not technologically innovative but which do increase productivity. Thus, capital-intensification of production, capital accumulation, and social differentiation can occur in the absence of technological innovation. This in no way alters the fact that small rural industries are affected, albeit in differing degrees, by fluctuations in the wider capitalist economy in such diverse areas as pricing of raw materials and producer's goods, in employment (e.g., demand for temporary or seasonal wage labor or for home pieceworkers), and in ideology (e.g., the valuation of labor-time; preference scales)(Cook 1982a:353-358; Deere and de Janvry 1979; Goody, ed. 1982).

Peasant-artisan industries may be anachronisms inserted in local or regional economies in which international capital shows only periodic, if any, interest; and their persistence may reflect local or regional idiosyncrasies. In the Oaxaca valley an example of a truly anachronistic industry is provided by metate making (Cook 1982a) which has persisted for centuries, without fundamental changes in its organization of production and exchange, to satisfy a traditional social demand from regional peasant and working class households. Despite the fact that modern capitalism has produced more efficient means (e.g., mechanized grinding mills) than the metate for grinding and processing corn and other foodstuffs, metates are still widely purchased. (One reason for this persisting demand seems to lie in rural cultural matrix

192

where the metate represents symbolically the traditional sexual division of labor and the establishment of new rural households, and functions ideologically to reinforce the traditionally subordinate position of women in the rural economy.)

At the other extreme, labor-intensive industries may be creatures of national or international capital as rejuvenated or introduced forms which appear to be regional precapitalist or peasant-artisan anachronisms, but which really function as appendages of the wider capitalist economy. In the Oaxaca valley, treadle loom weaving and embroidery provide examples of this pseudo-anachronistic type of industry. They have been rejuvenated or introduced, under the sponsorship of urban merchant capital, to satisfy a tourist-generated demand for handicrafts. Ironically, this demand is itself a by-product of factory industrialization in the metropolitan capitalist economies that virtually destroyed earlier forms of handicraft industry (Cook 1981; Novelo 1976:45 et passim; Garcia Canclini 1982:ch.III).

The Oaxaca valley brick industry represents still another type of labor-intensive industry. It bridges historical epochs and straddles different sections or levels of the division of labor. It employs an archaic production technology which combines a 16th century Spanish tool-kit with certain prehispanic elements. Its social relations are a syncretic mix of noncapitalist domestic economy, rural paternalism, and modern capitalism; its market structure and transport technology are predominantly urban capitalist. In previous chapters it was described how the brick industry, at the end of the 19th century, was firmly situated within the regional division of labor to supply limited quantities of bricks for rural and urban construction. Since then the industry has undergone a gradual internal transformation from seasonal peasant-artisan household organization to capitalist piecework as the market for construction bricks expanded in the nearby city.

Careful study of the results of recent research on rural industries in the Oaxaca valley leads to the conclusion that there are few processual regularities or tendential laws of motion which hold for local industrial units (e.g., one treadle loom weaving village) or for entire industries (e.g., all treadle loom weaving villages). It also shows that such regularities may hold for particular groupings of production units similarly involved in specific industries (e.g., all employer units which combine family and hired labor or which engage also in agriculture).

Cross-cutting and particularizing variables often intervene within and between industries to bedevil attempts at generalization. For example, what holds for proprietor-employer households in the brick industry often does not hold for proletarian households; and what holds for either of these groups may be inapplicable to independent worker-owner units. The same can be said for the treadle loom weaving industry, as well as for several others. Furthermore, many generalizations about the brick industry or the treadle loom weaving industry do not apply to the metate industry, the palm-plaiting industry, or to the embroidery industry. These industries are differentially inserted in the regional division of labor, and may have different relations of production, marketing patterns, and so on. Yet, to the extent that various industries begin to regularly employ hired labor the piece wage form is a common denominator between them.

Peasant Capitalist Industry, Merchant Industry, and Piecework

Indeed, there is a variety of piecework capitalism operating in both urban and rural branches of Oaxaca valley small industry. The rural branches (which include brickmaking, treadle loom weaving, and embroidery) are organized by peasant-artisan capitalists who, more often than not, achieved employer status by working their way up from either pieceworker or self-employed artisan status. The urban branches of this capitalist piecework sector(which include several different types of production from weaving and tinworking to leatherworking and jewelry-making) are organized either by craftsmen as extensions of a craft shop or by businessmen as extensions of retail or wholesale selling operations. A more detailed comparison of the conditions of capital and labor in these two branches, will provide a better understanding of the contribution of piecework capitalism to the development of the provincial economy.

A good point of departure is an interesting application of Marx's ideas about piece wages to contemporary Tunisian tailors which uncovers similarities between the "sweating system" in 19th-century England (established through the "interposition of middlemen between the capitalist and the laborers"), and the role patrons play between Tunis coat dealers and tailoring industry workers in a provincial town (Hopkins 1978:478). This parallels the situation existing within the Oaxaca valley embroidery industry where putting-out merchants often employ a series of commission agents who operate at the village level to recruit, supply, and pay outworkers (cf. Alonso 1983:165).

Also, in the basket industry Oaxaca City buyers-up make contracts for so much per basket of a particular type with one village master basketmaker who is then responsible for recruiting and paying other basketmakers in his village. As Marx said about this type of arrangement: "The exploitation of the laborer by capital is here effected through the exploitation of the laborer by the laborer" (1967:554). Finally, in the Oaxaca valley craft shops or brickyards where the employer is also a worker the situation approximates that in the Tunisian tailoring workshops where patrons push themselves to work just as hard as their pieceworkers because their income also depends on output (Hopkins 1978:478).

Differential wages among individual pieceworkers are typical not only in the brickyards but in other rural and urban industries where the piece wage system prevails. For example, the proprietor of a tin products manufactory in Oaxaca City with 45 workers responded as follows to a question asking him as to how much he paid his tinworkers per day: "Well, this varies a great deal. The head of my tinworkers earns 12,000 pesos (roughly 530 dollars) monthly. Then I have three who earn 4,000 pesos (178 dollars) monthly. The great majority earn between 2,000 and 2,500 pesos (90 and 110 dollars) monthly." He was then asked what the basis was for this differentiation and he responded: "Their output, because we base our salary on a commission per piece."

When asked if there was a basic salary for all of his tinworkers, this shopowner replied: "No. There are some workers who can earn a month's salary in a day. There's one worker, for example, who can make 350 tin boxes in one day--a product that we sell in large quantities. On the other hand, there is another worker who has a hard time making 24 boxes daily. It depends on their skill." The next follow-up question was whether, in fact, this employer paid workers per day or per piece, to which he responded as follows: "Almost by the piece. We pay them the minimum salary required by law and above that a commission by the piece so that they produce all that they can."[1]

It is clear from the available data on the economic consequences of the piece wage in this shop is that the time wage, apparently without being "lined-up" with a fixed "average" rate of worker output, was used to cover the minimum wage; and the piece wage was introduced to provide a material incentive for the intensification of production. It is the latter which seems to be of primary importance to Oaxaca piecework employers, rather than an overriding concern with the rate of exploitation (Cook 1984a).

What can be gleaned from the statistical data regarding the distribution of total product between capital and labor in these piecework industries (see Table 12)? The aggregate wage bill comprises a much lower percentage of the value of total product in the Oaxaca city manufactories (11%) than it does in either the embroidery (42%) or the brick industries (48%). On the other hand, the Oaxaca city manufactories had considerably higher capital costs than did the embroidery units or the brickyards. This translates into higher worker productivity in the city manufactories, as well as a much higher rate of exploitation of labor (P/W). This latter figure is indicative of the fact that higher productivity is not necessarily reflected in higher wages. The per capita average monthly wage was three times higher for the city manufactory pieceworker (32 dollars) than it was for the embroidery outworker (10 dollars), but it was well below the average monthly wage for the Santa Lucia brickyard pieceworker of 180 dollars. Incidentally, it was also below the monthly official minimum wage for Oaxaca City of 80 dollars (Murphy and Selby 1981:251).[2]

These apparent wage disparities require additional comment focussed on the difference in the total economic situation of urban and rural worker households in the Oaxaca valley. The mean wage for the city manufactory pieceworker in 1979 must be interpreted in the context of an urban economy in which the median monthly household income was 112 dollars (vs. 87 dollars for "poor" households) (Murphy and Selby 1981:253); and in which the median monthly household per-adult-equivalent income was 30 dollars (18 dollars for the "marginally poor" - Higgins 1983:173). Although the mean pieceworker wage is in line with these other figures, it is nontheless skewed to the low side because an undetermined percentage of the total work-force was casual or part-time. In the words of one weaving workshop proprietor: "When they want to work, they work all day; and when they don't want to work they don't come. We are short of workers but we have to manage. We lack human material. All of them want to be professionals. There are no longer many who want to be artisans."

Table 12. Monthly Costs, Value of Output, and Profits in Oaxaca Valley Piece Work Industries (values in dollars)*

	Means of production	Raw materials	Wages (W)	Value of product	Profit (P)	P/W
Oaxaca City	3,429	35,582	7,110	64,782	22,090	
(n = 15)	229	2,372	474	4,319	1,473	3.10
Embroidery	60	5,081	5,657	13,431	2,693	
(n = 30)	2	169	189	452	90	.48
Brickyards	---	429	2,376	4,965	2,160	
(n = 7)	30	61	339	709	309	.91

* Top values = aggregates; lower values = means

Among other things, this pattern of irregular work is associated with an urban situation in which "the majority of households have as many teenage and adult members working as possible" and where "there is a lack of unemployment because the majority of people are underemployed" (Higgins 1983:7). In other words, the craft pieceworker in the typical working class household in Oaxaca city is only one of several cash-earners. This is in marked contrast to the situation of brickyard households where the the pieceworker's wage is really a family wage since most members of the household directly participate in the production of bricks for which the wage is paid.

On the other hand, the low mean per capita wage for rural embroidery outworkers is a reflection of the sex and age composition of that population: a significant proportion (38%) of embroidery outwork is done by dependent, unmarried, and childless females--although a majority (51.5%) of the embroidery outworkers are married and have dependent children. Regardless of who performs it, embroidery work is poorly remunerated. Among fifteen outworker households for which detailed budget data is available, the highest hourly return was just under twenty-five cents and the lowest a paltry three cents.

From the perspective of the female embroidery outworkers the critical issue is not so much **low** remuneration as it is **no** remuneration. They have relatively few cash-earning alternatives which are so easily adaptable to daily household routines (Cook 1982a:64). That the Oaxaca valley countryside provides a fertile recruiting ground for outworkers, is demonstrated by the remarkable proliferation of the embroidery industry in the district of Ocotlán and elsewhere in the valley over the last decade.

In short, piecework industries in the Oaxaca valley have a wage structure which is bifurcated between the male and female labor force. Not only is there a differential in the average wages of men and women between industries, as for example between tin working and embroidery, but there is a difference within industries between male labor which is remunerated and female labor which is unremunerated, as for example in the brick industry. This conclusion takes on added significance in light of the fact that the average price of male labor-power in the Oaxaca valley, as indicated above, is itself undervalued. So, if men there can be said to suffer **super**exploitation, women such as embroiderers, thread-spinners and brick-yard workers suffer **hyper**exploitation (see Deere 1979:139; cf. Littlefield 1978:504).[3]

One final point should be made about the piece wage system in underdeveloped economies like that of the Oaxaca valley: it is incorrect to view it as linked to a unidirectional evolution from independent handicraft to capitalist manufacture, and to view the "freedom" of the direct producer under it as absolute. Marx observed that time and piece wages often coexisted in the same branches of industry and in the same shops (1967:551), and was scathing in his criticism of

198

the following statement made by Watts in 1865 (quoted in Marx ibid.): "The system of piece-work illustrates an epoch in the history of the working-man; it is halfway between the position of the mere day-laborer depending upon the will of the capitalist and the co-operative artisan, who in the not too distant future promises to combine the artisan and the capitalist in his own person. Piece-workers are in fact their own masters, even whilst working upon the capital of the employer." In short, under the piece wage system the equality between employer and worker is illusory (Hopkins 1978:477).

As argued above, in the Oaxaca valley it is equally illusory to consider the piece wage system as a systematic instrument for the maintenance of desig-nated rates of exploitation of labor by capital in labor-intensive industries. Rather it is the form of remuneration most suited to the general conditions of labor which confront employers, especially those in rural areas but those in urban areas as well. In other words, piecework probably is more conducive to the development of capitalist production than time work under conditions in which labor is still partly in-volved in or recently disengaged from simple commodity production.

Endofamilial Accumulation in Piecework Capitalism: Development Implications

Joseph Schumpeter (1950) criticized Marx for ridiculing the importance of saving by small proprie-tors as a mechanism of original or incipient capital-ist accumulation. While I disagree with Schumpeter's failure to link the origins of entrepreneurship to the labor process during later phases of capitalist devel-opment, I think his criticism of Marx on this point is valid. Furthermore, I believe that the following statement by Schumpeter (1950:16), which emphasizes the labor origins of proto-capitalists in Europe, has relevance for our understanding of small-scale, local-level capitalist development of the type found in the brick industry:

> Many a factory in the 17th and 18th centuries was just a shed that a man was able to put up by the work of his hands, and required only the simplest equipment to work it. In such cases the manual work of the prospective capital-

ist plus a quite small fund of savings
was all that was needed--and brains, of
course.[4]

On the basis of the foregoing analysis of data
from the brick industry (and also from the rural
treadle loom weaving industry), two additional elements can be added to Schumpeter's list: 1) family
labor; and 2) a supply of extra-household labor pre-
conditioned by involvement in simple commodity production to a system of payment by results. The crucial
point is that the development of piecework capital
from a basis in peasant-artisan household production
(through the process of endofamilial accumulation)
often occurs within village industries, and need not
be introduced from external sources.

A cautionary note is in order here. It is one
thing to study European economic history with a view
toward deriving possible insights or ideas about capitalist development in places like contemporary Oaxaca,
but it is quite another to assume that the former
established a trajectory which the latter can, should,
or must replicate. The heuristic approach is fruitful;
however, as the record of post-1945 economic development studies illustrates, the uncritical replication
approach is analytically sterile (Roxborough
1979:ch.2). The role of the entrepreneur in the British textile industry between 1750 and 1850 was important for the textile branch of British industry and
for the British economy; but it was also of world
historic importance because it directly contributed to
the transformation of British society (and of humanity
at large) to a new level of socioeconomic organization
in which industrial capital was dominant.

The rise of industrial capital to hegemony in
Britain had profound effects outside of Britain as the
histories of ex-colonies like India, Nigeria, or
Jamaica provide grim testimony: it irreversibly transformed the structure and dynamics of the world capitalist system. Given the subsequent evolution of
the international capitalist division of labor--in
which even the most advanced sectors of industries in
Third World countries are dependent upon transnational
corporations with their operational centers in the
U.S., Europe, or Japan--it is impossible for the "industrial revolution" to be replicated in the lesser
developed countries of Asia, Africa, or Latin America
today or in the future. The development trajectories

of these economies are enmeshed with the evolution of the global capitalist system whose control centers lie outside the boundaries of the Third World (Wallerstein 1974:3-11,346-357 and 1979; Wolf 1982:3-23, 296-309).

Small-scale industries in underdeveloped economies are enclaves or niches in a complex world system of hierarchically nested commodity-producing units and markets (Cooper 1980; Kahn 1980; Goody, ed.,1982). This situation should not inhibit our reconsideration of the merits of a position advocated by many scholars several decades ago, namely, that such industries can provide the basis for economically viable industrialization programs (Bauer and Yamey 1957:252-254)--with the important proviso that such programs devise policies designed to assure that direct producers receive equitable shares of the value their labor-power creates (Herman 1956:360).[5]

In tracing the precolonial structure of Indian craft production, its decline under British colonialism, and its revival under Gandhi's leadership, Milton Singer (1960) pointed to similarities in values between English and Indian craft producers and implied that the entrepreneurial capacities and developmental potential of the post-colonial craftsmen and their industries were seriously underestimated by eurocentric developmentalist approaches. As he stated in his conclusion (1960:275):

> What is an "industrial tradition"? Some of the things it is not are fairly obvious...An industrial tradition is not the factory system as it developed in England in the eighteenth and nineteenth centuries. Some elements of this form of economic organization will be found in newly developing countries, but there is no inherent necessity for the English experience to be recapitulated, nor is there any inherent reason why a factory system cannot coexist with cottage and small-scale industries in dispersed units. An industrial tradition is not a specific complex of values providing the motive force for industrialization.

With this statement Singer opened another dimension to rural industrialization in the Third World which has subsequently been ignored in the scholarly celebration of peasant economy with its agrarianization of the Third World countryside; namely, the impact of involvement in small industry by rural direct producers as an "industrial experience" which exposes them to some features of industrial capitalism prior to the proliferation of a factory proletariat (cf. Tilly and Tilly 1971:188; Nash 1967:148-49)). It must not be forgotten that in LDCs like India and Mexico a substantial proportion of the so-called peasants who circulate into new urban industries come from segments of the rural population with either long or intensive experiences in non-factory types of industrial commodity production (cf. Tilly and Tilly 1971:190). It is likely that rural industry provides many segments of the rural class of direct producers with an ideological and experiential repertory that could have a significant bearing on the course of future events in their local, regional, and national political economies.

In the last analysis, the future of small-scale, labor-intensive industries like those in the Oaxaca valley lies in a combination of external and internal forces, just as did their past. Nationally, advanced forms of industrial capital control the construction materials and textile sectors. Labor-intensive forms persist at the regional and local levels either because the market is not conducive to capital-intensive forms (e.g., the case of handicrafts) or because it is not attractive to capital-intensive enterprise, given the availability of low-cost labor to sustain the labor-intensive form (e.g., as in brick production).

Nevertheless, an economic future with higher degrees of capitalization is not totally preempted by or dependent upon external capitalist industry. Some of the enterprising weavers in the rural treadle loom industry might, with external assistance in production and marketing, develop a more capital-intensive clothing industry; and brickyard operators conceivably could develop more capital-intensive brickmaking enterprises by a combination of internal investment and loans. Indeed, more than one brickyard operator has already experimented with diesel-fueled burners, and the government has proposed a tentative plan for the reorganization and greater capitalization of regional brick production which would transform but not eliminate the present industry.

In conclusion, it is fitting to propose that small labor-intensive industries are not necessarily so retrograde as some scholars (e.g., Kautsky 1974:217 et passim; Baran 1973:316) have argued. In developing capitalist economies like Mexico such industries should not be arbitrarily dismissed as pawns of big capital (Cockcroft 1983:89,97-8) in a subsumed process of "permanent primitive accumulation" (Bartra 1974:23; cf. de Janvry 1981:37). Certain of these industries, especially those involving piecework, as they contribute to capital accumulation and class formation do play a moderately progressive role in improving over time the material life conditions of direct producers. These industries also provide an arena in which workers learn about their class interests and how to pursue them under the contradictory conditions of evolving provincial capitalism.[6]

NOTES

[1] The minimum wage was 70 pesos (3 dollars) daily.

[2] The mean return on capital invested--roughly equivalent to the marxist profit rate of surplus value/(constant + variable capital)--is higher in the brick industry (77%) than in Oaxaca city (52%) and embroidery (25%).

For reasons which are not entirely clear, estimates of rates of surplus-value realized by merchant-manufacturers in the Oaxaca valley are substantially higher than an independent estimate of 74% for Oaxaca City buyers of reed basket products (Bailón Corres 1980:108); and are much higher than estimates of rates realized by Yucatan hammock industry merchants studied by Littlefield (1978) where the rate for rural intermediaries was just over 15% and for city merchants about 54%. Like the Yucatan case, however, this rate soars for intermediaries in Mexico City and beyond, who regularly resell Oaxaca craft products at mark-ups of 200 to 300%.

[3] Alonso argues that domestic seamstresses in Mexico City are superexploited by Mexican monopoly capital among other reasons because "as domestic workers who receive none of the social benefits explicitly enumerated in the New Labor Law ... their salaries are lower than the minimum legal wage; they are always piece wages; they work normally more than eight hours a day; they do not receive any social benefits; and aside from the seasonal character of the clothing industry, their work is highly unstable" (1983:169-170).

[4] Schumpeter(1961:78 et. passim) introduced the concept of the "entrepreneurial function" which he defined as follows: "...to reform or revolutionize the pattern of production by exploiting an invention or...an untried technological possibility for producing a new commodity or producing an old one in a new way, by opening up a new source of supply of materials or a new outlet for products, by reorganizing an industry and so on...This function does not essentially consist in either inventing anything or otherwise creating the conditions which the enterprise exploits.

It consists in getting things done" (1950:132). He emphasized that entrepreneurs were not necessarily capitalists even though they clearly function vis-à-vis capitalist enterprises.

I am inclined to agree with Schumpeter's thesis that the entrepreneurial function performed its major historical role during the 19th century rise of industrial capital and has essentially ossified during the first half of the 20th century (it seems to be resurrected through the computer-related high technology movement currently underway). I disagree with his apotheosis of the private entrepreneur as a species of economic magician at the expense of the worker in the ascendancy of industrial capital.

5 Herman's 1956 article triggered an exchange between him (1957) and Spengler (1957) which revolves around the issue of the "capital accumulation potential" of "cottage industry", with Spengler cavalierly dismissing, a priori, labor-intensive development strategies because they "tend to bring very little surplus value (which he defines in Ricardian terms as net produce consisting of rent plus profits) into being" (1957:372). Herman astutely countered this argument by observing, a posteriori, that "Given the right market, cottage industry is not always a marginal subsistence occupation" (1957:372). Also noteworthy was Herman's separation of production for own-use from commodity production (cf. Staley and Morse 1965:5-8) based on the nature of the markets toward which production is geared, although he failed to snow how differences at the level of circulation relate to the structure of production. Moreover, his argument (1956:365) that mass production, standardization, and assembly-line organization are not only possible but are characteristic of some branches of non-factory industrial commodity production has escaped many other writers on the topic.

6 In a brief yet thought-provoking essay Enrique Semo (1984) poses and answers the following question with reference to the contemporary Mexican political economy: "Is the weakness of the social sector (vs. the state) and of medium and small enterprise owing to its intrinsic non-viability or to obstacles created by the State-monopoly capital alliance?" In arguing for a new development trajectory in which small and medium en-

terprise are "transformed into active economic subjects" Semo points out that during the past three
decades State policy has been based on a development
model which gives priority to the expansion of large
private and government enterprises (1984:39). A new
strategy, based on the expansion of small and medium
enterprise, would by contrast "widen the internal
market, reduce unemployment, make income distribution
less unequal, and strengthen national independence"
(ibid.).

Heilbroner was shortsighted and superficial in
his dismissal of such a strategy for Third World
development due to the time factor: "If the underdeveloped countries had time, they could build an industrial capital sector much as the West originally did,
by the slow process of accretion from handicraft. But
time is what lacks above all in the race for development" (1963:82).

APPENDIX 1. REVIEW OF THE OAXACA VALLEY SMALL INDUSTRIES PROJECT

With regard to the primary empirical data corpus --collected directly by project staff in specific research sites through the use of pre-tested census forms, interview schedules, and observational and other formats supplementary to these--the scope of the project embraced twenty villages in three political districts (Ocotlán, Tlacolula, Centro) of the Oaxaca Valley. These data cover but are not limited to the economic, social, and cultural aspects of production and exchange in the selected localities. This corpus also includes other data, collected through the use of a separate interview schedule, dealing with a series of craft-producing and -selling enterprises in Oaxaca City and in the outlying towns of Ocotlán de Morelos, Mitla, and Tlacolula de Matamoros. At this level the data pertain to the following units of analysis: (1) individual commodity-producing units (mostly household-firms but also including small to medium sized commercial firms and small capitalist commodity-producing units which employ several full-time wage laborers; (2) discrete village-based branches of regional industries (e.g., the Santa Lucía del Camino branch of the brick industry, the Xaagá branch of the treadle loom weaving industry); and (3) an aggregate unit made up of several localized branches of particular regional craft industries, for example, treadle loom weaving (5 villages), backstrap loom weaving (4 villages), embroidery (10 villages), and palm weaving (2 villages).

Let me say a few words about the rationale and the comparative analytical possibilities of the 20-village household survey component of the project. The survey generated data which make possible comparative analyses between several localities within a particular branch of production (e.g., weaving and brickmaking) based in one or more localities. I decided early in the project to concentrate on the districts of Ocotlán, Tlacolula, and Centro (Oaxaca City and a series of rural satellite communities including Santa Lucia del Camino) because these are the districts which have the highest incidence of craft production in the "Central Valleys" region (Cook 1978 and 1982a: ch.8).

While some important rural industries were not included in the survey (e.g., pottery), most of them were; and the data collected for local branches of these industries are, in most cases, representative of the entire regional industry. This is especially true where the project surveyed leading or other important localities in a particular regional industry, as was the case with backstrap loom weaving (Santo Tomas Jalieza and three other localities), treadle loom weaving (Teotitlán del Valle and three other localities), embroidery (San Juan Chilateca and nine other communities), palm weaving (San Lorenzo Albarradas and Santo Domingo Albarradas), and brickmaking (Santa Lucía del Camino).

No localities were surveyed which did not have households participating in a regional craft industry. However, the survey covered a random sample of households in each locality surveyed and, as it turned out, one-third of these were not involved in craft production. While these households may not be statistically representative of non-craft households in districts or localities not covered by the project, I do think that something can be learned about such households by making a separate analysis of these data. Moreover, a comparative analysis of these and the craft-producing households in the localities surveyed should make an important contribution to our knowledge about the regional division of labor (without assuming that the 20 villages surveyed comprise a microcosm of the regional population).

As a perusal of the remaining parts of this Appendix shows, the household survey represents only one component of the primary data corpus. In the qualitative sense, the most important data were collected through a combination of observation, structured and unstructured interviewing, and archival work. Unfortunately, it was not possible to collect these kinds of data in every community surveyed but we were able to do so for each major industry included in the survey. Those industries in which the best integration of various kinds of primary data was achieved are the brick industry, the treadle loom weaving industry, and the palm weaving industry. A less complete yet adequate integration was achieved in the wooden utensils industry, the backstrap loom weaving industry, and the embroidery industry.

The main data gathering instrument in the twenty village household survey was a pretested, stuctured census form which was organized into the following sections: Resident Members of the Household (name, relation, sex, age, birthplace, civil status, languages, schooling); Socioeconomic Data on Resident Household Members (occupation, position in occupation, type of work, time dedicated to occupation, form of payment, income); Housing (8 questions); Family Budget (5 questions); Agricultural Data (6 questions); Instruments of Labor (7 questions); Animal Raising (7 questions); Relations of Production in Agriculture (7 questions); Non-Agricultural Commodity Production (both principal and secondary occupations--50 questions on details of means of production, labor process, circulation of products, relations of production and exchange).

In addition to the data collected by administering the principal household census form, which was subsequently coded into more than 250 variables for computer processing, the primary project data corpus consists of the following components:

1. Transcribed texts of tape-recorded, structured interviews with 160 craft producers (74 men, 82 women) from eight different villages and towns in three districts (Ocotlán, Tlacolula, and Centro) and representing the following occupations: backstrap loom weaving, treadle loom weaving, embroidery, woodcarving, palm weaving, broom making, rope making, brick making, mescal distilling, basket making, fireworks making, sandal making, blacksmithing, and carpentry. The basic format for these tape-recorded interviews includes 48 questions (mostly open ended) organized into seven sections as follows(see Appendix 3 for the questions asked in the brick industry study): Occupational History and Current Occupational Situation (14 questions); Occupational Ideology (8 questions); Product Valuation (2 questions); Civil-Religious hierarchy participation/attitudes (4 questions); Economic Ideology (12 questions), Class Consciousness (8 questions). In addition to this basic interview schedule (which includes several optional questions for respondents who were females and/or employees and/or self-employed producers) special versions were designed and used, taking into account industry-specific conditions, in interviews with mescal-distillers, brickmakers, and brickmaker´s wives.

209

2. A specially designed interview schedule was administered to 31 intermediaries in the embrodiery industry in five localities in the district of Ocotlán as follows: San Antonino del Castillo (11), Ocotlán de Morelos (8), San Juan Chilateca (7), San Martín Tilcajete (4), and San Pedro Guegorexe (1). This schedule has a total of fifty questions distributed under the following headings: Biographical Data (15 questions); Products Sold (listed by place of origin and mode of acquisition); Products Bought (7 questions); Products Manufactured (4 questions); Means of Production (listed by type, quantity, where and when acquired, cost); Employees (5 questions); Sales (3 questions); Wholesale Operations (4 questions); Retail Operations (2 questions); Capitalization and Organization of Business (5 questions); Attitudes (4 questions).

3. The interview schedule described above was also administered to 72 craft business proprietors in Oaxaca City; 47 of these interviews were tape-recorded and have been transcribed. The respondents can be categorized by type and/or location of their business as follows: pottery workshops - 6 interviews (4 recorded); weaving workshops or **mantelerías** - 11 interviews (7 recorded); miscellaneous workshops - 7 interviews (all recorded as follows: 2 tinsmiths, 1 leather worker, 1 knife-maker, 1 rope maker, 1 sandal maker, 1 shirt-maker); stall keepers in the artisans' market - 11 interviews; stall keepers in the main market ("Central de Abastos") - 7 interviews; stall keepers in the "20 de Noviembre" market - 14 interviews; store proprietors - 21 interviews (all recorded).

4. Fifteen detailed household budget studies in four different villages (Santo Tomás Jalieza, San Pedro Guegorexe, Xaagá, and Santa Lucía del Camino) ranging from four to ten weeks each using a form requiring daily itemizing by the informant of income and expenditures together with tasks performed.

5. Observational studies, field notes, and preliminary field reports for each of the localities and industries surveyed. The field notes and observational studies are most important in the case of treadle loom weaving in Xaagá, palm harvesting and weaving in San Lorenzo Albarradas, ixtle fiber production in Santo Domingo Albarradas, and brickmaking in Santa Lucía.

APPENDIX 2. PROBLEMS IN DEFINING AND SAMPLING THE COMMUNITY

One measure of urbanization in Santa Lucía is the difficulty encountered in compiling a list of heads of household for purposes of selecting the sample for the survey. In the typical rural village in the Oaxaca valley one customarily finds that the authorities (the Municipal President in the case of municipalities like Santa Lucía) have a fairly accurate and up to date list of all heads of household and, consequently, have a good idea of the total population of the village. However, in Santa Lucía we were forced to compile a composite list from separate and incomplete lists obtained from the municipal government, the ejido office, and the local school and our experience was that no one had a reliable basis for making a solid estimate of the settlement's total population.

In addition to this difficulty, another was immediately confronted. A decision had to be made whether to focus only on Santa Lucía proper (i.e., the **cabecera**) or to also include in our survey other settlements within the municipality which were spatially separate from the **cabecera**. The longer we spent in Santa Lucía, the more we realized that the boundaries between the **cabecera** and the other settlements were tenuous and, in fact, were dissolving as the separate population clusters coalesced. Therefore, we decided to define Santa Lucía, for purposes of our study, as one settlement with four residential sections. These are: Center (**Centro** - the central sector with stores, a bus stop, government offices, church, school, and the largest residences); **Rancho Nuevo** (a rural settlement located several hundred yards south of the southern residential perimeter of the center and separated from it by agricultural fields); **Colonia del Bosque** (a sprawling, rapidly growing, and primarily working class residential area about five blocks to the west of the core of the center; and the Brickyard Zone several blocks to the east of the center where the kilns, patios, and clay pits are located and where many brickworker families reside (see Figure 3).

Excluded from "Santa Lucía" for purposes of our study was the settlement of San Francisco Tutla--an agency of the municipality of Santa Lucía--located across the highway to the east of Santa Lucía center.

211

The 1980 roster of **ejidatarios** listed 133 names which shows a marked decline since 1925 when there were 249 heads of household listed as eligible to receive ejido allotments. This decline in the number of **ejidatarios** contrasts with the increase in the general population which in 1960 was 644 (Santa Lucía proper) compared with 1211 in 1970.

Our final composite list had 370 households representing the three major residential areas, with those residing in the brickyard zone being excluded for lack of information. This situation was remedied only through subsequent field work. Consequently, the survey was conducted in two phases. The first phase proceeded according to a 10% random sample of the 370 households drawn from the composite list and resulted in 32 completed census forms; the second phase entailed surveying households in the brickyards where we had established rapport, together with surveying several brick industry households which did not reside in the brickyards, and yielded 24 completed forms. In other words, the second phase of the survey covered only brick industry households.

APPENDIX 3. BRICK INDUSTRY AND OTHER INDUSTRY HOUSEHOLDS COMPARED

The data presented in Table 13 provide a basis for comparing brick industry households with other industrial households in the Oaxaca Valley. Regarding the household and occupational variables, the most notable contrast is the larger mean household size for the brick industry households (7.2 vs. 5.9 for the other five groups of rural households) which also translates into a higher average consumer/worker ratio (3.5 vs. 2.2). Also, there is a higher proportion of nuclear (and a lower proportion of extended) households in the brick industry population (81% to 9%) than in the other rural industry populations (71% to 16%). That this latter difference is apparently not attributable to urbanization seems to be indicated by the fact that the town-dwelling population has a higher ratio of extended to nuclear households (73% nuclear to 27% extended) than does the combined rural population.

Nevertheless, urbanization does seem to be a relevant factor underlying the larger average size for the combined town and brick industry households in comparison with the rural craft households (6.6 vs. 6.0). It also appears to have some role in explaining the higher consumer/worker ratio for these households (3.2 vs. 2.2), as well as the slightly higher average number of years of schooling of their heads. The most striking statistic here, however, is that the average for the entire sample is just over three years of schooling per household head. There is little difference between these groups regarding the number of paid workers and the number of occupations per household; they average around two paid workers and four occupations each, which gives an overall indication of the extensiveness of their involvement in wage labor and commodity production.

There are several marked differences between the brick industry and town industry households, and the rural craft households. It is clear, for example, that brick industry and town industry households have much higher weekly incomes than do the rural households. The average weekly income for the five rural industry groups was 17 dollars compared with 34 dollars for the town artisans and 60 dollars for the brick industry

213

TABLE 13. SELECTED SOCIAL AND ECONOMIC VARIABLES FOR 710 CRAFT HOUSEHOLDS IN 23 OAXACA VALLEY COMMUNITIES GROUPED BY INDUSTRY.

Type of Industry	Household Size	% Type N	E	Household Head Age	No. Yrs. School	No. of Paid Workers	No. of Unpaid Workers	No. of Occupations in Household	Consumer/Worker Ratio	Weekly Household Income (pesos)[1]	Living Conditions Index (mean)	Weighted Value of Land (mean has.)[4]	1979 Harvest (kilos)	Corn No. of Months Bought in 1979[4]	Total Value of Agric. Means of Production (pesos)[1] Owned	Rented	Agricultural Wage Labor (Mean Man-Days) Hired	Worked	Total Value of Owned Animals (pesos)[1]
Embroidery (5 villages) N = 77	6.4	75	12	42	3.0	2.1	0.8	4.0	2.4	406	4.0	1.7 / 2.4 (>0, N=58)	200 / 566	7.0 / 7.2	2624 (<0, N=23)	545	77 (>0, N=13)	67 (>0, N=15)	4612 (>0, N=67)
Treadle Loom Weaving (6 villages) N = 177	5.4	76	19	44	3.7	1.4	1.4	4.3	2.2	607	2.2	1.3 / 1.8 (>0, N=110)	35 / 395	10.0 / 8.5	2729 (<0, N=28)	543	15 (>0, N=30)	48 (>0, N=59)	2435 (>0, N=121)
Mixed Crafts[2] (6 villages) N = 232	6.0	63	22	45	2.7	2.3	0.7	4.5	2.2	260	3.1	1.8 / 2.2 (>0, N=208)	200 / 332	8.0 / 7.3	626 (>0, N=124)	476 (>0, N=110) 80 0	39 (>0, N=33)	53 (>0, N=49)	6062 (>0, N=205)
Town Crafts[3] (2 towns) N = 37	6.0	73	27	53	3.5	1.6	1.1	3.2	2.9	772	3.9	1.5 / 2.1 (>0, N=9)	0 / 136	0 / 3.6	6250 (>0, N=2)	0	86 (>0, N=5)	30 (>0, N=3)	1861 (>0, N=18)
Palm & Ixtle/ Rope (2 villages) N = 108	5.3	75	13	47	3.2	1.9	1.2	4.0	1.9	261	3.3	1.5 / 3.3 (>0, N=91)	500 / 806	5.0 / 5.1	10198 (>0, N=68)	76	31 (>0, N=25)	54 (>0, N=30)	10178 (>0, N=75)
Backstrap Loom Weaving (1 village) N = 44	6.5	69	13	47	2.8	1.8	1.5	3.9	2.1	388	4.0	1.5 / 2.6 (>0, N=30)	200 / 289	8.0 / 7.2	5525 (>0, N=17)	300	55 (>0, N=16)	N.D.	5875 (>0, N=35)
Bricks (1 village) N = 35	7.2	83	9	42	4.0	1.8	1.3	4.3	3.5	1348	4.3	1.0 / 1.7 (>0, N=21)	0 / 342	10.0 / 7.0	3400 (>0, N=3)	1513	14 (>0, N=5)	7 (>0, N=2)	3954 (>0, N=19)

1 All values are means.
2 Occupations include wood carving, broommaking, backstrap loom weaving, lime making, metate making, basketmaking, embroidery, thread spinning and mescal distilling
3 Occupations include carpentry, sandal making, candlemaking, mescal distilling, metate making, brick making, and blacksmithing.
4 Upper value = median; lower value = mean

214

households of Santa Lucía. This striking income advantage in the brick industry is accompanied by a less striking but also higher ranking on the Living Conditions Index (see Chapter 2).

The advantage accruing to the brick industry households from these two variables is, to some extent, offset in many rural households by possession of land and the ownership of agricultural means of production. Some 78% of the rural households are landed as opposed to only 60% of the brick industry households and 24% of the town artisans. The average amount of arable possessed by the rural households is significantly larger (1.6 to 1.0). Moreover, 41% of the rural households own agricultural means of production in comparison with only 14% of the brick industry households. The data also show that the rural households are substantially more involved in corn production and animal raising. These data support the thesis that the separation of agriculture from industry has proceeded much further in Santa Lucía than it has in communities more distant from the city.

A study of the distributions throughout the entire sample for key economic and agricultural variables discloses two basic patterns: a normal distribution with a majority of households clustered in the center and a distribution skewed toward the lower values. Generally speaking, these two types of distribution for wealth-related variables reflect populations with a predominance of either independent landed "middle strata" households (i.e., normal distribution) or of land-poor or landless households which comprise a rural proletariat (i.e., the skewed distribution). An estimated 26% of the rural households surveyed participated in agricultural wage labor (the best indicator of rural proletarian status), compared with only 11% in the town sample and 6% in the Santa Lucia brick industry households (Table 13, next to last column).

It is significant that only the brick industry households display a bimodal pattern regarding the frequency distributions for the Living Conditions Index This indicates that there is a higher degree of class polarization in this industry. The treadle loom weaving industry presents by far the most skewed distribution. This probably reflects the relative land poverty of its peasant-artisan households and the

215

landlessness of the hired weavers who, like the hired brickmakers are paid weekly by piece rate.

REFERENCES CITED

Alonso, J.A., 1983, "The domestic clothing workers in the Mexican metropolis and their relation to dependent capitalism" in **Women, Men, and the International Division of Labor**, (J. Nash and M. Fernandez-Kelly, eds.), Albany: State University of New York Press.

Alonso, J. (ed.), 1982,**El Estado Mexicano**, Mexico, D.F.: Editorial Nueva Imagen.

Bailón Corres, M., 1980, "Artesanías y capital comercial en los valles centrales de Oaxaca," in **Sociedad y Política en Oaxaca 1980** (R. Benítez Zenteno, ed.), Oaxaca: Instituto de Investigaciones Sociales, UABJO.

Baird, P. and E. McCaughan, 1979,**Beyond the Border**, New York: NACLA.

Baran, P.A., 1973, **The Political Economy of Growth**, Pelican.

Barkin, David, 1975, "Mexico´s Albatross: the U.S. economy", **Latin American Perspectives** 11, (2):64-80.

Barkin, D. and G. Esteva, 1979, **Inflación y Democracia, el Caso de Mexico**, Mexico, D.F.: Siglo Veintiuno.

Bartra, R. 1974, **Estructura Agraria y Clases Sociales en México**, México, D.F.: Ediciones Era.

Bartra, R., 1978, **El Poder Despótico Burgués**, Mexico, D.F.:Serie Popular Era.

Bauer, P. and B. Yamey, 1957, **The Economics of Underdeveloped Countries**, Chicago: University of Chicago Press.

Baumol, W. and A. Blinder, 1982, **Economics: Principles and Policiy**, 2nd edition, New York: Harcourt Brace Jovanovich.

Beals, R. L., 1975, **The Peasant Marketing System of Oaxaca, Mexico**, University of California Press.

217

Benería, L. and G. Sen, 1981, "Accumulation, reproduction, and women's role in economic development: Boserup revisited", **Signs: Journal of Women in Culture and Society** 7,(2):279-298.

Blanton, R.E. and S.A. Kowalewski, 1981, "Monte Alban and after in the valley of Oaxaca", **Supplement to The Handbook of Middle American Indians,** (ed. J.A. Sabloff), Austin: University of Texas Press.

Blanton, R.E. et.al., 1981, "The valley of Oaxaca." In **Ancient Mesoamerica, A Comparison of Three Regions,** R. Blanton et.al., Cambridge: Cambridge University Press.

Bottomley, A., 1965, "The fate of the artisan in developing economies", **Social and Economic Studies** 14,(2):194-203.

Braverman, H., 1974, **Labor and Monopoly Capital,** New York: Monthly Review Press.

Chayanov, A.V., 1966, **The Theory of Peasant Economy,** Homewood, Ill.: Irwin.

Childe, V.G., 1951, **Man Makes Himself,** New York: Mentor.

Cockcroft, J.D., 1983, "Immiseration, not marginalization: the case of Mexico", **Latin American Perspectives** X:86-107.

Cohen, G.A., 1978, **Karl Marx's Theory of History, A Defence,** London:Clarendon Press.

Cook, S., 1976 "Value, price, and simple commodity production: the case of the Zapotec stoneworkers", **Journal of Peasant Studies** 3,(4):395-427.

Cook, S., 1977, "Beyond the Formen: towards a revised marxist theory of precapitalist formations and the transition to capitalism", **Journal of Peasant Studies** 4, (4):360 - 389.

218

Cook, S., 1978, "Petty commodity production and capitalist development in the `central valleys´ region of Oaxaca, Mexico", **Nova Americana** I:285-332.

Cook, S., 1981, "Crafts, capitalist development, and cultural property in Oaxaca, Mexico." Inter-**American Economic Affairs** 35,(3):53-68.

Cook, S., 1982a, **Zapotec Stoneworkers, the Dynamics of Rural Simple Commodity Production in Modern Mexican Capitalism.** Lanham, Md.: University Press of America.

Cook, S., 1982b, "Craft production in Oaxaca, Mexico", **Cultural Survival Quarterly** 6,(4):18-20.

Cook, S., 1984a, "Merchant capital, craft production, distribution relations and capitalist development in the Oaxaca valley, Mexico", paper presented at the Annual Meeting of the Society for Economic Anthropology, Davis, California.

Cook, S., 1984b, "Rural industry, social differentiation, and the contradictions of provincial Mexican capitalism", forthcoming in **Latin American Perspectives.**

Cook, S., 1984c, "Peasant economy, rural industry, and capitalist development in the Oaxaca valley, Mexico, **Journal of Peasant Studies** (October).

Cook, S. and M. Diskin (eds.), 1976, **Markets in Oaxaca**, Austin: University of Texas Press.

Cooper, E., 1980, **The Wood-Carvers of Hong Kong,** Cambridge: Cambridge University Press.

Dalton, G., 1974, "How Exactly Are Peasants `Exploited´? **American Anthropologist** 76:553-61.

Dalton, G., 1975, "Putting a cat among the red herrings: a reply to Newcomer and to Derman and Levin", **American Anthropologist** 77:338-341.

Dalton, G., 1976, "Exploitation of peasants: A reply to Dunn", **American Anthropologist** 78:643-645.

Dalton, G., 1977, "Further remarks on exploitation: a reply to Newcomer and to Derman and Levin", **American Anthropologist** 79:125-134.

Deere, C.D., 1979, "Rural women's subsistence production in the capitalist periphery, in **Peasants and Proletarians,** (ed.by R. Cohen, P. Gutkind and P. Brazier), New York: Monthly Review Press.

Deere, C.D. and A. de Janvry, 1979, "A conceptual framework for the empirical analysis of peasants", **American Journal** of **Agricultural Economics** 61:601-611.

Deere, C.D. and M. León de Leal, 1981, "Peasant production, proletarianization, and the sexual division of labor in the Andes", **Signs: Journal of Women in Culture and Society** 7,(2):338-360.

de Janvry, A., 1981, **The Agrarian Question and Reformism in Latin America,** Baltimore: Johns Hopkins.

Dobb, M., 1963, **Studies in the Development** of **Capitalism,** New York: International Publishers.

Dobb, M., 1975, **Theories of Value and Distribution Since Adam Smith.** London: Cambridge University Press.

Dobb, M., 1976, "From Feudalism to Capitalism," in **The Transition from Feudalism to Capitalism,** (P. Sweezy, et.al.), London: New Left Books.

Eckstein, S., 1977, **The Poverty of Revolution,** Princeton University Press.

Firth, R., 1979, "Work and Value", in **Social Anthropology of Work,** (S. Wallman,ed.), London: Academic Press.

Fuentes, C., 1969, "Viva Zapata", **New York Review of Books** XII,(5):5-12.

Galeski, B., 1972, **Basic Concepts in Rural Sociology,** Manchester: Manchester University Press.

García Canclini, N., 1982, **Las Culturas Populares en el Capitalismo.** México, D.F.: Nueva Imagen.

Ghosh, S.K., 1984, "Marx on India", **Monthly Review** 35,(8):39-53.

Goody, E.N., 1982, "Introduction", in **From Craft to Industry** , (edited by E.N. Goody), Cambridge: Cambridge University Press.

Goody, E.N. (ed.), 1982, **From Craft to Industry,** Cambridge University Press.

González Casanova, P., 1980, "The economic development of Mexico", **Scientific American** 243,(3):192-205.

Graburn, N.H.H. (ed), 1976, **Ethnic and Tourist Arts: Cultural Expressions from the Fourth World,** Berkeley: University of California Press.

Graburn, N., 1982, "The dynamics of change in tourist arts", **Cultural Survival Quarterly** 6,(4):7-14.

Gudeman, S., 1978, **The Demise of a Rural Economy,** London: Routledge and Kegan Paul.

Gulati, L., 1982, **Profiles in Female Poverty.** Oxford: Pergamon Press.

Harnecker, M., 1974, **Los Conceptos Elementales del Materialismo Histórico,** México, D.F.: Siglo Veintiuno.

Harris, O. and K. Young, 1981, "Engendered structures: some problems in the analysis of reproduction", In **The Anthropology of Pre-Capitalist Societies,** (J. Kahn and J. Llobera, eds.), New York: Humanities Press.

Hart, K., 1982, "On commoditization", in **From Craft to Industry,** E. Goody, ed., Cambridge: Cambridge University Press.

Heilbroner, R., 1963, **The Great Ascent,** New York: Harper.

Hendricks, J. and A.D. Murphy, 1981, "From poverty to poverty: the adaptation of young migrant households in Oaxaca, Mexico", **Urban Anthropology** 10,(1):53-70.

Herman, T., 1956, "The role of cottage and small-scale industries in Asian economic development", **Economic Development and Cultural Change,** July:356-370.

Herman, T., 1957, "Cottage industries: a reply", **Economic Development and Cultural Change,** July:374-5.

Higgins, B., 1959, **Economic Development: Problems, Principles, and Policies,** New York: Norton.

Higgins, M., 1983, **Somos Tocayos,** Lanham, Md.: University Press of America.

Hindess, B. and P. Hirst, 1975, **Precapitalist Modes of Production,** London: Routledge and Kegan Paul.

Hobsbawm, E., 1969, **Industry and Empire,** Pelican Books.

Hopkins, N., 1978, "The articulation of the modes of production: tailoring in Tunisia", **American Ethnologist** 5,(3):468-483.

Howard, M. and J. King, 1975, **The Political Economy of Marx,** London: Longman.

Hughes, H., 1980, "Achievements and objectives of industrialization", In **Policies for Industrial Progress in Developing Countries,** (J. Cody et.al., eds.), Oxford University Press.

Hunt, E. and H. Sherman, 1975, **Economics: an Introduction to Traditional and Radical Views,** 2nd edition, New York: Harper and Row.

International Labor Organization (ILO), 1951, **Payment By Results,** Geneva: ILO.

Iñigo Aguilar Medina, J., 1980, **El Hombre y La Urbe, La Ciudad de Oaxaca,** Mexico, D.F.:SEPINAH.

Kahn, J., 1980, **Minangkabau Social Formations,** Cambridge University Press.

Kautsky, K., 1974, **La Cuestión Agraria,** México, D.F.: Siglo Veintiuno.

Keddie, J. and W. Cleghorn, 1980, **Brick Manufacture in Developing Countries,** Edinburgh: Scottish Academic Press.

Kirkby, A., 1973, **The Use of Land and Water Resources in the Past and Present Valley of Oaxaca, Mexico,** Memoirs of the Museum of Anthropology, no. 5, Ann Arbor: University of Michigan.

Kowalewski, S.A. and L. Finsten, 1983, "The economic systems of ancient Oaxaca: a regional perspective", **Current Anthropology** 24, (4):413-442.

Krader, L., 1975, **The Asiatic Mode of Production,** Assen, the Netherlands: Van Gorcum.

Kriedte, P., Medick, H., and J. Schlumbohm, 1981, **Industrialization Before Industrialization,** Cambridge University Press.

Lackey, L., 1982, **The Pottery of Acatlán, A Changing Mexican Tradition,** University of Oklahoma Press.

Lamphere, L., 1979, "Fighting the piece-rate system: new dimensions of an old struggle in the apparel industry", in **Case Studies on the Labor Process,** (A. Zimbalist, ed.) New York: Monthly Review Press.

Landes, D., 1969, **The Unbound Prometheus,** Cambridge University Press.

LeClair, E.E., Jr., 1968, "Economic theory and economic anthropology", in **Economic Anthropology: Readings in Theory and Analysis,** (ed. by LeClair, E.E.,.Jr. and H.K. Schneider), New York: Holt, Rinehart & Winston.

Lenin, V.I., 1964, **The Development of Capitalism in Russia.** Moscow: Progress Publishers.

Levy, D. and G. Szekely, 1983, **Mexico, Paradoxes of Stability and Change,** Boulder: Westview Press.

Littlefield, A., 1978, "Exploitation and the expansion of capitalism: the case of the hammock industry of Yucatan", **American Ethnologist** 5:495-508.

Littlefield, A., 1979, "The expansion of capitalist relations of production in Mexican crafts", **Journal of Peasant Studies** 6,(4):471-488.

Lomnitz, L., 1975, **Como Sobreviven Los Marginados,** Mexico, D.F.: Siglo Veintiuno.

Malinowski, B. and J. De La Fuente, 1982, **The Economics of a Mexican Market System,** London: Routledge and Kegan Paul.

Mandel, E., 1970, **Marxist Economic Theory,** Vol.1. New York: Monthly Review Press.

Martínez Ríos, J., 1964, "Análisis funcional de la `guelaguetza agricola´", **Revista Mexicana** de **Sociología** 26 (1):79-125.

Marx, K., 1967, **Capital,** Volume 1, New York: International Publishers.

Medick, H., 1976, "The proto-industrial family economy: the structural function of household and family during the transition from peasant society to industrial capitalism", **Social History** 1, (3):291-315.

Medick, H., 1981, "The proto-industrial family economy", in **Industrialization Before Industrialization,** P. Kriedte et.al., Cambridge University Press.

Mendels, F.F., 1972, "Proto-industrialization: the first phase of the industrialization process." **Journal of Economic History** 32:241-261.

Mendieta y Nuñez, L. (ed.), 1949, **Los Zapotecos.** México: Universidad Nacional Autónoma de Mexico.

Mintz, S., 1964, "Peasant market places and economic development in Latin America", The Graduate Center for Latin American Studies, Vanderbilt University, Occasional paper no. 4.

Moguel, R., 1979, **Regionalizaciones Para El Estado de Oaxaca, Analisis Comparativo.** Oaxaca: Centro de Sociología,U.A.B.J.O.

Moore, W.E., 1951, **Industrialization and Labor**, Cornell University Press.

Murphy, A. and H. Selby, 1981, "A comparison of household income and budgetary patterns in four Mexican cities", **Urban Anthropology** 10,(3):247-67.

Nash, M., 1967, **Machine Age Maya**, Chicago: University of Chicago Press.

Nolasco, M., 1972, **Oaxaca Indígena**, Instituto de Investigación e Integración Social del Estado de Oaxaca. Serie: Investigaciones, num. 1.

Nolasco, M., 1981, "Oaxaca, una ciudad mercado", in **Cuatro Ciudades, El Proceso de Urbanizacion Dependiente**, Mexico, D.F.:INAH.

Novelo, V., 1976, **Artesanías y Capitalismo en México**. México,D.F.: SEP-INAH.

Paz, O., 1961, **The Labyrinth of Solitude**, New York: Grove Press.

Paddock, John (ed.), 1966, **Ancient Oaxaca, Discoveries in Mexican Archaeology and History**, Stanford University Press.

Popkin, S., 1979, **The Rational Peasant**, Berkeley and Los Angeles: University of California Press.

Popkin, S., 1980, "The rational peasant", **Theory and Society** 9:411-471.

Ramírez Brun, R., 1980, **Estado y Acumulación de Capital en México 1929-1979**. México, D.F.: UNAM.

Redfield, R., 1941, **The Folk Culture of Yucatan**. University of Chicago Press.

Reyes Osorio, S. et.al., 1974, **Estructura Agraria y Desarrollo Agrícola en México**. México, D.F.: Fondo de Cultura Económica.

Reynolds, C., 1970,**The Mexican Economy**, New Haven: Yale University Press.

Roxborough, I., 1979, **Theories of Underdevelopment.** Atlantic Highlands, N.J.: Humanities Press.

Sanders, W.T., 1972, "Population, agricultural history, and societal evolution in Mesoamerica", in **Population Growth: Anthropological Implications,** (ed. by B. Spooner), Cambridge, Mass.: MIT Press.

Schneider, H.K., 1974, **Economic Man.** New York: The Free Press.

Schumpeter, J.A., 1950, **Capitalism, Socialism, and** Democracy, New York: Harper.

Schumpeter, J.A., 1961, **The Theory of Economic Development,** Oxford.

Scott, J., 1976, **The Moral Economy of the Peasant,** New Haven: Yale University Press.

Semo, E., 1984, "Estado o sociedad", **Proceso** 383 (5 March):38-39.

Shapiro-Perl, N., 1979, "The piece rate: class struggle on the shop floor. Evidence from the costume jewelry industry in Providence, Rhode Island", in **Case Studies on the Labor Process,** (A.Zimbalist, ed.), New York: Monthly Review Press.

Singer, M., 1960, "Changing craft traditions in India", in **Labor Commitment and Social Change in Developing Areas.,**(W.E. Moore and A.S. Feldman, eds.), New York: Social Science Research Council.

Slotkin, J., 1960, **From Field to Factory,** Glencoe, Illinois: Free Press.

Spengler, J., 1957, "Cottage industries: a comment", Economic Development and Cultural Change, July: 371-73.

Staley, E. and R. Morse, 1965, **Modern Small Industry for Developing Countries,** New York: McGraw-Hill.

Stavenhagen, R., 1978, "Capitalism and peasantry in Mexico", **Latin American Perspectives** V,(3):27-37.

Sweezy, P., et.al., 1967, **The Transition from Feudal-ism to Capitalism** (3rd printing), New York: Science and Society.

Sweezy, P., et.al., 1976, **The Transition from Feudalism to Capitalism** (new, expanded edition), London: New Left Books.

Taylor, W.B., 1972, **Landlord and Peasant in Colonial Oaxaca**, Stanford University Press.

Tilly, C. and R. Tilly, 1971, "Agenda for European economic history in the 1970s", **Journal of Economic History** 31:184-198.

Tilly, L., 1981, "Paths of proletarianization: organization of production, sexual division of labor, and women´s collective action", **Signs:Journal of Women in Culture and Society** 7,(2):400-417.

Tilly, R., 1983, "Flows of capital and forms of industry in Europe, 1500 - 1900", **Theory and Society** 12,(2):123-142.

Wallerstein, I., 1974, **The Modern World System**, New York and London: Academic Press.

Wallerstein, I., 1979, **The Capitalist World-Economy**, Cambridge University Press.

Warren, B., 1980, **Imperialism, Pioneer of Capitalism**, London: New Left Books.

Weber, M., 1961, **General Economic History**, New York: Collier Books

Welte, C., 1976, "Appendix: Maps and Demographic Tables," in **Markets in Oaxaca**, (S. Cook and M. Diskin, eds.), Austin: University of Texas Press.

Wolf, E., 1955, "Types of Latin American peasantry: a preliminary discussion", **American Anthropologist** 57,(3):452-478.

Wolf, E., 1966, **Peasants**, Prentice-Hall.

Wolf, E., 1969, **Peasant Wars of the Twentieth Century.** Harper and Row.

Wolf, E., 1982, **Europe and the People Without History**, Berkeley: University of California Press.

Wolf, E. and E. Hansen, 1972, **The Human Condition in Latin America**, New York: Oxford.

World Bank, 1981, **World Development Report 1981**, Oxford University Press.

Young, K., 1978, "Modes of appropriation and the sexual division of labour: a case study from Oaxaca, Mexico", in **Feminism and Materialism**, (A. Kuhn ánd A. Wolpe, eds.), London: Routledge and Kegan Paul.

AUTHOR INDEX

SUBJECT INDEX

Land tenure, 29, 37
Land use, 37, 59-60, 109, 155, 156, 162
Land value, 118, 150, 166
Landlessness, 16, 17, 18, 22, 36, 41, 51, 139, 214-6
Living conditions index, 44, 121, 214-5
Loans, 5, 52, 55, 129, 140, 141, 142, 166, 169, 180,
    202. See also Credit

Maize. See Corn
Manufacture, 3, 5, 25, 26, 56, 198, 204
Manufactory, 13, 106, 129, 195, 196
Marginal analysis. See Marginalism; Marginalist economics
Marginalism, 113, 115. See also Marginalist economics
Marginalist economics, 113-6, 149. See also Margin-
    alism
Market(-s, -ing), 5, 12-14, 17, 19, 23, 36, 38, 40,
    44, 78, 89, 90, 92, 113, 114, 115, 117, 130, 131,
    133, 134, 135, 136, 140, 144, 149, 152, 179, 186
    193, 194, 201, 202, 205, 206
Market economy, 26,
Marx (-ist, -ism), 3, 25, 108, 113, 115, 124, 125,
    126, 127, 149, 151, 194, 195, 198, 199, 204
Means of production, 21, 46, 57, 120, 162, 214-5
Metate industry, 12, 13, 23, 28, 111, 152, 192, 193,
    194
Mexican clothing industry, 191-2, 204
Mexican economy, 4-7, 27, 153, 203, 205
Mexico City, 37, 48, 168, 191, 192, 204
Migrant labor, 5, 40, 183
Migration, 7, 9, 39-40
Migratory labor. See Migration; Migrant labor
Milero defined, 56
Minimum wage, 128, 129, 196, 204
Noncapitalist production, 13

Oaxaca City, 9, 14, 16, 18, 19, 23, 29, 33, 35, 36,
    40, 44, 48, 52, 57, 59, 84, 97, 106, 126, 128,
    129, 133, 135, 136, 168, 174, 176, 185, 195, 196,
    197, 204, 207
Oaxaca valley, 4, 7, 9, 15, 20, 22, 27-8, 30, 33, 36,
    37, 39, 44, 51, 57, 59, 84, 109, 111, 116, 153,
    167, 172, 188, 189, 192, 193, 194, 195, 196, 198,
    199, 202, 204, 207
Occupation(-al), 9, 19, 20, 22, 45, 46, 47, 50, 51,
    52, 101, 157, 158, 159, 205, 213-4
Own-use production, 6, 26, 153, 156, 172, 173, 205
    See also Subsistence

PAN (National Action Party), 18, 30
Paternalism, 140, 141, 142, 148, 193

Value, 44, 113, 114, 115, 116, 117, 120, 124, 129, 139, 143, 149, 150, 151, 187, 198, 201, 204, 205. See also Labor value

Wage (hired) labor, 3, 9, 12, 13, 16, 18, 24, 26, 38, 39, 40, 44, 54, 139, 155, 166, 172, 173, 178, 179, 191, 192, 194, 213-6
Wage-price spiral, 133
Wealth, 6, 136, 159, 162, 163, 166, 174, 215
Weaving industry, 12, 28, 36, 56, 124, 160, 187, 188, 189, 193, 194, 197, 200, 214, 215-6
Weber(-ian), 1, 25, 165
Women's roles, 71, 167-73, 188-9, 193, 198, 199. See also Female labor; Sexual division of labor
Work, 17, 18, 22, 23, 34, 36, 37, 40, 46, 47, 48, 49, 51, 52, 53, 54, 55, 62, 69, 70, 71, 77, 78, 79, 84, 90, 91, 115, 120, 121, 125, 126, 127, 128, 140, 141, 142, 143, 145, 146, 147, 148, 152 155, 156, 157, 159, 160, 161, 163, 164, 165, 166, 168, 169, 170, 171, 172, 173, 180, 181, 182, 185, 186, 187, 188, 189, 197, 199, 204.   See also Employment; Female labor; Labor; Occupation (-al)
Workshop, 12, 36, 191, 195, 197. See also Manufacture; Manufactory